TO

"Advocate 6"

Thanks sincerel[y]

for making

study happen!

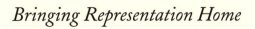

Bringing Representation Home

Michael A. Smith

Bringing
Representation
Home

State Legislators among
Their Constituencies

University of Missouri Press
Columbia and London

Library of Congress Cataloging-in-Publication Data
Smith, Michael A., 1970–
    Bringing representation home : state legislators among their constituencies /
Michael A. Smith.
        p.   cm.
Includes bibliographical references and index.
    ISBN 0-8262-1452-5
    1. Legislators—United States—States.   2. Representative government and
representation—United States—States.   I. Title.
    JK2488 .S65 2003
    328.73—dc21

                                                                        2002152704

Text designer: Foley Design
Jacket designer: Susan Ferber
Typesetter: The Composing Room of Michigan, Inc.
Printer and binder: Thomson-Shore, Inc.
Typeface: Adobe Caslon

THIS BOOK IS DEDICATED TO THE MEMORY OF

Candice Richie

ONE OF THE BEST STUDENTS I HAVE EVER TAUGHT

Candice was one of those remarkable students whose class participation, intense questions, and genuine thoughtfulness made me into a better teacher

Contents

Acknowledgments

Special thanks to Richard J. Hardy and Valerie Heitshusen for all their guidance and support in this endeavor. Thanks also to Peter Hall, Catherine Holland, and Garry Young.

Bringing Representation Home

1

Studying Representation

> [I]n spite of many centuries of theoretical effort, we cannot
> say what representation is.
>
> —*Heinz Eulau, "Changing Views of Representation"*

For this study, I took my cue from Heinz Eulau. Instead of asking, "What is representation?" I asked, "How can we discover what representation is?" I focused on its actual practice. To that end, I interviewed and observed twelve state representatives over the course of two legislative sessions.[1] I thus discovered how state legislators define their approaches to representation by *doing it*. This study attempts to show what representation is in practice, not what it is in theory. Generalizations are offered, but they are grounded in discussions of actual representatives going about their tasks. In confronting my chosen question, I have not taken Professor Eulau's insight so seriously as to be frightened away from the first question. After all, representation is fundamental to democracy. But, as Eulau points out, theoretical effort alone is not sufficient to answer the question "What is representation?"

A caveat: this project is not based on the assumption that there is a single answer to that question. Hanna Pitkin has thoroughly discredited such a notion. According to her, *representation* is a term that encompasses a range of approaches and answers, each of which is

---

1. The study was conducted in 1998 and 1999 in Kansas City and surrounding areas. See Appendixes I and II for details on the methodology and site of the study.

based on a different set of assumptions and posits a different set of implications. A few prominent scholars have stressed the value of understanding representation through the eyes of representatives themselves. These include Richard F. Fenno Jr., Malcolm Jewell, and Donald D. Searing. All of these scholars have used interviewing to discover how legislators approach their tasks. Fenno added participant observation (he calls it "soaking and poking"). I used both techniques. Fenno, Jewell, and Searing have somewhat different opinions on the value of constructing a "role theory" to explain representatives' approaches to their tasks. But they all agree that the best way to define representation from a representative's perspective is to ask the representatives themselves.[2] I agree too.

How do representatives themselves approach representation? My own study began with my inclination to believe that representatives do not define representation through explicit assumptions, hypothesis-testing, imagined states of nature, or metaphysics. Rather, representatives define representation through its actual practice. They shape and refine their definitions as they put them into use. The definition-in-use of representation is not an academic exercise in which definitions are specified first, then applied to specific cases. Rather, the approach to representation and its actual practice evolve together in the representatives' experiences. This study tracks that process, relying heavily on descriptions of twelve state representatives presenting themselves to constituents. From the descriptions, I draw generalizations. Thus I construct a typology of roles, not based on the representatives' roles within the system, but from the representatives' own understandings of their districts and their careers. These variables, in turn, shape their home styles.

What is home style? According to Fenno, it is the symbolic presentation that a representative makes at home, in seeking political support from his or her constituents. I see it as an approach to the state legislator's four tasks, as specified by Jewell. These tasks are: communication with constituents, policy responsiveness, allocation of resources for the district, and service to constituents. Jewell con-

2. Hanna Fenichel Pitkin, *The Concept of Representation;* Richard F. Fenno Jr., *Congressmen in Committees;* Richard F. Fenno Jr., *Home Style: House Members in Their Districts;* Malcolm E. Jewell, *Representation in State Legislatures;* Donald D. Searing, *Westminster's World: Understanding Political Roles.*

cludes that all state representatives must complete each task in order to be successful. But Heinz Eulau and Paul D. Karps also note that a legislator must be *symbolically responsive* to his constituents.[3] That is, he must also present his work to his constituents. What has the representative done? How has he done it? How does he respond to the needs of constituents—and which constituents? What will he do in the future? To whom does he address his presentation of himself? All of these questions must be answered in order for a representative to develop an effective home style. In Figure 1, I model the term *home style* as a symbolic responsiveness to constituents regarding the legislator's accomplishment of Jewell's four tasks.

Home style is a variable. Different legislators present themselves in different ways. Some of the variation in home style is almost certainly idiosyncratic. But in my study I observed certain key variables that each legislator interpreted in shaping his home style. Several of these variables reflect the representative's perception of his district, and another is the representative's own ambitions beyond the statehouse.

Many of these legislators delighted in telling me that they "fit their districts." But what does it mean to "fit"? In my observation, the legislators' perceptions of the key variables shaped their home styles. In my open-ended interviewing, they discussed their districts in terms of three variables: socioeconomic status, metropolitan or rural location, and political competitiveness. These responses were remarkably similar to those of Fenno's congressmen. Like Fenno's congressmen, all these state legislators believed that they must respond to the district's needs ("fit"). Their understandings of those needs were based in large part on their perceptions of these three variables. Further, they believed that there was a great deal of variation in these areas in different districts across the state.

In addition to the district variables, the legislators' own ambitions also shaped their home style. For example, those that had ambitions for higher office generally worked much harder to draw publicity to themselves, because they believed that this publicity would "spill over" into neighboring districts, thus building name recognition there

---

3. Fenno, *Home Style*, 55; Jewell, *Representation in State Legislatures*, 18; Heinz Eulau and Paul D. Karps, "The Puzzle of Representation: Specifying Components of Responsiveness," 68.

Figure 1: A Model of Home Style

● District characteristics   ● Rep's ambition

  ● Metropolitan/rural

  ● Socioeconomic status (income and growth)

  ● Political competitiveness

↓   ↓

Home style:
Rep's own articulation of his or her role, grounded in past experience and future expectations of the above variables.

Components   ● communication   ● policy responsiveness   ● resource allocation   ● service

too. Those who had no future political ambitions, by contrast, were less aggressive in placing issues on the agenda. They tended to take other approaches. Some of these less-ambitious legislators relied heavily on their own judgment to make policy choices: an approach resembling the style of Edmund Burke. Others in the less-ambitious column chose to wait until constituents placed issues on the agenda. Then they responded.

In grouping this data, I have reintroduced the concept of representational roles. In so doing, I am not proposing to restore the institution-heavy "role theory" of authors such as John C. Wahlke et al. I am not assuming that roles are norms of behavior that are defined by institutions alone. Rather, I group data into roles only on the basis of the representatives' own approaches as observed during my interviews and extensive trips to their home districts. As Jewell points out, institutions are influential in constraining a representative's approach to his role, but they are not entirely deterministic.[4] Different representatives take different approaches to completing their tasks within the

4. John C. Wahlke, Heinz Eulau, William Buchanan, and LeRoy C. Ferguson, *The Legislative System: Explorations in Legislative Behavior,* 10; Jewell, *Representation in State Legislatures,* 15–16.

institution. They also take different approaches to presenting their work to constituents. The roles I discuss stand for representatives who developed similar themes in their home styles. And home style, in turn, is shaped by a representative's own understanding of his district ("fitting the district"), as well as by his own ambitions.

Three roles of representation are offered here: *Burkean, advocate* (subdivided into in-district and beyond the district), and *ombudsperson*. At home, Burkeans focus on presenting themselves as experienced, levelheaded, and knowledgeable, and take a "whole-state" orientation to public policy. They also stress character and experience. Advocates, by contrast, work hard to "socialize the conflict."[5] They raise concerns and bring them to their constituents' attention. Advocates take the lead in putting issues on the agenda. In-district advocates emphasize issues that arise in the district and neighboring communities, while advocates beyond the district take a citywide or statewide orientation, stressing issues that affect the larger community but taking stands they believe are particularly popular in the district. Ombudspersons are most concerned with listening to constituent demands, then responding to them. Such demands include both casework and district-specific policy needs. All of these legislators do casework, listen to constituents, and justify their votes and bills to organized groups of constituents. But they also have different home styles that are centered around achieving those tasks and letting constituents know what they have accomplished. Each role that I propose is a way of relating to the district and securing reelection.

Chapter 2 engages the debate over "role theory." I discuss the poverty of the functionalist approach to roles, which does not allow sufficient latitude for variation. Representatives develop their own approaches to presenting themselves, and there is more variation in those approaches than we can understand from a functionalist standpoint. Instead, I take my cue from Searing and propose to construct roles from the representatives' own understandings of their environmental constraints and career plans. Like Fenno, I ground my theory in the symbolic interactionist school of sociology, which posits that a subject's self-understandings develop out of his interactions with

5. E. E. Schattschneider, *The Semi-Sovereign People: A Realist's View of Democracy in America*, 3.

other people. The symbolic interactionist school has developed a "grounded theory" methodology, in which the study of processes and the development of generalizations evolve together in research. I read Fenno as an application of grounded theory and follow his lead. I quibble with Searing's argument that symbolic interactionism ignores both the power of institutions and the importance of actors' preexisting biases. In fact, I argue that Fenno's work appropriately accounts for both of these elements as well as the subjects' interactions with other people. All of these things together shape the representatives' "presentation of self," to use Erving Goffman's term.[6]

Chapters 3 through 6 provide descriptions of the twelve representatives, grouped by the home-style roles that I observed during the study. These chapters offer "more of the same," in Searing's words: more discussion of the representatives' perceptions of their districts, their own ambitions, and the tasks of representation. All of this information is presented from the representatives' own perspectives: an "over the shoulder" approach.[7] Each of these chapters has a concluding section that discusses the ways the different types of representatives present themselves at home in terms of Jewell's four tasks.

Chapter 7 draws hypotheses from the model proposed in this chapter, and evaluates them in light of the twelve cases discussed in chapters 3 through 6. In the first part of Chapter 7, I discuss the concentric circles of constituency that state representatives face. Unlike Fenno's congressmen, whose largest "circle" was the district itself, these representatives must also orient themselves beyond the district, particularly in metropolitan districts. This spillover into neighboring districts is inevitable due to the fact that many school districts, municipalities, and organized interest groups lie in more than one statehouse district. Furthermore, spillover is important in developing a constituency if one plans to run for an office with a larger district, such as state senate.

The second part of Chapter 7 develops hypotheses that relate district characteristics and the representatives' political ambitions, considered as independent variables, to home style, considered as a dependent variable. Four hypotheses emerge. First, representatives from financially struggling, metropolitan districts of moderate or low socio-

6. Erving Goffman, *The Presentation of Self in Everyday Life.*
7. Searing, *Westminster's World,* 27; Fenno, *Home Style,* xv.

economic status tend to be in-district advocates. Second, legislators from politically competitive, well-off metropolitan districts are most likely to be ombudspersons. Third, those with ambition for state senate seats are often in-district advocates. And fourth, those with no political ambition beyond the statehouse are more likely to be Burkeans or ombudspersons.

The last part of Chapter 7 considers a new constraint on legislators' progressive ambitions: term limits. Early evidence from this study indicates that term limits do not fundamentally alter representatives' progressive ambitions, but they do create a "day of reckoning" by which the legislators must act on their ambitions or step aside—at least temporarily—from politics.

The appendix provides details about my approach to data collection and the site of the study. My methods were qualitative and closely resembled Fenno's "soaking and poking," with the notable exception that I preferred to tape-record interviews and use the resulting data together with my field notes from participant observation. The metropolitan area chosen for this study is obviously not a true random sample, but the diverse group of districts in that area reflect many of the challenges facing contemporary state representatives around the country. Two rural districts that lie entirely outside any standard metropolitan statistical area (SMSA), as defined by the U.S. Census, were also included in this study.

As Searing points out, there is little hope left for a grand, "covering law" theory of political roles.[8] That is, there is no role theory that can be understood apart from an extensive, qualitative engagement with the representatives' own understandings of the contexts that shape their behavior. But perhaps this is just as well. Eulau warned us that theoretical inquiry alone has not gotten us far in answering the question "What is representation?" Following the lead of Searing, along with that of Fenno and Jewell, I have asked the representatives themselves to tell me how they approach representation. Informed by the proper literature, theory, and methods, I believe this will help us make more progress than theory alone when it comes to understanding representation.

8. Searing, *Westminster's World*, 24–28.

2

Constructing Roles from the Representatives' Perspectives

Literature and Methods

[T]he core problem involved in representation is the relationship that exists between representative and represented.

—*Heinz Eulau, "Changing Views of Representation"*

This study does not make any grand claims for "role theory." The twelve state legislators' roles emerge as groupings of the data, informed by my own experiences interviewing and observing them in their home districts. In Chapters 3 through 6, I group the descriptions and analysis of each representative's behavior in terms of a predominant role. The roles are described in those chapters. These generalizations emerged from my own observations and subsequent descriptions of how the representatives present themselves to their constituents.

Existing Literature: Roles and Interactions

My work here is informed by, but not identical to, the theoretical orientation found in Donald D. Searing's seminal study of British Members of Parliament (MPs). Like Searing, I conceptualize a legislator's behavior as a sort of role, constrained by both institutional arrangements and personal goals. Like Searing, I do not seek to develop a "role theory" which can serve as a general "covering law," which in turn purports to explain political behavior apart from the situations that shape it.[1] Instead, I follow his example by developing generalizations through a rich description of the data.

Searing critiques prior attempts at "role theory" rather harshly. He begins with what he calls the structural approach, which he associates with a number of older studies, most notably that of John C. Wahlke, Heinz Eulau, William Buchanan, and LeRoy C. Ferguson. Wahlke et al. label their work "a functional view of representation" because it is derived from the function of the representative in the political system. According to Searing, the weakness of this approach is that it "emphasizes the dominance of institutions over individuals" in constructing roles. Wahlke et al. write: "Institutions, it has been said, are regularities or uniformities of behavior. The concept of a role associated with a position of membership in any institutionalized group refers to precisely those behavioral uniformities or regularities which constitute the institution."[2]

Searing charges the structuralist literature with "two important but unacceptable assumptions. . . . The first is that there will normally be widespread consensus about how any given role should be played. Actually, such consensus varies enormously from one role to another. It is a variable. The second . . . is that the individual's role-related attitudes and behaviors are determined by the expectations of his or her associates. Again, the power of such expectations is surely a variable that differs across different roles and institutions."[3]

According to Searing, the structural approach takes institutions seriously—too seriously. In attempting to derive representational roles from the representatives' function within the system, Wahlke et al. get only half of the picture. They ignore variations that are based on the subjective experiences and interpretations of the actors themselves. Later in their careers, Wahlke and his coauthors moved away from their functionalist formulation. In Eulau's words: "We have come to know what representation is not. . . . Our conceptions of representation are obsolete."[4] Even the title of Eulau's essay, "Chang-

1. Searing, *Westminster's World,* 7.

2. Ibid., 9; Wahlke et al., *Legislative System,* 268, 10.

3. Searing, *Westminster's World,* 9.

4. Heinz Eulau, "Changing Views of Representation," in Heinz Eulau and John C. Wahlke, eds., *The Politics of Representation: Continuities in Theory and Research,* 52.

ing Views of Representation," suggests doubts about his and his coauthors' earlier formulation. Eulau and the others came to embrace the view that studies of representation must be grounded in the interactions between representatives and represented (as shown in the quotation that begins this chapter). According to Searing, however, the interactionalist literature overcorrects for the excesses of functionalism. Richard F. Fenno Jr., for example, discards the idea of roles altogether.

Searing traces the origin of the interactionalist literature, including Fenno's, to the symbolic interaction school of sociology. This school, associated with the philosopher George Herbert Mead, emphasizes social interactions as the core of self-understanding. Fenno relies heavily on the symbolic interactionist tradition for his own theoretical grounding. In *Home Style: House Members in Their Districts* (1978), he cites Erving Goffman, whose approach bears notable similarities to the symbolic interactionist one. Goffman's "presentation of self" concept compared everyday social interactions to the behavior of stage actors. According to Goffman, everyday "actors" expect some response from others in reaction to their own behavior. The anticipated reaction shapes the behavior. From this interactionist standpoint, Fenno writes: "Goffman does not talk about politicians; but politicians know what he is talking about. The response they seek from others is political support. And the impressions they try to foster are those that will engender political support."[5]

This quotation shows the link between goal-oriented activity and the interactionist approach. David R. Mayhew sees a legislator's goals as being central to his own behavior. Mayhew argues that the goal of reelection drives legislative behavior not because reelection is a legislator's only goal, but because his other goals cannot be obtained effectively without remaining in office for several terms.[6] The interactionist school encompasses the goal-orientation theory posited by Mayhew and others. In the Fenno quotation above, politicians engage in interactions with constituents, motivated by the goal of political support. In trying to obtain support, they develop their understandings of their constituencies through interactions with others. Their

5. Goffman, *Presentation of Self*, 1–16, 238–55; Fenno, *Home Style*, 55.
6. David R. Mayhew, *Congress: The Electoral Connection*, 16.

presentation of themselves is done in pursuit of that goal. Yet they cannot simply return home and present themselves to their constituents. Instead, they must gather information from their constituents through interaction. That information-gathering process, in turn, shapes the legislators' approach to presentation. Particularly when they are new to the seat, or when the district seems to have changed a great deal, legislators must ask themselves several questions, such as: What do people seem to expect from me? Which people are watching me within the district? Are these people part of clearly identifiable groups within the constituency? How do they perceive me now? What is particularly important to them? What is less important? If the district seems to be changing, how does my approach fit with the changes? How is my own presentation of myself changing? How do constituents perceive these changes?

Fenno's use of the term *political support* instead of *reelection* is valuable for my own study. Many of the state representatives I studied have political ambitions beyond the statehouse. Most plan to remain state representatives for only a few terms. Thus reelection goals may be overridden by broader political ambitions, particularly if the house seat seems relatively safe for the incumbent. These broader ambitions, in turn, require more expansive approaches than those narrowly focused within the district. In Chapter 7, I give more sustained treatment to the phenomenon I label "spillover," in which representatives appear at functions sponsored by jurisdictions and organized groups (such as school districts and local chambers of commerce) that encompass not only the representative's own statehouse district, but neighboring communities as well. Thus they seek political support that goes beyond reelection to their current seat.

Interaction, motivated by the goal of political support, is a trial-and-error process. This is particularly noticeable when watching a newly elected state representative try out different approaches to see what works and what does not. The representative whom I call Ombuds 2, elected to an open seat during my study, was the hardest one to categorize in my typology. This was because he was a whirlwind of activity, trying out different approaches that varied widely. He worked hard for organized groups of people back home, who in turn would give him feedback about local issues. Some of these groups met only sporadically, while others gathered regularly. He took a Burkean stance in his suburban newspaper column, advising constituents during veto session that "I have read each bill carefully and will vote upon each based on my best judgment." He also took on an advocate's role, successfully lobbying the governor to sign a moratorium on use of the controversial gasoline additive MTBE. He responded quickly and effectively when local government and neighborhood groups asked for his intervention to prevent rezoning for a proposed trailer park. There, too, he prevailed. He avoided controversies that seemed to divide the district, such as concealed-carry permits for handguns. Yet with all his activity, Ombuds 2 still is not quite sure what will serve him best in his reelection campaign. In our interview, he based his reelection hopes on his ability to listen and respond, particularly regarding sensitive local issues such as those involving school districts. With some reluctance, I categorized him as an ombudsperson, but his home style is likely to develop further in subsequent terms—if he is reelected in his highly competitive district.

Other legislators also made reference to the trial-and-error process of developing home style. For example, Advocate 6 mentioned that she used to schedule town hall meetings before deciding that low turnout made them "a waste of time." For his part, Advocate 5 made big plans for a competitive first election, bringing in a national consultant. But when that consultant looked at the district's voting history, he advised Advocate 5 that no aggressive campaign was necessary. The district is so Democratic that the general election would not be much of a threat. After this quick judgment, the consultant moved on to more interesting races, leaving Advocate 5 to run a scaled-down campaign of door-knocking and leaflets in an election he was unlikely to lose. Thus Advocate 5 learned early on, through trial and error, that he need not focus many resources on general elections. Though he continues to raise money each election cycle, he now gives a great deal away to other Democrats in more competitive races. He now uses fund-raising not to defeat a Republican challenger, but to develop ties to other Democrats who can help him in the house and to help Democrats win marginal seats in other districts, thus retaining the party's statehouse majority. This trial-and-error process is important to legislators as they develop their home styles and the understandings that shape them.

Like Fenno, I draw generalizations regarding the interactions of

legislators and constituents as well as the goals that shape that behavior. These generalizations are drawn from the descriptions and
analysis of legislator-constituent interactions. Searing, however, is
dismissive of symbolic interactionism, charging it with "neglecting
the broader institutional contexts within which such negotiations oc-
cur" and "not adequately credit[ing] people with their own independent standpoints."[7] Searing prefers what he labels the motivational
approach. According to him, the motivational approach is the best
way to account for the role of institutions as well as for individuals'
own standpoints. Those standpoints, in turn, may be formed apart
from both the individuals' roles within a system and their interactions
with others. But Searing is too quick to dismiss the similarity of the
motivational approach to Fenno's work. Searing's categories are a bit
misleading. In fact, Fenno's work can accommodate his concerns.

Prior to *Home Style,* Fenno published a work that explicitly ac-
counted for institutional variation and measured its impact on those
working within institutions. Searing portrays Fenno's 1973 book
Congressmen in Committees as follows: "This interest in goals was developed furthest in [that book], where Fenno dismantled purposive
roles to investigate the specific 'personal political goals' within them,
goals like influence in the House and reelection."[8] Fenno does, in
fact, scrap the idea of purposive roles, and thus jettisons Wahlke et
al.'s functionalist baggage. But this does not mean that Fenno ignores
institutions.

In *Congressmen in Committees,* Fenno seeks to overthrow previous
"one-size-fits-all" approaches to studying committees. He suggests
that each committee has its own, unique set of both resources and expectations, which in turn affect the development of legislators' roles
on any given committee. He writes that "committees differ in all
the[se] respects . . . —their influence in congressional decision making, their autonomy, their success on the chamber floor, their expertise, the control exercised by their chairmen, and their domination by
the executive branch. If such is—even partially—the case, the need
for a new set of generalizations is obvious."[9]

---

7. Searing, *Westminster's World,* 10.
8. Ibid., 11.
9. Fenno, *Congressmen in Committees,* xiv.

Here, Fenno presents his research in terms of the committees' function in the House—an institutional variable. Fenno does not reduce institutions to the behavior of those within them. He takes institutions seriously in their own right: "Of the various clusters of outsiders, the four most prominent are: members of the *parent House,* members of the *executive branch,* members of *clientele groups,* and members of the two major *political parties*—or, more operationally, the leaders of each. These four elements make up the environment of every House committee. Each has an interest in committee behavior coupled with a capacity to influence such behavior. *But their interests and their capacities are not the same for all committees.*"[10]

In this passage, Fenno describes institutions in terms of their capacities for influencing behavior. He includes these capacities together with the other factors under the broader subheading of "environmental constraints."[11] This approach is remarkably similar to Searing's own. Fenno does not use the word *institutions,* but this does not mean that he disregards the concept. In fact, it plays an important part in his analysis. Fenno does incorporate institutional variables, as part of the "environmental constraints" in his model. Together with member goals, such constraints shape decision rules, which in turn shape processes and decisions. In other words, interactions are constrained by institutions and other environmental factors.

Fenno studies institutional variables less in *Home Style* than in *Congressmen in Committees,* because the respective subject matters are different. In *Home Style,* Fenno studies congressmen working in their home districts. Of course, there are a number of institutional factors that may shape their behavior at home—for example, all U.S. congresspersons represent single-member districts, nearly all work within a two-party system, and all are reelected every two years by plurality vote. However, these are not variables. They are the same for every case Fenno studied. When legislators are at home, the formal institutions make for a sort of background. However, they do not vary from legislator to legislator, and thus they are

10. Ibid., 15 (emphasis of the four clusters is Fenno's; emphasis on the last sentence is mine).
11. Ibid., xv.

not the study's focus. Fenno does deal with the power of institutions in *Congressmen in Committees.*

Searing's second point—that interactionism is too dismissive of pre-existing biases—also slights Fenno. In fact, Fenno demonstrates that a representative cannot simply shape himself to a new set of social and political expectations when the environment changes. In *Congress at the Grassroots* (2000), Fenno discusses the career of Jack Flynt, who represented the 6th congressional district in Georgia from 1954 to 1978.[12] In *Home Style,* Fenno used the term "person to person" to describe Flynt's approach. In part because of his background and experiences growing up in his small-town, conservative district, Flynt felt naturally comfortable with his local orientation. He relied on being personally known by and acquainted with his constituents, whom he generally called by their first names. Flynt's service in the House revolved around bringing federal money home for local projects. He rarely discussed policy at home, focusing instead on visibility by stopping to exchange small talk with constituents, attending local gatherings, and generally presenting himself as a "good old boy." As Flynt's district changed from rural to suburban, he was unable to change his own presentation of himself to meet the expectations of the growing population of impersonal, policy-oriented suburbanites. He watched his reelection margins dwindle until he was nearly defeated by a political newcomer named Newt Gingrich. Flynt retired during the next election cycle, and was replaced by Gingrich. Fenno uses the example of Flynt to make the point that legislators are not simply the creations of their immediate interactions with others. They have their own personalities, biases, and routines of presenting themselves to others. For example, Flynt was not able to adjust his home style to accommodate a changing district.

Indeed, no social actor is simply a creation of his interactions with others. And institutions matter as much as one's preexisting biases and established routines. But Fenno and the interactionist school cannot be dismissed hastily. Fenno focuses on institutions when they are variables in his study, as in *Congressmen in Committees.* When institutions are a relatively fixed background, and other variables come into play, Fenno does not emphasize institutional factors as variables.

12. Richard F. Fenno Jr., *Congress at the Grassroots: Representational Change in the South, 1970–1998,* 1–2.

Further, he does not simply reduce actors to creations of their own social interactions.

My study, like Fenno's, traces home style to variables related to both the home district and the legislator's own ambitions. There is only minor to moderate variation in the institutional background of these legislators' home styles. All the legislators in my study represent single-member districts of between 20,000 and 35,000 people (district populations are smaller in Kansas than in Missouri), all are in session about half a year, and all have similar institutional resources to communicate with their constituents, such as a limited budget for sending mail home. Keith E. Hamm and Gary F. Moncrief classify both Missouri and Kansas legislatures as hybrids that lie somewhere between the professional legislatures, which have extensive resources, and the citizen legislatures, where legislative pay, duration of sessions, and staff are minimal. There is some variation here. Peverill Squire measures Missouri's General Assembly as somewhat more professionalized than Kansas's legislature.[13] But the variation between these two states pales in comparison to the variations Squire measures among all fifty states. Only three Kansas legislators participated in my study, so there is not a good sample size from that state for comparison to the nine Missouri representatives.

Presumably, institutions do affect state legislators' behavior in their home districts. (In the third part of Chapter 7, I discuss an important new institutional variable that constrains legislators in some states: term limits.) However, they are not treated as variables in this study. Different subjects call for different adaptations of symbolic interactionism. On behalf of my own work, and Fenno's, I quibble with Searing's dismissal of the interactionist approach. But this should not distract the reader from a larger point. Searing, Fenno, and I all share a common, methodological focus. Each of us seeks to develop generalizations about the legislator's role, not from a preexisting canon of literature, but from descriptions and analysis of legislators' behavior. My own engagement with this data led me to reintroduce roles as a way of drawing generalizations and hypotheses from my obser-

13. Keith E. Hamm and Gary F. Moncrief, "Legislative Politics in the States," 145; Peverill Squire, "Legislative Professionalization and Membership Diversity in State Legislatures," 72.

vations. I am not reintroducing roles in an attempt to restore the "functionalist" perspective of Wahlke et al., which overemphasizes the system and does not sufficiently account for the interactions that shape the role. Like Searing, I emphasize that roles must be reconstructed from the representatives' own perspectives, quotes, and behavior. Searing even suggests that his generalizations may be tested by discussing them with the representatives themselves! He writes: "I will therefore be pleased when MPs say, 'nothing new here' to the reconstructions of the roles with which they are most familiar. But it also requires 'more of the same'—more statements, more quotations, more information to make the interpretations as persuasive as they can be in their own terms."[14]

Fenno also grounds his work in the self-interpretations of legislators. But in *Home Style,* the focus moves to their perceptions of constituency. Fenno writes: "*What does an elected representative see when he or she sees a constituency?* And, as a natural follow-up, *What consequences do these perceptions have for his or her behavior?* The key problem is perception."[15]

Like Fenno, I interviewed the legislators and traveled extensively with them in their home districts. My first goal was to find out what they see at home. My second was to determine how what they see shapes their behavior. And, like both Fenno and Searing, I derived my generalizations during the collection and subsequent analysis of data, rather than forming predetermined hypotheses to test with set rules of inference. This rich engagement with qualitative data is a more fundamental part of Searing's work than his quick, cursory division of "role theory" into the aforementioned three camps.

None of the legislators in my study ground their views of effective representation in political theories derived apart from political activity. For all of them, effective representation is a continuous activity of processing and refining information through their own preexisting biases (and the biases themselves may also change over time). This approach to representation is not derived from explicitly stated assumptions, formal data analysis, or hypothesis-testing. For these legislators, defining representation is a process grounded in its actual practice.

14. Searing, *Westminster's World,* 27.
15. Fenno, *Home Style,* xiii (Fenno's emphasis).

This is not meant to insinuate that legislators are explicitly performing investigations in political science. Legislators must make sense of the variables that influence their own behavior, but it is the academic's job to read the preexisting literature, draw samples, analyze data, develop generalizations, refine existing theories, and offer reflections on what has been learned. As Searing points out, the legislator's role is generally implicit in his behavior. The political scientist's task is to make it explicit. Rarely do legislators stop to reflect on what their activities have to say to political science. After all, they are just doing their jobs. But in doing the job, each representative develops an approach that resembles grounded theory. These approaches involve a continuous sorting of information to develop generalizations. Those generalizations are intended to help one get the job done, not to speak to an academic discipline and its students. That is why I call representation a grounded *process* but not grounded *theory*. The scholar creates the theory while observing the legislator go about the process.

As previously mentioned, Fenno chose to discard the idea of a "role theory" and thus jettison Wahlke et al.'s functionalist baggage. Turning to the statehouses, Malcolm E. Jewell also avoids constructing roles (though Searing puts some of Jewell's earlier work in the same "structuralist" school as Wahlke et al.'s "role theory"). In *Representation in State Legislatures* (1982), Jewell stresses the tasks that must be undertaken by contemporary state representatives. As outlined in my previous chapter, these tasks are: communication with constituents, policy responsiveness, allocation of resources for the district, and service to constituents.[16] Jewell notes that state representatives must complete all four tasks in order to do their job effectively. He argues that the tasks derive from both public and institutional expectations toward the legislators in the system. I propose to reintroduce the concept of roles as *approaches to accomplishing these tasks*. The approaches, in turn, are grounded in a representative's understanding of the district, as well as in his political ambitions.

Jewell's focus on these four tasks moves his research agenda away from the functionalist tradition. Like Searing, he stresses that a leg-

---

16. Jewell, *Representation in State Legislatures*, 18.

islator's understanding of others' expectations is a variable. He writes: "If the legislative institution is characterized by representation, the norms of that body may influence the role perceptions and behavior of its members [but a] recognition of the utility of studying representation as a characteristic of the institution need not lead us to abandon the effort to understand representation as it is practiced by individual legislators. That is the central focus of this study: the legislator's perspective on representation." Jewell in fact begins his book with this point—that a recognition of institutional norms need not preclude the study of variation in legislators' approaches to those norms. He writes on the first page: "I found that there is no average legislator and no set of answers to the question about representation that might be considered typical. But examples of a couple of interviews will suggest the range of meanings that are associated with the term *representation*."[17]

Heinz Eulau and Paul D. Karps suggest a similar list of tasks. However, they add a different one: "symbolic responsiveness" to constituents. Jewell sees that task as the basis of home style, as described by Fenno; in addition, Jewell proposes to put symbolic responsiveness under his heading of "communication with constituents" rather than list it as a separate task.[18] I quibble with this decision, because the effective representative must present herself at home in terms of all four tasks. Granted, symbolic responsiveness—including home style—shapes a representative's approach to communication, which Jewell describes in terms of attending meetings and forums, campaigning, writing letters, and related activities. But as Fenno demonstrates, a successful home style also means a responsiveness to the policy needs of the district (as he perceives them), a struggle for a resource allocation that is in the best interests of the district, and a successful approach to constituent service requests. Simply attending meetings, campaigning, and writing letters is inadequate without the other three tasks—it is the other three that provide the substantive activities about which the representative communicates. It is true that some of Fenno's subjects used communication techniques that were

17. Ibid., 15–16, 1.
18. Eulau and Karps, "Puzzle of Representation," 66–67; Jewell, *Representation in State Legislatures*, 20–21.

simple name-recognition efforts and not related to the other three tasks. For example, one printed and distributed shopping bags featuring his picture. But Fenno also noted that some House members had "issue-oriented" styles of presenting stands on key issues to constituents (policy responsiveness), that several stressed "bringing home the bacon" for the district (allocation of resources), and that some emphasized a "one-on-one" style that included being responsive to casework requests (constituent service).[19] In my own research, I found that state representatives do, in fact, respond to all four of Jewell's tasks. But the ways in which they presented these tasks to constituents, and the tasks which they chose to stress, varied among the legislators I studied.

What are the causes of this variation? Many representatives in my study, like those in Fenno's, liked to say that they "fit the district." But what does it mean to "fit"? In *Home Style*, Fenno gives sustained treatment to the ways in which perceptions of the home district shape a representative's home style. In my study, I observed several district-level variables to be important to a representative's development of a home style. Those variables are socioeconomic status, metropolitan/rural distinctions, and political competitiveness. Like Fenno, I observed the representatives' *perceptions* of these variables, not objective indicators. The districts in my study varied significantly on all three of these district-level variables. There were inner-city, gentrified urban, inner- and outer-suburban, and rural districts. Some were mostly wealthy, some poor, and several middle-income. Certain districts featured close, two-party competition in races for state representative. Others had an overwhelming supermajority of one party. Several of the representatives had faced close, competitive elections when first elected. A few anticipated competitive elections in the future. Others were elected and reelected by huge margins. They expected these margins to continue. All of these variables influenced their home styles.

The model's other independent variable is the representatives' ambitions beyond the statehouse. The reelection incentive for legislators' behavior has become a truism in political science. Kaare Strøm suggests that roles can be reintroduced into legislative studies only if

19. Fenno, *Home Style*, xii, 91–101, 106, 61–69.

they are treated as goal-oriented. Like Fenno, Mayhew suggests that legislators have goals besides reelection—specifically, prestige and good public policy.[20] However, reelection is crucial to accomplishing these other goals. A short tenure in the house makes it difficult to accomplish much.

Stressing the reelection imperative, Fenno traced congresspersons' behavior to their respective career stages. Further study led him to distinguish between "expansionist" and "protectionist" career stages, each of which is a way of securing reelection.[21] Fenno was studying congressmen who had, or expected to have, long careers in the House. Some had served for several decades. I did not find these long careers in the statehouse, however. According to Burkean 1 (one of my subjects), the average tenure of a Missouri state representative is only five and a half years. Further, Missouri's legislators are now constitutionally limited to serving eight years in each house. Even in Kansas, where there are no term limits, state representatives rarely anticipate long careers in their present public service. Many in my two-state sample, however, had progressive ambitions. Several of them mentioned the possibility of a state senate run in the near future. One of them won an at-large city council seat during the study. Another announced his exploratory candidacy for state insurance commissioner. A few suggested that they might someday run for Congress. And finally, some subjects told me that they had no ambitions for public office beyond the statehouse. Like the district-level variables, a representative's ambition shapes his home style as he incorporates it into an effective approach, not only for the purpose of reelection to the house, but quite possibly as a springboard to another political office.

Taken together, these variables shaped the home style of each of the twelve representatives. The representatives interpret their districts' needs, and their own ambitions, in order to form their individual responses to representation. A representative's home style is a role based on his interpretation of the independent variables. The interactionist school teaches us that environmental and personal factors are developed into interpretations by the actors themselves. In sum,

---

20. Kaare Strøm, "Rules, Reasons, and Routines: Legislative Roles in Parliamentary Democracies," 157; Mayhew, *Congress,* 15–16.
    21. Fenno, *Home Style,* 171–76.

the key variables are those characterizing the home district (metropolitan or rural, socioeconomic status, and political context), as well as the representative's progressive ambition (not only whether or not he has such ambition, but for what type of office). Hypotheses are developed after the descriptions of the roles and the representatives' approaches to them—an approach I believe is consistent with grounded theory. These hypotheses, in turn, link the independent variables to the chosen roles. But to jump to the hypotheses now would bypass the process by which the representatives themselves come to understand their districts and their own ambitions, and how these variables shape their home styles—and that is what forms the very basis of my categorization of the legislators as Burkeans, advocates, and ombudspersons.

3

Burkeans

Deliberate, decide, justify: this is the Burkean's approach. For the Burkean legislator (including Edmund Burke himself), the process of making decisions and representing constituents must go, in order, through those three stages. John Wahlke, Heinz Eulau, William Buchanan, and LeRoy Ferguson seem to imply that the "whole-state" orientation precludes any attention to the district.[1] This is incorrect. The Burkean uses his own background, tenure, and actions as justifications for reelection back home. He tells constituents that he is the best person for the job, then offers the reasons why, often citing examples from his service in office or in the community. Burke's own "Speech to the Electors at Bristol" exemplifies such an approach. Many times the issues discussed are not confined to the district. The representative I call Burkean 2 boasted to constituents about his work on restructuring school districts in the most sparsely populated part of the state, hundreds of miles away. Constituents knew little about this issue and most of what they did know came from him. But for Burkean 2, this type of service exemplified his actions for the whole state. He told constituents that he had worked to educate children more effectively while using taxpayer dollars more wisely. Likewise, Burkean 1 spent a great deal of time at home discussing his support for tougher license requirements for teenage drivers. He did not point to any specific district interests, but rather claimed that his policies would benefit the state as a whole. "How does this affect my district?" was not a major concern for Burkean 1. For these two legislators, as for Burke himself, service to the district was synonymous with service to the state. Yet they stressed that the district's

1. Wahlke et al., *Legislative System.*

voters deserve an explanation for the legislator's decisions made on their behalf.

Qualification to serve is also a major Burkean theme. These qualifications revolve around the issues of character and experience. These two legislators had been active in the community before running for the legislature. Further, both had been in office for several terms. Each argued that his character and expertise gave him an advantage over challengers. They maintained that the most qualified people should make the policy decisions. Burkean 1 chose to emphasize the character theme, pointing to his strong grounding in family and church. "They're my guiding light," he said of the two institutions. During this time of presidential impeachment, Burkean 1 went home and attacked the character and judgment of President Clinton regarding personal matters. When among friendly audiences (such as religious conservatives), Burkean 1 liked to contrast his scandal-free tenure and that of his conservative colleagues with the embarrassing actions of the current U.S. president. In so doing, he reinforced the theme that good character is essential to good representation—and that he had the character to make wise judgments for the good of the state.

Burkean 2 chose instead to emphasize experience, stressing his background as an academic. While it was rare for me to discover Ph.D.'s in the statehouse, Burkean 2 was proud to be an exception. He did not downplay his higher-education background. In fact, he even suggested that more Ph.D.'s should consider running for office, and thus bring an academic perspective to lawmaking. As chair of the house Education Committee, he offered his own background as one of his qualifications for the job.

Tenure in office is also essential, according to what these Burkean legislators told constituents. Each said that being in office for a few years gave them wisdom and expertise. To this end, each of them strongly opposed term limits, which are law in Burkean 1's state but not in Burkean 2's.

These two Burkeans' districts contrasted somewhat. While Burkean 1 represented an area that was stable, well-off, suburban, and growing, Burkean 2's district was made up of small towns and farms just beyond the edge of suburban sprawl. As far as I know, these two legislators never met one another. But there was a consistent theme in the way they described their districts: to use Burkean 1's words, each had "fewer problems" and constituents who were "less concerned." As we shall see in the next chapter, this contrasts with Advocate 2's "changing" district and Advocate 3's "crumbling" district. Of course, the descriptions in these chapters revolve around the legislators' *perceptions* of their constituency. There are no statistical abstracts featured here.

It is clear that the two Burkeans perceived stability in their districts. While Burkean 1 said his constituents were less concerned, Burkean 2 emphasized that he would not want to represent Advocate 3's inner-city area, or even Advocate 4's suburban district. He told me his own small-town voters "are more fun to be around. They take themselves less seriously. They have a live-and-let-live attitude." The theme here, again, was that these constituents were relatively easy to represent and not too demanding. The community itself was stable.

All districts make specific, local demands on legislators. But the Burkean representatives believed that they faced fewer such demands than many of their colleagues. Still, a population of active constituents came to local meetings, expecting an accounting of how their legislator spent his time in the capitol. Further, many of these citizens were active in key interest groups, such as the chamber of commerce, the Rotary, and schoolteachers' organizations. Thus they influenced other, less active members of those groups, and had a say in endorsements.

The Burkean approach appeared to fit these legislators' perceptions of their respective districts. The active subpopulation of voters there wanted accountability, but they did not need to be consulted on every issue, nor did they generally flood their representatives with demands for casework and other requests.

In this chapter, I will discuss Burke's concept of representation, and how it shaped his own home style; the home styles of two Burkean representatives who deliberate, decide, and justify; and, finally, how Malcolm Jewell's four tasks of representation are approached by Burkeans.

Burke's Three Steps of Decision-Making

Sir Edmund Burke was a theorist and legislator. He believed that accumulated wisdom and experience, not abstract philosophies, are the keys to effective representation.[2] Burke's "Speech to the Electors at Bristol" exemplifies his philosophy of representation. Hanna Pitkin points out that Burke linked the district's interest with the proper behavior of its representative. She writes: "Burke conceives of broad, relatively fixed interests, few in number and clearly defined, of which any group or locality has just one. These interests are largely economic, and are associated with particular localities whose livelihood they characterize, and whose over-all prosperity they involve."[3]

Pitkin also points out that for Burke, these interests were not in the eye of the beholder. Rather, it is the task of the good Burkean representative to know these interests and to serve them. Pitkin states that the most effective representative is the one who has the wisdom and experience to do this. She describes Burke's concept of interests as follows: "The true interest of any group, or for that matter of the entire nation, has an objective reality about which one may be right or wrong, about which one may have an opinion. The intelligent, well-informed, rational man, who has studied and deliberated and discussed the matter, is the man most likely to know the true interest of any group."[4]

In Burke's view, effective representation of interests is the task of good representatives. These interests may, indeed, be local in nature. But Burke, like James Madison, rejected the idea that a dominant faction could effectively understand and articulate interests for the good of the state.[5] Regarding proposed legislation to ostracize Roman Catholics, Burke said in his speech: "Nor do I believe that any good constitutions of government, or of freedom, can find it necessary for their security to doom any part of the people to a permanent slavery. Such a constitution of freedom, if such can be, is in effect no more than another name for the tyranny of the strongest faction, and factions in republics have been, and are, full as capable as monarchs of the most cruel oppression and injustice."[6]

Burke did not depend on factions for effective representation. Instead, he argued that the accumulated, practical experience of the rep-

2. George J. Graham Jr., "Edmund Burke's 'Developmental Consensus,'" 29.
3. Pitkin, *Concept of Representation*, 174.
4. Ibid., 176.
5. James Madison, "Federalist 10," 43.
6. Burke, "Speech to the Electors at Bristol," 134.

resentative is the more effective means to discover and serve the objective interest. He saw deliberation as central to the representative's task. In fact, in Burke's view, the representative is often the most knowledgeable person on the subject, and must not be swayed by short-term fluctuations in public opinion. Over the longer term, the constituents will have time to do their own deliberating. Then they will be more likely to see the wisdom of the legislator's position. But short-term passions are likely to sway constituents away from a clear, rational understanding of the underlying, objective interest. Thus the representative must remain true to the interest and not be swayed by immediate opinions. Burke told his own electors: "I did not obey your instructions: No. I conformed to the instructions of truth and nature, and maintained your interest, against your opinions, with a constancy that became me. A representative worthy of you ought to be a person of stability. I am to look, indeed, to your opinions; but to such opinions as you and I must have five years hence."[7]

Burke therefore suggested that a representative should not always be beholden to public opinion, inclined as it is to being swayed emotionally. Thus he suggested that public opinion is not an effective guide to representation. Furthermore, in a diverse district, it is probably not even possible to represent public opinion effectively, because that opinion is too divided. Burke said: "I could wish, undoubtedly, if idle wishes were not the most idle of all things, to make every part of my conduct agreeable to every part of my constituents. But in so great a city, and so greatly divided as this, it is weak to expect it." The Burkean legislator believes that his own wisdom is a better guide than short-term fluctuations in opinion. Yet this does not mean that he is disconnected from the district. As Burkean 2 told me, "The voters deserve an explanation." Burke's speech presented just such an explanation, as did the many appearances the two Burkean legislators made back home. Burke opened his speech as follows: "I am extremely pleased at the appearance of this large and respectable meeting. The steps I may be obliged to take will want the sanction of a considerable authority; and in explaining anything which may appear doubtful in my public conduct, I must naturally desire a very full audience."[8]

7. Ibid., 103.
8. Ibid., 91, 89.

Here he suggests that electors confer authority when they hear their representative justify his decisions. The representative relies on his own judgment to make decisions, but his authority to do so ultimately comes from his constituents. Since authority is conferred on the representative by the represented, the justification of his actions is essential to his job. His explanations are not a mere courtesy, but rather an integral part of his job. Without those explanations, authority has not been maintained and the task of representation is incomplete.

Burke's opening comments are consistent with two ideas that together form a rational approach to representation. First, he suggests that a representative should be expected to explain his conduct. It is a natural part of his job. Neglecting to do so would mean shirking his duties. Second, Burke's comments are consistent with a rational reelection strategy. In defending his behavior before his electors, the representative has the opportunity to persuade them that his actions have indeed been in their own interest. His speeches allow him to discuss the district's interest and to show how his actions have served it.

Burke did not shy away from controversy. He anticipated that public opinion would be both emotional and divided. He was prepared to accept a mixed reaction to his own behavior. Yet he sought the opportunity to justify his choices and articulate the district's interest before being judged by the electors. Burke's "Speech to the Electors" exemplifies the three-step process of deliberate, decide, and justify. That process also describes the home styles of the two Burkean representatives. The steps must be completed in the prescribed order; deliberation precedes rational decisions, allowing for a reflection of the true interests of the community, or the state as a whole. To Burke, deliberation was distinct from emotional reaction. While the former is time-consuming, the latter is immediate. It is only through the longer process of accumulating knowledge and wisdom that the best decision can be reached regarding objective interests. Emotional reaction short-circuits the process. Burke considered not what his constituents' opinion was at the moment, but what it was likely to be, for example, in five years. Because interests are objective, he further suggested that the opinions of the electors and the elected would eventually come into harmony. Given enough time to deliberate, both would move closer to a correct realization of the interest of the district and the interests of the nation as a whole.

Decision marks the division between deliberation and justification. Since Burke did not find it useful to collect public opinion before making a decision, it was not necessary to return home to canvass the district before deciding. He told the electors, "I canvassed you through your affairs, not your persons."[9] A representative need not poll the district, but he must understand the district and its interests in order to be effective. That is, he must fit the district. Only after making his decision should the representative return home to justify it.

Deliberate, decide, justify is a system that allows the Burkean representative both to rely on his own accumulated wisdom and judgment and to link local voters into the electoral process. It holds that representative accountable to the district. Deliberation ties his actions to the district's interest. The voters then have the opportunity to deliberate on those actions, asking themselves if those actions fit the district's objective interest. Thus the relationship between the representative and the represented is crucial. It can be built most effectively if deliberation and decision precede justification. As Burke's own speech shows, such justification is an essential part of the representative's job. My observations convinced me that in the hands of a competent Burkean representative, serving an appropriate district through the approach of *deliberate, decide, justify* can be a sound reelection strategy.

Burkean 1: The Suburban Burkean

[Y]ou elect me because of who I am. I'm going to come down here and make some decisions. If you don't like a decision I make, let somebody else [do it.] So I don't get hung up on . . . 'how does this affect my district?' My district elect[s] me based on who I am to come down here and make some decisions. . . . You don't elect somebody down here that's gonna take a poll, because if you do, you don't need me down here. And so that's my attitude.

—*Burkean 1*

9. Ibid., 95.

Burkean 1 has limited patience when it comes to political theories. Happy to help me with my study, he was nevertheless unsure about the value of academic theory in general. "A lot of time, theory doesn't cut the mustard," he told me. "Theory and reality are two different things." It is particularly appropriate that this legislator's style is described by Burke: another practical politician who criticized his contemporary political theorists. Like Burke, Burkean 1 believes he was sent to the capitol to do what is best for the state (though "the state" obviously has a different meaning here—a subunit of a nation-state instead of the nation-state itself). Like Burke, Burkean 1 did not get "hung up on" how a given decision would affect his district. This makes for a sharp contrast with most of the other subjects of this study. During our interview, Burkean 1 argued that his district's wealthy, secure status allowed him to act as a Burkean legislator.

Burkean 1 reinforced his home style with two themes: respect in the capitol and a unique approach to constituent service. On the first point, he stressed his ten years in office. In a statehouse where the average length of tenure is five and a half years, Burkean 1's decade in office gave him an advantage in "historical-institutional knowledge" (his phrase, not mine, but very appropriate for political theory). Burkean 1 said, "I've been here a while and I think they [other house members] respect my judgment." He continued: "I'm not one who will speak on the house floor a lot, but when I do, it gets quiet. People want to listen to what I've got to say." In addition, before election to the statehouse, Burkean 1 served on his local, suburban city council. According to him, this gave him a head start on his current job—in particular, it prepared him for dealing with constituent service requests and helped him build name recognition among active constituents. At home, Burkean 1 sometimes stressed his conservative stands on controversial issues. Some of these issues were not related to pending house legislation. For example, he was outspoken in denouncing President Clinton for his extramarital affair and resulting legal troubles. Meanwhile, in the capitol, he did not vote a strict party line. He sometimes departed from the conservative approach. Most notably, he rarely consulted his district to make up his mind on day-to-day concerns.

Burkean 1 did not believe that his relationship with his home district was central to effective representation. Note the quotation above:

"I don't get hung up on . . . 'how does this affect my district?'" After our interview, he asked me if I was sure that I wanted to follow him in his home district. As an alternative, he invited me to "shadow" him while he went about his business in the capitol. He was not initially convinced that following him in his district was the best way to study him. I insisted, and he turned out to be quite welcoming and supportive of my project. His constituents were too. But Burkean 1 clearly focused on the capitol, not his home district, as the place where serious state decisions were made. His point of view on this topic gives further insight into the Burkean legislator at work.

Burkean 1 did not have unlimited patience for his constituents or for my questions. I breezily introduced a new topic by suggesting that his constituents might ask, "What do we pay you for?" I was emphatically corrected when he said, "I would tell them, 'You offend me by coming down and saying you're paying me.' Because if you multiply it out, I'm probably making less than minimum wage from what they're paying me. So, ask me the question, saying, you know, in your job, 'If I've got a problem, how can you help me?' And I'd be willing."

This quote highlights several elements of Burkean 1's presentation to his district. The first concerns the limits to his patience. He tried to help, but would not invest unlimited time and effort. As he said in the quotation above, "If you don't like a decision I make, let somebody else [do it]"—in other words, his constituents were free to send someone else to the capitol to make the decisions they wanted him to make. The second element is that Burkean 1 was frustrated by the low pay of Missouri state representatives: about $23,000 per year as of 1998. "You need to give me a raise," he told me. But the most important element is the way in which he reframed my question. For him, the relationship with his constituents was one of constituent service—"If I've got a problem, how can you help me?"—but not consulting the district to make up his mind on the issues. Moreover, even for casework, his patience had its limits.

Burkean 1 is a Republican. His electoral base included large sections of the two largest towns in his suburban district: *New Town*, his home, and neighboring *West Heights*.[10] He felt so secure in his "homogenous" base that he referred to these towns as "*my* New Town

10. The italics indicate a pseudonymous place name. See Appendix IV.

and West Heights." He spent more effort cultivating support in other parts of the district, where his name recognition was weaker and Democrats were more popular. Two days after our interview, I observed him in working-class *Springfield*, at the edge of the district. He and other state and school officials were giving awards to the local wrestling team, the state champions. At that gathering of several hundred people, mostly students, Burkean 1 was the only African American in the gym. But he looked right at home as he stood with the others to congratulate his young constituents and solicit applause for the team from the students in the bleachers.

Making appearances in certain sections of the district was part of Burkean 1's electoral strategy. After his first election, he looked at his voting percentages precinct by precinct. Though pleased to have won by ten points overall, he was not satisfied. He concentrated his name-recognition efforts on those areas where he did most poorly. Not only did he congratulate the high-school wrestlers each year, but he also appeared in innumerable parades. He also spoke to classes of fourth-graders, again targeting the parts of the district where he got the fewest votes in his first election. In addition to helping educate students, he hoped word would get out among teachers and parents, enhancing his name recognition. While he put emphasis on certain places, he did appear at events throughout the district. The places he targeted most were both working-class and Democratic. Burkean 1 was pleased with the results. Though he had to refocus on different precincts due to early-1990s redistricting, he was leading or drawing even with the Democrats in the working-class parts of the district, while leading overwhelmingly in the wealthier, more Republican areas.

When Burkean 1 first ran for state representative in his overwhelmingly white district, some people asked him about his campaign literature. They said, "Are you sure you want to put your picture on there? They'll know you're black!" Burkean 1 replied, "What you see is what you get!" He did put his picture on the literature and won by ten points. He did not think that his Democratic opponents had made race an issue, though some "renegades," he said, tried to "play little racial games" from time to time. One year, someone wrote a racial slur on a "Burkean 1 for state legislature" sign. According to Burkean 1, this worked in his favor. He stressed that the Democratic candidates did not play these "racial games," only a handful of people who acted on their own. "It turned people off," he said. That year, he won by a larger margin than before.

His personal appearance was a striking aspect of Burkean 1's self-presentation. Near the end of our interview, he proudly pointed to photos of his grandchildren and praised them, just as one would expect a good grandparent to do. Nevertheless, I was shocked. Burkean 1 looked much too young to be a grandparent. I had assumed that his own children were perhaps high-school age, maybe younger. He looked fit and healthy, and dressed very well. Like most legislators, he wore a suit to work at the capitol. At many in-district gatherings, he wore a sport coat over a sweater. The only time I saw him dressed casually was when he was speaking to the fourth-graders. He wore a clean, white "Burkean 1 for state representative" T-shirt (even though it was not an election year) under the unzipped jacket of a name-brand athletic warm-up suit. When he told the children that he was a grandfather, several of them shouted back, "You don't look it!" He thanked them for the compliment and moved on. All legislators pay some attention to their appearance, but among them, Burkean 1 stood out as especially sharp. Even his choice of clothes presented Burkean 1 as a professional man who took his job seriously.

His everyday appearance was important, because he never knew when he might meet a constituent. He stayed in an inexpensive motel during the legislative session and, like most legislators, he went home every weekend. He told me, "No matter how important you feel down here, when you go home you still have to take the trash out. You've got to mow the lawn." Of going home, he said, "It's a very humbling experience." While he went to in-district meetings regularly, he also told me, about interactions with constituents, that "the most significant part of it is probably informal." Many people recognized him and stopped to chat. He even told a story of being pulled over by a police officer who just wanted to thank him for having his grade-school-age daughter come to the capitol to be "page for a day." (Burkean 1 was easy to spot on the highway, because he chose to display the optional state representative license plates on his car.) The officer said that his daughter was so proud that she took every houseguest into her room to see her "page for a day" certificate. When schoolchildren visited him in the capital, he sent them home with a packet of coloring books, as well as maps (for the parents), all supplied to his office by various state agencies. Finally, he sent a community service directory to all households in the district, in order to help constituents reach government officials (including himself) and keep emergency numbers handy. This also helped with name recognition.

Among the congressmen he studied, Fenno found that the type of district represented (homogenous or heterogeneous) affected the home style of its representative. Burkean 1 would probably agree. Although there was some diversity of income level, most of his constituents were securely middle-class. Burkean 1 argued, "When you represent a district that's upper-middle-class, upper-middle-income, they have fewer problems. They are less concerned." Thus the wealth and homogeneity of his district allowed him to adapt a Burkean style, and also resulted in fewer constituent service problems: "You're going to have your isolated situations, where people are going to have some specific needs, but as a whole, I think . . . I'm fortunate."

A former party whip, Burkean 1 saw party affiliation as a pragmatic decision. "To be honest . . . I'm not a party person," he said. Busy with his outside job at a local greeting-card company, he did not have time to go to local party meetings. He regarded those meetings primarily as social gatherings. He discussed the party switch that most African Americans made in the twentieth century: moving from Republican to Democrat. Then he made his central point:

> The black community [asks], "Why do you want to be a Republican?" I say, "[Do] all white folks put . . . their eggs in one basket, or have you got white folks that are Democrats, Republicans, and Independents?" "Well, they're all of them." So I say, "Well, why should all black people be Democrats?" "Oh." And I say . . . "I have a good example of that: 1994. When Republicans took over Congress, darn, we don't have any blacks that are chairmen of committees anymore, do we? That's because we don't have any blacks that are Republicans . . ." So, they're starting to understand.

As mentioned, Burkean 1's district was overwhelmingly white; in his words, it was "98 percent non–African American." Yet, after announcing that he is not a party person, he ended by concluding that being a Republican was a pragmatic decision to help the African American community, which was mostly outside his district. During our interview, he stressed his dissent from the party on statehouse votes concerning affirmative action, day care, and, in the 1980s, divestment from South Africa. He called himself a "three-quarter-tank conservative" and criticized other Republicans who "get that tunnel vision" and refuse to depart from the "full conservative" party line, even when good judgment calls for it. In this case, we were discussing a bill that had been proposed to offer state subsidies for day care in public schools. Burkean 1 supported the bill on the grounds that it would speed people off welfare by giving them affordable child care. Most statehouse Republicans, particularly those from rural districts, opposed the bill. (The bill passed in the 1998 session and the governor signed it into law.)

Burkean 1 did maintain his conservative credentials at home. In 1998, I attended two legislative forums with him on separate weekends. At both, he made a point of attacking the Canadian health care system for its "government health care" and "long waiting lines." According to Burkean 1, another representative sponsored a bill every year to create a Canadian-style health care system in Missouri. That bill is "always DOA," he told one chamber group. If he did not think that Canadian-style health care is a salient issue in Missouri politics, then why did he bring it up? Apparently, it was his way of reassuring his conservative constituents that he was probusiness, that he was on their side. It served a rhetorical function. Some of his colleagues saw Burkean 1 as a moderate Republican. Another representative I interviewed said that Burkean 1 "might as well be a Democrat" given his voting record. But by attacking the political left on a "DOA" issue like socialized health care, Burkean 1 could shore up his conservative support.

Following Burkean 1 in 1999, I watched him take a more combative stance on hot-button social issues. This highlights the value of "home style" research. I would never have seen this side of him if I had just interviewed him. Of all the representatives I interviewed, only one or two mentioned the controversy surrounding President Clinton's extramarital conduct and the ensuing impeachment trial. The story of the White House affair had just broken when I interviewed Advocate 1, for instance, and he made vague, disapproving references to it. Several other representatives said that their constituents "don't want me to embarrass them," which might have been a comment on Clinton's troubles. Of all these representatives, only Burkean 1 focused on this issue with constituents. He was disgusted and made no secret about it.

His most outspoken moments came at "Legislative Appreciation Sunday," held at an evangelical Christian church just outside the district. Several Missouri legislators, including Burkean 1, Advocate 6, and Rep 1, were in attendance. All were Republicans. Clinton's impeachment trial had just concluded, with a sharply divided Senate voting for acquittal on all charges. In a service attended by over a thousand parishioners, the pastor made clear his church's conservative stands: against abortion, opposed to the teaching of evolution in public schools, and critical of the American Civil Liberties Union. The pastor also let parishioners know that House Speaker Dennis Hastert was a personal friend. Next, each elected official in turn thanked the pastor and stated a concern for family values. Advocate 6 was somewhat broad in her speech, stressing her faith as a Catholic but avoiding specific stands on the issues. Rep 1 read a poem by a southern Missouri judge that denounced the teaching of evolution in public schools and the legalization of abortion. In addition, Rep 1 said that a recent poll showed that 68 percent of the state's residents—including his own constituents, he noted—advocated the separation of church and state. "They don't think we should be here today," he said. Then he added, "Did you see that letter in the [local newspaper]? It simply said, 'Two thousand years ago they took a poll. Most chose Barabbas over Jesus.'" Thus Rep 1 set a theme: conservatives were outnumbered, but right. Burkean 1 picked up on it, and when his turn came, he delivered the punchline:

> It would not surprise me if the ACLU filed suit against us for being here today. Greetings from our church, things are going well. . . . Today, society is about labels—your house, where you live and work, your church. People let those form their opinions. One constituent wrote me comments on my newsletter. It was meant to insult, but I took it as a compliment. He wrote, "Your far-right politics doesn't serve us. You're for less government at the expense of progress." To which I say, "Right on, brother, amen!" [Applause]
>
> The lack of morals today is serious. The worst is Bill and Monica! The world is in awe of them. It reminds me of an old

hymn, "Yield not to temptation . . ." Monica's lipstick color is
now a popular new shade: people want to wear the same lipstick
as her. What is the world coming to?

God bless you, America. [Sustained applause]

President Clinton's behavior, though ignored by most other representatives in this study, provided Burkean 1 with a new way to solid-
ify his conservative credentials and personal character. He attacked
Clinton in front of a supportive crowd. Before church, Burkean 1 and
Rep 1 appeared as guests on the pastor's local radio show, where I
heard them stress their opposition to abortion and assisted suicide, as
well as their disgust with Clinton. The impeachment issue did not
relate directly to Burkean 1's job in the statehouse. He did not vote
on the President's impeachment. Burkean 1 stressed his ideological
leanings with constituents, but did not ask their opinions on day-to-
day legislation. For him, reelection was a referendum on character,
and, thus, fitness to serve in office.

The above exchange also highlights Burkean 1's close working relationship with Rep 1. Both were Republicans, representing neighboring suburban districts. Their political views varied somewhat. Rep
1's voting record was closer to that of a "full-tank" conservative, compared to Burkean 1's "three-quarter-tank" record. Yet they worked
closely together, appearing as a team at many legislative forums. By
stressing where they agreed, these exchanges gave Burkean 1 chances
to burnish his conservative label with his suburban constituents. The
"Proposition B" (concealed-carry firearms) debate offered Burkean 1
another such opportunity.

A supporter of concealed-carry, Burkean 1 had little patience for
those on the other side of the debate. Before the election, he wore his
"Yes on B" button when he spoke to chamber of commerce and school
district forums (he attended both with Rep 1, who also supported a
"yes" vote). I watched as he confidently told each group of constituents
that "B" would pass with at least 60 percent of the vote. In fact, the
proposal was narrowly defeated due to high turnout and a strong "no"
vote in suburban areas. Prior to the election, Burkean 1 not only predicted passage, but denounced those who were opposed to the proposition. Editorialists in the local daily newspaper advocated a "no" vote,
worrying over the possibility that those convicted of certain nonfelony
crimes would get concealed-carry permits. At a chamber meeting,

Burkean 1 mentioned the newspaper editorialists by name, and accused them of "lying" to "scare people" about the issue. He also denounced the governor for his opposition, adding, "Liberals want the government to do everything, and then you have no rights." Finally, he took on some law-enforcement agencies that endorsed a "no" vote, saying that "police officers are for this, it's the top brass that's against it." Burkean 1 may have departed from "full-tank" conservativism on a few issues, but on some of the most emotional and contentious ones he made clear his strong conservatism. This outspokenness was much more visible to me in 1999 than in the previous year.

Though he was strongly conservative on some issues, Burkean 1 stressed his prerogative to depart from the party on key votes. A good Burkean, he let his own judgment, not constituent preferences or party discipline, determine his votes. He did not follow a responsible-party model. In addition to his conservatism on hot-button issues and his desire to provide some balance for the black community, there is another reason why Burkean 1 might have chosen to be a Republican. He assessed the district's political makeup as follows: "I would say the political mix is over 50 percent Republican. The next group are people that consider themselves being independent. I would say maybe 30 percent independent, and less than 20 percent Democrat." Thus, Burkean 1's party choice was likely to give him an advantage in a Republican district. But the core of his representational strategy was the Burkean strategy, not partisanship. He shored up support for his own integrity so he could "come down here and make some decisions" for the district.

Constituent service was important for Burkean 1, as for all the representatives I studied. He was especially grateful for the longtime experience of his legislative assistant, who was invaluable in meeting these requests. Yet his approach to constituent service also contrasted with that of many others. Advocates 3 and 4, for example, both told me that they had never had to say "no" to a constituent—not yet, anyway. By contrast, Burkean 1 did not hesitate when he felt it necessary to say "no." During our interview, he said:

> Now, like that letter I just got done. A lady . . . was upset because she had applied for unemployment compensation and she was denied. So I checked with the Department of Labor, and

they said she was denied it because she was not fired. She quit her job. And the referee for the Department, whoever looks at it, said, "Hey, you don't qualify for unemployment compensation when you quit your job, period." So I wrote her a letter trying to explain all that to her. She sends me another little letter, getting snotty, saying, "I'm a registered voter." I don't care about you being a registered voter. If I won by one vote, maybe I would be concerned, but I didn't win by one vote. I won by four thousand votes. But that's not the point, the point is that I'm trying to help her, and she's getting an attitude about it. So I . . . will just tell her that there are limits to what I can do.

Burkean 1 said that his next letter to that constituent would be the last one he sends her. He was the only one of the twelve legislators I interviewed to tell me how absurd constituent requests can be. "In this job," he said, "[a] lot of weird things happen to you." He went on, "I had a lady once, she'd call my house every weekend because she went out to the lake and she said the water patrol and the highway patrol was shooting at her. And, as I start to inquire, I found out this lady didn't have all her furniture. She was a few pieces shy of having a full house. The lady had a mental problem."

After that incident, Burkean 1 started ignoring the woman's complaints. In addition to this story, he told me one about a neighboring legislator: "She has a constituent that calls her up periodically, even calls her down here, and he's got aluminum foil on his head to keep the zap gun from his neighbor from penetrating his brain." It may be that Burkean 1's efforts toward name recognition resulted in more requests, including a few that were unreasonable or strange. John R. Johannes found that congressmen with more seniority get more casework requests. This might also apply at the statehouse level. Burkean 1's conservative leanings may play a role, too. Patricia K. Freeman and Lilliard E. Richardson Jr. found that among state legislators, those who favor limited government tend to do more constituent service work.[11] At any rate, though, Burkean 1 was willing to help, but also much bolder about saying "no" than others I interviewed.

11. John R. Johannes, "The Distribution of Casework in the U.S. Congress: An Uneven Burden," 532; Patricia K. Freeman and Lilliard E. Richardson Jr., "Exploring Variation in Casework among State Legislators," 48.

There was a strong pride and confidence in Burkean 1's self-pre-sentation. This was clear from both his physical appearance and the way he discussed his qualifications. He saw himself as well qualified to "make some decisions," and he would not spend endless time with eccentric or stubborn constituents. In the quotation above, it can be seen that Burkean 1's confidence was based in part on his electoral security. He admitted that he might be more responsive to difficult constituents if he had won by one vote. But since he did not, he had the confidence to set limits with constituents. He believed that most were pleased with his leadership. He argued that his reelection mar-gins demonstrated that. Finally, it should be noted that the story about the man with aluminum foil on his head has become some-thing of a legend: Advocate 1 mentioned it to constituents during a legislative forum. But the context was different. Advocate 1 was us-ing the story primarily for its entertainment value, while Burkean 1 mentioned it in order to stress that there were limits to his constituent service.

As noted, Burkean 1 also had limited tolerance for constituents who expressed their views. Like most Missouri legislators, Burkean 1 sent a newsletter out every year with a mail-in survey on pressing issues. He used the surveys primarily in two ways. First, he looked at the constituents' self-reported party identification, to get an idea of what the partisan breakdown was in the district. Second, he read the open-ended comments. Many constituents wrote things like, "I ap-preciate your asking me." But here again, Burkean 1 refused to use the comments in deciding his views on the issues. He told me, "I had a person say, 'Well, you voted this way, and it don't reflect me,' and I say, 'It probably reflected somebody else in the district.'" In his afore-mentioned church presentation, Burkean 1 pleased his conservative audience by criticizing one constituent's negative comments. Of course, he kept the writer's identity anonymous.

Burkean 1 had clearly used the incumbency advantage to build up secure reelection margins. A strong Burkean legislator, he relied on his own judgment to make key votes, while showing his constituents his ideological leanings on hot-button social issues and his support for business. He was comfortable with the "good old conservative val-ues" of the Republican party, but would not let party loyalty eclipse his own judgment on important votes. He presented himself as a veteran, family man, church founder, and public servant. An opponent of term limits, he stressed that decisions should be made by those most qualified and experienced, such as himself. He believed he had the moral character and support at home to make decisions, and did not hesitate to contrast himself with others—even the President of the United States—whom he believed did not. Further, he relied on his own judgment, not on a circle of advisors, to decide how to build name recognition and trust in the district. Studying his behavior and self-presentation provides insight into how a Burkean legislator from an upper-middle-class, suburban district can "come down here and make some decisions." The next legislator to be discussed, Burkean 2, also relied on character and judgment to make decisions and then justified them to constituents. Yet his district, and his approach, contrast somewhat with suburban Burkean 1.

Burkean 2: The Commonsense Burkean

Edmund Burke is a friend of mine. I've spent a good deal of time with him. I follow many, if not all, of his ideas. I find a good deal of the Burkean influence in American political leadership, such as, well, the Founding Fathers.

I believe in virtual representation as often as I do in actual representation. I don't believe in asking my folks how I should vote on many issues. I will frequently try to read the impulses that are there on issues, but more often than not, I think I have been sent to [the capital] to exercise common sense, to—again, this goes right back to what I said earlier, which is a very imprecise way of doing business, but— . . . to do the right thing, and to be a free moral agent.

—Burkean 2

Recently, state legislators have begun communicating with the public through E-mail and World Wide Web sites. But it is rare indeed to meet a representative whose official web page cites the works of Plato and Burke! Nor do we usually expect legislators to mention V. O. Key during interviews. Burkean 2 is that unusual representative.

I discovered him by reviewing the websites posted by legislators in his state. I followed Burkean 2's E-mail link and requested his participation in the study. He agreed readily, and we met soon afterwards in his district. Clearly, Burkean 2's citation of political theory is the most explicit of any representative in the study. This is easily traceable to his background: a Ph.D. in American history and employment as a professor and as president of two small, private universities (one in another state and one in his district).

Burkean 2's academic background shows when he presents himself. He is eminently articulate and quotable. "If you were to ask some other people in the house in [this state], 'What is it about [Burkean 2] that is different?' I would bet you that most of them would say, 'His vocabulary,'" he told me. When Burkean 2 first came to the house, Advocate 4 nicknamed him "Dr. Strangeword" because of his verbosity. According to Advocate 4, Burkean 2 sometimes used terms that went over his colleagues' heads. His fellow legislators often said that they had to cut their remarks short in order to make more time for Burkean 2. I observed one state senator joke about this at a forum, and Burkean 2 told me that this was not an isolated incident. Even his constituents seemed to tease Burkean 2 about his longwindedness.

Burkean 1, the professional, embodied the Burkean notion of representation, but he never mentioned the British theorist by name. In contrast, Burkean 2, the professor, cited Burke often and worked hard to integrate Burkean ideas into his own political practice. In representing the interests of his district, Burkean 2 often struggled with state agencies and others on behalf of constituents. Ever the good Burkean, he saw that those in the district, and others, have a common interest with the state. He labeled that interest "common sense," and he addressed it through constituent service.

Common sense is Burkean 2's theme. His presentations of himself revolve around it. The theme provides a link between this highly educated former college president and his small-town constituents. One of his favorite books is Philip K. Howard's *The Death of Common Sense: How Law is Suffocating America,* which he cited in detail during our interview. Howard argues that government works too hard to micromanage public policy in both the private and public sectors, with regulations that are overly detailed. According to Howard, this leaves little or no room for individuals to exercise discretion or adjust to circumstances when implementing the law. Burkean 2 agrees with Howard, and he often cites examples of how government and academia are suffocating individual judgment. Howard's book consists mostly of stories showing how government programs fail due to overregulation. Burkean 2 likes to add his own stories to Howard's, illustrating this death of common sense.

During the interview, Burkean 2 became quite heated as he discussed his frustrations with bureaucracy. In one case, Emergency Medical Technicians (EMTs) were disciplined for "performing surgery" without the proper licensing. The "surgery" consisted of cutting a V shape in a patient's ingrown toenail to relieve pressure. The EMTs were Burkean 2's constituents. Burkean 2 railed against the agency official who disciplined them, and he worked hard and successfully to get that official removed from his job. "There's another case [of the death of common sense]," he told me angrily. "You know, some people just cannot restrain themselves when they get a little authority!"

Burkean 2 often juxtaposed his hard work in defense of common sense with the actions of the "damn fools" who oppose it. He got upset when discussing a local water-treatment plant. The biggest town in his district needed a new plant to keep up with demand. However, the permit to build it was held up in environmental disputes. As he told it:

> The latest order that came down, about three weeks ago, was to build two new facilities, two new wastewater-treatment plants. One would be used for about a two-year period . . . while they build the other one, which would be the long-lasting, the durable one. . . . The argument was over two things. One was the possibility that a rare mollusk was in that river. They didn't find any. They've not seen any evidence that it was there, but the environmental conditions were such that it must be there. Now, that's a damn-fool notion! That's, that's number one—that's a Death of Common Sense Award right there! The other was that we're dealing with something like two parts per billion of a chemical, and it's a . . . herbicide. Now two parts per billion approximates—we can't be very precise with this—but it approximates one teaspoon of liquid stirred into a railroad tank car of

liquid. . . . Well, I just, I went with the city people over to the Secretary's office in [the Department of Health and Environment] and I said, 'I'm here to talk with you about reasonableness.' In ten minutes I left, and I was able to prevail, again largely because of common sense.

While most "damn fools" were in the bureaucracy, some were liable to be Burkean 2's own colleagues. During our interview, he referred to a fellow legislator as "the biggest damn fool I have ever seen!" In the extended quotation above, he refers to his idea for a "Death of Common Sense Award," which he discussed with me in some detail. His idea was based on former U.S. Senator William Proxmire's famous "Golden Fleece Awards." Proxmire gave his awards to government agencies that he believed were wasting taxpayers' money. If Burkean 2 ever implements his plan for a Death of Common Sense Award, it will be given to government agencies or employees who, in his eyes, overregulate their own subordinates, local governments, and the populace in general. He told me: "I have thought very seriously of . . . having a scroll or something prepared that confers the citation of various and sundry folks for having contributed to the death of common sense. . . . Well, [I may] come up with a Death of Common Sense Award one of these days!" I followed up, asking, "Who's going to get the award?" He replied: "Well, there would be many candidates. There would be no dearth of candidates for that award. Government has a way of shooting itself in the foot, particularly the bureaucracy."

By stressing the death of common sense, Burkean 2 often reframed simple constituent-service issues into ideological struggles on behalf of the state's people. While many other legislators I met quoted Tip O'Neill's maxim "All politics is local," Burkean 2 believed that he was doing more than just constituent service. He was, in fact, struggling to bring common sense back into a process where it sometimes seemed absent. He told me that he liked to restrain the government's excesses. He also believed that "government will take care of itself. It doesn't need any help." He therefore directed his constituent service toward restraining abuses by the bureaucracy.

Burkean 2 talked about the death of common sense when he met with constituents. Before our interview, I observed him speaking at two legislative forums. They occurred on two different weekends, in two different parts of the district. At each, he stressed his opposition to the state's long, detailed constitution. He told constituents that the U.S. Constitution is a better model due to its brevity. The issue arose while he stated his opposition to a legislature-initiated referendum. If approved, it would have changed provisions of the oil severance tax that are written into the state constitution. Burkean 2 did not believe that the oil severance tax should be in the constitution at all. Instead, he felt, it should be handled by regular legislation. (The voters rejected the provision in 1999.) He also mentioned the long state constitution during our interview. He told me: "In [this state], we try to get every damn thing moving into the constitution! We have not learned our lesson!" This follows closely Howard's argument: too many details are encoded into law, making it harder to adjust to circumstances. For Burkean 2, as for Howard, this adjustment process is the essence of common sense, and legislators and bureaucrats have yet to "learn their lesson" about leaving room for discretion.

Burkean 2 is quite serious in his dedication to Burkean principles, as evidenced in the quotation above in which he states that his constituents chose him to be a "free moral agent." He demonstrated just how serious he is about this when asked to sign a no-new-taxes pledge. He refused, saying he wouldn't "handcuff myself." The taxpayers' association wooed him for several election cycles, noting that they had given him a 94 percent approval rating. In the face of this pressure, he became more adamant still. He defended his prerogative to be a "free moral agent." He told me: "It is not only, anymore, 'no,' it is, 'Hell no, and don't ask me again!'"

This decision left Burkean 2 with a new responsibility—how would he explain his approach to his constituents? Few constituents in any district seek higher taxes. Further, small-town Kansas is known for a generally conservative approach to taxes and government.[12] Burkean 2 justified his decision to voters by pointing to something they all care about: highways. Instead of explaining his decision in terms of abstract political theory, as he did with me, he told his constituents about it in concrete terms. He said, "We're not going to

---

12. Marvin Harder and Carolyn Rampey, *The Kansas Legislature: Procedures, Personalities, and Problems,* 79.

have . . . a major highway campaign, highway program, without new taxes." Here he discovered a statewide interest, but one of special concern in his district. He used this to justify his broader, Burkean approach to the tax pledge.

Both the north-south and east-west arteries of Burkean 2's district were two-lane highways, connecting the two major towns he served with each other, the nearby metropolitan area, and the larger college town a few miles away. Accidents were common, with occasional fatalities, and there was strong sentiment for widening the roads to four-lane, divided highways. Constituents believed that this would reduce accidents that occurred when vehicles crossed the center line into oncoming traffic. (Ombuds 4's district, over a hundred miles away in another state, had a very similar problem.) At one forum, I observed a constituent tell Burkean 2 that she wanted to see the road widened because a relative was killed on it several years ago. I observed more constituents ask him about the highways than about any other issue. During the course of my research, the Kansas Legislature passed a highway program that included the money to widen these roads. The governor signed the bill into law. It did include gasoline-tax increases. Burkean 2 had left himself free to vote for the rare tax increase he thought was needed both statewide and back home. Having helped the highway program pass, it remained to be seen how Burkean 2 would justify his Burkean approach to constituents in the future.

"The voters deserve an explanation" for tough votes, Burkean 2 told me. A Burkean to the core, he relied on his own judgment to make the tough decisions. But his long-winded comments at legislative forums were intended to tell constituents why he voted as he did. Another good example of his approach occurred when conservative house Republicans sponsored a bill to eliminate the sales tax on food. Burkean 2, a Republican himself, understood the appeal and the value of this bill. It would be good for both Kansas agriculture (important in his district) and lower-income taxpayers. Burkean 2 believed that his district was slightly below the median in terms of family income. Because sales tax on food is regressive, eliminating it would be especially valuable for the less-well-off in the district. Still he voted no. He explained to his constituents that the bill would have led to a revenue shortfall and massive cuts in education spending. Once again he found a specific "hook" on which to justify his Burkean decisions back home.

Like Burke, Burkean 2 believed that interests deserve representation in the legislature. During our interview, he lauded V. O. Key's work on pressure groups. "I think pressure groups are a good thing in society," he told me. "They're not to be deplored." He got along particularly well with the Farm Bureau. Agriculture is important to his district, and he often listened to the bureau articulate the needs of Kansas farmers. In return, the bureau approved of his voting record, gave him high ratings, and supported his reelection. But Burkean 2 also cited James Madison, saying that government should divide the influence of pressure groups.[13] He argued that there was a strong Burkean influence in our nation's founders. There is a simultaneous embrace and skepticism toward democracy evident in both the Burkean style and *The Federalist Papers*. Democracy and the representation of interests are celebrated, but also require sources of control. Of course, the Federalists argued that representative democracy, bicameralism, and separation of powers acted as the checks.

Lately, some scholars have taken Burke to task for his elitism. It has been suggested that Burke's notion of deliberation toward good policy leads to entrenched control by a political and social elite.[14] While these criticisms may be valid, it must be emphasized that Burkeans do not equate the political and social elite with the moneyed elite. Both Burkeans in this study support higher pay for state legislators. Other legislators I interviewed did not bring up this topic. Higher pay would ensure that those most qualified can serve regardless of their personal financial circumstances. The two Burkeans did not assume that those with independent sources of wealth are the ones most qualified to participate in deliberative democracy. For them, being a member of the elite is a matter of character, experience, and work background, not personal wealth. (Nor, they felt, does formal education necessarily confer good judgment. The legislator that Burkean 2 called "the biggest damn fool I have ever seen" was highly educated, but, according to Burkean 2, had no common sense.) As mentioned, Burkean 1 told me, "You need to give me a raise." Burkean 2 added his own lament, pointing out that the pay is so low "you can't make a living in the legislature," and that it is "more and

13. V. O. Key, *Politics, Parties, and Pressure Groups;* Madison, "Federalist 10."
14. Lynn M. Sanders, "Against Deliberation," 359.

more a full-time job." It should be noted that Missouri legislators make somewhat more money than their Kansas counterparts.[15] However, neither state's legislators are as well paid as they would be in private-sector careers. Burkean 2 liked the idea of a "people's house" instead of a full-time, professional legislature. But he also believed that the pay should be sufficient to attract the best and brightest into public service. He said that at present, that is not the case.

The common-sense theme was also reflected in Burkean 2's work as chair of his state's House Higher Education Committee. He voted for a slate of moderates to lead the house, and was the first person offered a committee chair by the new leadership. Not surprisingly, political strategy played a role in his selection. He told me, "The secret is to vote for the winners." But there was another important factor in his assignment as education chair. Burkean 2 understood that it was his résumé, not the characteristics of his district, that got him the chairmanship. As a Ph.D. and past university president, he was deemed particularly qualified for the job. His district did have two small, private universities. There was also a community college and, of course, public-school districts. Yet his district was little different in this regard from any number of others across the state. The area included no major state universities. Contrast this situation with that of Ombuds 3 and 4, both of whom sat on the Education Committee because their districts included major state university campuses. They were put on the committee, in essence, to represent the interests of their districts. This brings the Burkean approach of Burkean 2 into sharper focus; even his own party leadership chose him due to his personal background, not the district he represents. As Pitkin points out, Burke believed that interests should be represented, but he did not always tie these interests to characteristics of the representative's home district.[16] It would be hard to find a better illustration of this aspect of Burkean representation than Burkean 2's appointment as education chair.

Burkean 2's leadership of the Education Committee was not tied to his district on a day-to-day basis. Given his reliance on Burkean principles, an examination of his chairmanship gives further insight

15. Hamm and Moncrief, "Legislative Politics in the States," 145.
16. Pitkin, *Concept of Representation*, 168–89.

into a trustee legislator at work. Burkean 2 told me that he had to work hard and be fair while leading the Education Committee. Yet he also had a strong philosophical bent. He had attended academic meetings featuring lectures by conservative scholar William Bennett, whom he quoted with approval. He came back to his common-sense theme, this time criticizing professional educators. He argued that they were removing the substantive content of education and replacing it with pedagogical methodology, to the detriment of students' learning. He told me that the principles of school accreditation in Kansas were "not clearly stated," and placed the blame for this squarely on the shoulders of professional educators. He continued: "There's a perverse style of English in there, if that's what it is. It's very difficult to read and understand. It is filled with gobbledygook. There are terms that professional educators use that very few other people understand, and I'm not certain the professional educators do."

Burkean 2 went on to say that he had "very quietly waged a battle" to translate these standards into plain English—common sense—once again. He had no kind words for the standards, telling me, "I'm not sure we know what the hell we're doing." I watched him proudly tell constituents that he had pushed through a bill to end open-admission practices at Kansas's larger state universities. Smaller state universities would be open-admission while the larger campuses would set higher academic standards.

The theme of setting high standards for the universities fits nicely with the Burkean approach. Burkean 2 even told me that poetry should be chosen for the classroom on the basis of its having survived several hundred years of scrutiny—that Shakespeare should have precedence over Maya Angelou (then adding, "Why not study them both, but certainly [study] Shakespeare more"). He went on to say, however, that as education chair he did not involve himself in day-to-day curriculum decisions. Still, such views give yet another glimpse into his philosophy and his Burkean approach: a high regard for tradition and a reluctance to change the curriculum. He denounced a proposal to offer diversity education classes at a nearby state university. Regarding the term *diversity education*, he asked me rhetorically, "What the hell does that mean? What does it mean?" Here again he showed esteem for tradition and established ways of teaching, and a strong opposition to what he saw as change for the sake of change.

However, he noted again that he did not generally get involved in ordinary curriculum decisions.

When the Kansas School Board voted to remove evolution from the recommended science curriculum in K-12 public schools, Burkean 2 opposed their move. In a meeting that received media coverage, he discussed the possibility of switching from an elected school board to an appointed one in order to avoid incidents like this in the future. The idea of reining in the excesses of democracy also embodies Burkean principles. In general, Burkean 2 had plenty of criticism for both the "education lobby" and the right-wing advocates of no-new-tax pledges and removing evolution from the curriculum. But in criticizing either the left or right, he maintained that decisions should be made by those most qualified.

Back home in his small-town district, Burkean 2's biggest reelection problem came from the district's population center. Two towns anchored the district: *Easton* and *Prairie Town*. Prairie Town was the larger town; Burkean 2 lived over twenty miles away in Easton, home of the small university he once headed. Because the population center of his district was some distance away, he faced a representational challenge. Every election, his Democratic opponents came from in or near Prairie Town, and argued that the district should have a Prairie Towner as its representative. Burkean 2 struggled, winning huge margins in *Easton County* while drawing nearly even with each opponent in *Prairie County*. He did not win elections overwhelmingly, but he seemed to hold the seat effectively. There seemed to be some rivalry between the two counties. I watched as Burkean 2 discussed highway problems in his district at a Prairie Town forum. He mentioned that some drivers were reckless on the local highways, and that he was recently passed in a no-passing zone. "I didn't see the county tag on the license plate . . ." he began, but before he finished, several voices in the crowd called out, "Easton County!" I could not ascertain why the Prairie Countians distrusted the drivers in the neighboring county. It might have had to do with young drivers going to and from the major college town in Easton County, just beyond Burkean 2's district.

Burkean 2 spent a lot of time visiting Prairie Town. He attended as many coffees as he could, and often stopped on the street to chat with constituents. Prairie Town has a caught-in-time, small-town feel, with downtown storefronts advertising farm-implement dealers, small local banks, all-American cooking, antiques, and the like. There is no shopping mall or discount store nearby, and the downtown does not have the seedy look of many other small towns where shopping opportunities have moved away. This provided a good place for Burkean 2 to be seen, and he visited Prairie Town whenever he could. What he did not do, however, was knock on doors. He worked hard to find other ways to gain name recognition. He told me:

> People who are effective in this business of winning elections will tell you that there's no way to win an election without going door-to-door. Well, I probably am living proof that that is not the case. I don't, however, recommend that you make much out of the fact that you didn't go door-to-door. Don't talk about it. If you're not going to do it, at least don't talk about it. I've found that newspaper advertising, thirty-second radio spots, thirty-second cable-TV spots, appearances at public gatherings, and those kinds of things help you get name recognition.

Burkean 2 also appeared at county fairs and parades, much like Ombuds 4, the other small-town/rural representative in the study. These kinds of appearances seem to be particularly important for rural representatives, though they do sometimes happen in urban communities. Burkean 1 often appears at "skillet days" and other parades in his outer-suburban district. Ombuds 3, one of the urban representatives I followed, also appeared in a parade, held in celebration of a gentrified city neighborhood's history and pride. Still, the comments and activities of Burkean 2 and Ombuds 4 seem to show that rural representatives have more unique opportunities to reach constituents. Advocate 4 hypothesized that his rural colleagues were much better known than the suburban legislators. This should come as no surprise. There are fewer legislators crowded into a rural area. Radio and even television airtime is more affordable. Unlike urban and suburban representatives, rural legislators do not have to rely so heavily on going door-to-door or using direct mail. By way of contrast, urban and suburban legislators often face communities in which the largest gathering places are shopping malls, not public squares. Burkean 2 had prevailed against Democratic opponents that do knock on doors, though not by a safe margin.

Even with his power and prestige in the house and name recognition at home, Burkean 2 did not expect the district to keep him in office forever. He saw two problems coming down the road. First, a department-store chain had opened a large distribution center in Prairie Town. This brought new workers to the community. These blue-collar employees were unionized, and most appeared to favor Democrats. In general, Democrats appeared to be highly competitive in the district. In spite of his lifetime membership in the National Education Association, Burkean 2 did not have close relationships with unions. "When I became a member, NEA was not a trade-union organization," he explained. He saw unions as the backbone of the Democratic party. As a Republican, he did not want to switch parties. He was very much a part of the moderate Republican delegation in the house, and he was quite comfortable there. Burkean 2 told me the story of an opponent who switched parties. This person ran against him unsuccessfully in the Republican primary, then ran as a Democrat, but lost just as badly in the general election. Burkean 2 argued that voters don't usually trust those who switch parties, because they look like opportunists.

Because of the partisan split in his district, Burkean 2 could not rely on his party label to get reelected. This situation sharply contrasts with that of many of the urban-area legislators, such as Burkean 1 and Advocates 2 and 5, whose party labels helped them enormously. Nor did Burkean 2 depend too heavily on the state GOP organization, embroiled as it was in infighting between its moderate and conservative wings. The party helped him with direct mail from time to time, but generally speaking, he took his reelection strategy into his own hands. To justify his decisions in the house, he stressed his judgment on statewide issues. When necessary, he tied them to local concerns. But he did not emphasize party stands.

The second problem Burkean 2 faced was an ambitious young college student in the district. This student had served as one of Burkean 2's interns just a few years ago, then won the mayoralty of Prairie Town. Now only twenty-one years old, this young man had impressed Burkean 2. In fact, Burkean 2 feared that his ex-intern was planning to run against him. "My neat trick, if I can pull it off, is to get out of here under my own steam before he decides to whip me!" he told me. As mayor, his possible opponent had name recognition and support in the district's population center. Burkean 2 speculated that the young man would run as a Republican and that the primary between the two of them would be very close. However, Burkean 2 thought he might have one more successful race in him. The house leadership had an education agenda for which they needed his help. Most notably, the school districts in the most sparsely populated part of the state, far away from Burkean 2's district, would perhaps need some consolidation. Also, the state's community college system had recently been restructured. More legislation would possibly be needed to implement these changes. The house leadership had asked Burkean 2 to stay around for three more sessions. This would mean serving out his current term, then running one more time.

Burkean 2 was considering his political future as this study went to print. But he had no plans to seek other elected offices. Like Advocate 3, he does not think state senators have nearly as much fun as house members. Burkean 2 stressed that the house is the "people's house," closer to the constituents. For him, the house has a special relationship to the people it serves, because most house members are not career politicians. Further, he noted that the people have more of a voice in the house, where sixty-three votes must be amassed to get a bill passed. The senate is a much smaller body, and coalition-building is not nearly so central to its functioning, he said. These thoughts are similar to Advocate 3's comments. Advocate 3 told me that the senators act more as individuals, not coalition builders (or coalition members). He told me that "the senate is about power," a remark that contrasts the senate with Burkean 2's view of the house as the "people's house." Burkean 2 has spent his own time in the house restructuring education policy, pushing for common sense, and struggling against "damn fools." He is living proof that an academic political theorist can be a politically viable candidate and officeholder in the modern era. For him, that's just common sense.

Conclusion

Jewell's lists of the four tasks that an effective modern state legislator must address are: communication with constituents, policy responsiveness, allocation of resources for the district, and constituent service. Burkean 1 did not see allocation of resources for the district as a major concern in his community, which was already prosperous and stable. But otherwise, the two Burkeans I observed worked to accomplish the four tasks and to present their accomplishments to the electorate at home.

I began this chapter with the Burkean's three-step system of deliberate, decide, justify. For these legislators, communication with constituents took the form of justifying a decision and the resulting action. They focused on explaining not just what they did, but why they did it, and how that decision benefited the state. Thus, communication was essential. As Burkean 2 said, "The voters deserve an explanation." Both Burkeans relied on their own judgment to make decisions, but they also went home to discuss their decisions. Each of them also often discussed his personal qualifications—character and experience—to make said judgments.

Burkeans ensure policy responsiveness with a focus on the state's overall good. Both Burkeans held committee leadership positions—Burkean 1 on motor vehicles and traffic safety, Burkean 2 on education—and both sponsored a substantial amount of legislation. They prided themselves on their work and believed that their expertise would lead to good decisions. Again, here they stressed a whole-state orientation. They presented themselves as qualified citizens elected from their particular districts to craft legislation that would be responsive to the needs of the whole state. They also sponsored fewer district-specific bills and projects than many of their counterparts.

When it came to allocation of resources for the district, Burkean 1 simply did not believe his district needed much from him. Thus he did not concern himself with district-specific projects. He invited me to join him at many meetings, but only one of them focused primarily on district-specific issues. It was sponsored by the Department of Transportation and dealt with highway projects in growing suburban areas, including his own and neighboring communities. I was at the meeting, but Burkean 1 was not. He had a last-minute scheduling conflict and decided not to attend. Burkean 2, by contrast, confronted district problems more often. Such problems included, for example, environmental permits for the new water-treatment plant. He worked hard to be responsive to district needs. Yet this academic "friend of Burke" was also careful to emphasize the benefit that his work had for the whole state—specifically, reining in "damn fools" who were a hindrance to common sense and thus making state government more responsive. In general, the Burkeans' whole-state orientation makes allocation of resources for the district a somewhat difficult issue, but it can be negotiated, as Burkean 2's approach shows. Some Burkeans might serve districts that are not particularly needy and that already have the state resources they seek. Burkean 1 believed this was the case with his community; thus, his approach fit the district.

Burkeans do their share of constituent service. But Burkean 1 stressed that his patience for such casework was limited, and he got fewer requests than many other legislators. Burkean 2 fit casework into his broader theme of restraining the "damn fools" and thus serving the whole state. When casework came in, Burkean 2 did not just address the specific request and get it resolved. He tried to get to the root of the problem and fix it. For example, he got the overzealous agency official removed from his job.

The two Burkeans took divergent approaches to progressive ambition. Burkean 1 was anxious for redistricting. He kept open the possibility of running for state senate or even Congress. Burkean 2, by contrast, wanted only to serve in the "people's house." Once he was done there, he did not plan to seek any other elective office. But whatever their ambitions, these Burkeans approached the legislator's job with a heavy reliance on their own character and judgment. They completed the tasks that a modern legislator must. They did not neglect the district. But throughout the process they continued to "deliberate, decide, justify." Whenever possible, they presented themselves as servants for the interests of the whole state.

4

In-District Advocates

Advocates place issues on the agenda instead of waiting for them to bubble up. In E. E. Schattschneider's words, they "socialize the conflict."[1] Advocates see themselves as community leaders. They do not wait for issues to come to them. They work aggressively to organize media appearances, forums, and other events that draw attention to their communities. While some of my other subjects discounted the value of town-hall meetings, I watched Advocates 2 and 3 draw hundreds of people to their town halls to discuss "hot" local issues (highways and violence, respectively). Further, those constituents were joined by local television and newspaper reporters.

The advocates described in this chapter all harbored progressive political ambitions. Advocate 1 suggested to me that he might run for either state senate or Congress, depending on upcoming redistricting. He was hoping for a new senate district to be drawn after the census, one that would be more Democrat-friendly. Advocate 2 had already announced his candidacy in his community's state senate district. Advocate 3 was planning to run for state senate when the incumbent retired, and Advocate 4 was considering a candidacy for state insurance commissioner. These advocates' seeking of publicity was an approach not only to reelection but also to building up name recognition throughout a larger area. State representatives must often cross district boundaries to serve school districts, cities, or towns, each of which may be only partially within their district. Thus, the in-district advocate's work builds name recognition in adjoining areas. This can help enormously in a state senate campaign or a run for some other higher office.

1. Schattschneider, *Semi-Sovereign People,* 7.

All of these advocates were defensive. They often found themselves representing communities that were in some sense struggling. They saw the quality of life in their districts as threatened by outsiders, or by forces that were difficult to control. For Advocates 1, 2, and 4, this meant feeling overlooked in favor of growing suburbs nearby. This was exemplified in Advocate 2's fight to keep open access to local roads after a major road-construction project. Advocate 3 focused on representing an urban community that was an anomaly in his state. Advocate 4 argued that he was preserving stability and quality of life in the face of changing growth patterns within his county.

Most of these legislators had seen substantial "white flight" out of their communities. Many younger, middle-income whites had left the communities of Advocates 1, 2, and 3. In the districts of Advocates 1 and 2, a different demographic group was moving in to replace them—mostly blacks in flight from the inner city. In Advocate 3's district, no one was replacing those who left. As a result, vacant housing was one of the major issues in his community. Advocate 2, who is white, and Advocate 3, who is black, served school systems that were predominantly African American. Each had to respond to the challenges that racial divisions posed to their communities.

Advocates 1 and 2 had large portions of senior citizens—more than 50 percent of the voting-age population—in their districts. Advocate 3's district had a great deal of inner-city poverty, including many senior citizens and young, single-parent families. There were few middle-class, two-parent families in his district. As their constituents aged, Advocates 1 and 3 emphasized senior-citizen issues such as pensions, health care, and insurance costs. Advocate 4 mentioned such concerns to me as well.

Most of these legislators saw little growth in property values in their areas. Advocate 4's wealthier district was the anomaly here. Property values were growing in his district, but Advocate 4 remained concerned. His community had a disproportionate number of senior citizens, leading to uncertainty as to who would occupy these homes in the coming decades. During a schoolteachers' meeting, one speaker mentioned that Advocate 4's celebrated school district was losing enrollment. I was surprised, and passed a note to Advocate 4 asking for an explanation. "We are losing the older kids to the districts [in the outer suburbs]," he wrote back. Thus, even he could be a little defensive about property values and stability in his area.

None of these districts showed significant population growth, and these advocates worried that their areas would lose political power as the metropolitan area grew around them and redistricting loomed. Advocates 1, 2, and 4 all harbored some fear that in the middle-class rush to the outer suburbs, their communities might one day become crumbling, low-property-value, high-crime areas such as Advocate 3's. For Advocate 4, whose district was still well maintained and middle-class, this fear was less pronounced. Still, he told me that constituents expected him to "keep out blight, which seems to have been very active in [Advocate 3's county]." (Advocate 3's county bordered Advocate 4's.)

This chapter shows how in-district advocates struggle to keep their communities viable. In the process, they build name recognition for themselves in preparation to run for other offices. If Burkean 1 represents constituents who are "less concerned" and "have fewer problems," these advocates' constituencies are *more* concerned. Their legislators must react to any number of problems, current or anticipated. The following descriptions show how four state representatives met these challenges.

Advocate 1: The Consummate Politician

When folks in [the capital] ask me what the people are like in *Grove City*, I tell them: "pro-gun, pro-life, pro–public education, and pro-labor."

I'm going to be political. But I'm a politician, and that's my right.

—*Advocate 1, speaking with constituents*

Advocate 1 is not ashamed to be a politician. He enjoyed the spotlight and made acquaintances easily, often stopping to chat with strangers. There was always another hand to shake, another friend to make, another local meeting to attend. He often referred to himself as "a politician"—even when he was among constituents. Though he was well aware that some hold lawyers in disdain, he also pointed proudly to his outside career as an attorney. He believed that lawyering made him well qualified to make state laws. The one-time president of his high-school class, and later of the school board, he was a party man, a delegate, and a trustee. Like most representatives in this study, Advocate 1 was a blend of representational styles, taking the approach that John Wahlke et al. label *politico*.[2] But this label does not give an in-depth understanding of representational strategy. Constituents and other representatives often told me that Advocate 1 was a "consummate politician" (and one constituent added, "with a heart of gold"). He was particularly adept at working within different models of representation. Thus the *politico* label does fit Advocate 1, but it does not provide a rich understanding of his behavior. Following him over two years, to at least a dozen appearances in his district, provided me with the chance to watch him move among his constituents. I label him an *advocate* because most of the time at home, he raised issues and placed them on the agenda. He frequently related these issues specifically to the district's well-being and argued that his background qualified him to represent that particular community. Further, he presented himself as a community leader.

With an undergraduate degree in political science, Advocate 1 easily framed his discussion of representation in terms of political theory, though I never prompted him to do so. During our interview, he said:

> I think there [are] two parts to legislators. There are some legislators down here, and this goes back to a political science debate, [who think that] you represent your constituents to the best of your ability. Or, are you here as their voice, and whatever they say isn't really that big of an issue, because you know more? You know they've trusted you with this decision. Those are two political science thoughts. . . .
>
> Clearly, what I do on the Judiciary Committee on a day-today basis has no impact on Grove City. Insurance, probably the same thing. . . . Social services, not quite the same. Appropriations, well, I help appropriate funds for buildings and growth.
>
> But you also sponsor legislation. I've got a bill now that's in-

2. Wahlke et al., *Legislative System*, 277–80.

quiring into insurance companies that sell nursing home cover-
ages, to be rated . . . Great bill for my district, and for senior citizens. But . . . it is a combination.

After more discussion, he picked up where he left off, saying: "I
think there's a combination. On issues like hog farming that don't affect my district (there are no hog farms in my district), I try to do
what's the best thing. If it is something that affects your district, you
do what affects your district. If my district doesn't want a railroad
train going through the district, I'm going to fight a railroad train. If
they want a railroad train coming through the district, I'm going to
try to help them get a railroad train."

Advocate 1 discussed partisanship later in the interview. But on
hog farming, he showed Burkean leanings. The same was true of
many issues that arose in committee. Advocate 1's constituents were
not particularly affected by some of these issues and he used his own
judgment to decide. Many legal changes that moved through the Judiciary Committee, for example, affected the entire state. Yet the legislation had no disproportionate impact on his own community, so
he took a "whole-state" approach. When acting as a Burkean (particularly in Judiciary), Advocate 1 relied on his background. As an attorney, he argued, he was more knowledgeable than some about legal processes. Thus he had special qualifications. When I asked him
about his committee requests, he said, "Of course, being a lawyer, I
chose Judiciary!" But he did not spend much time discussing these
types of issues at home.

Advocate 1 occasionally acted as an ombudsperson. He collected
the opinions of community leaders, letting them speak for the district. Then he voted the (perceived) will of his constituents. One example of this was the railroad controversy. I sat in as Grove City's
mayor, city manager, city attorney, and an alderman met to discuss
strategies for stopping the railroad expansion. All agreed that the
train should not come to the district because it would bring noise and
traffic problems. The city would also incur major expenses related to
upgrading certain railroad crossings, currently unused. Advocate 1
promised to pursue their antitrain agenda as zealously as he could,
telling them that he would "pound this issue—thump my chest about
the social and economic impact of this." He did not participate in the

articulation of what the district's interests were (at least not at first). But once local leaders took a stand, he promised to be their mouthpiece in the capitol. In this case, Advocate 1 counted on city officials to relay the conscience of the district. Yet his discussions at home rarely focused on the train issue. When meeting with constituents, he preferred to talk about issues on which he could take the lead. The political process of negotiating, debating, and defending constituents' interests was where Advocate 1 really thrived. Though occasionally an ombudsperson, he generally preferred a more aggressive presentation of himself when he was in front of more than just one or two constituents.

Advocate 1 generally adopted an advocate strategy at home. When meeting with constituents, he took the lead in articulating issues that were of special importance to the district. For example, he knew that his district had a large and growing portion of retirees. He worked to represent their best interests whenever he could—hence his nursing home bill. In general, he had a strong sense of the district's best interests. The inner-suburban community was populated by blue-collar families seeking to enroll their children in the local public schools and escape the nearby inner-city school district. Advocate 1 believed that the well-being of the schools was central to the stability of the aging community. In both local and state policy, he stressed education, which one would expect from a former school-board president. Yet as his community aged, retirees on fixed incomes often turned against the property taxes that funded local schools. Here, Advocate 1 moved into the advocate role: articulating the district's best interests, then using his politician's skills to try to build support among his constituents. In the older, working-class suburbs that he represented, he worked to sway voters toward support for the local schools. "You have to remind them that there is a continued need to make a city—a community—grow through public education," he told me. "You ask them the same rhetorical questions: why did you move here in the 1960s? Because of the public schools. We wanted property taxes. We wanted the tax. And it's kind of an education process."

As an advocate for the schools, Advocate 1 interacted with constituents and tried to forge a new consensus or restore an old one on the issue he cared about most passionately. It was an active process for him. It depended on his interactions with constituents. He did not simply reflect the consensus, he tried to create it. It could be frustrating. During the first busy day I observed him with his constituents, he did not get a single question or comment about the local schools, even when he attended a school-board event. The only school issues raised concerned the inner-city school district, outside Advocate 1's district. Constituents were concerned about an expensive, drawn-out desegregation lawsuit in the inner-city district. Thus being a responsible delegate involved "an education process" of trying to "remind" voters to support his cause. He was not always successful.

Advocates and ombudspersons each tend to focus on district-specific interests. Advocate 1's stand on local school issues is an example. But advocates try to *build* consensus, while ombudspersons try to *reflect* consensus. Consensus-building involves more agenda-setting activity, both in the district and beyond it. The idea is to educate constituents, work with them, and ultimately make, restore, or preserve a consensus. Consensus-reflecting, while still a lot of work, involves less activity in the district. When reflecting consensus, representatives use key contacts to relay a pre-made consensus to the representative, then work to get that consensus enacted in the capitol. Advocate 1 did not have to remind constituents, or educate them, about the railroad. He sat back and let local officials tell him what they wanted to accomplish. Then he worked toward their goals in the state capitol. In meeting with larger groups of constituents in chamber and school forums, Advocate 1 rarely discussed the train issue. Instead he talked about issues such as the local schools. As the district aged, he had to continually stump for his educational priorities, even when on his own home turf.

Advocate 1 took a strong stand when it came to his party. He was reelected quite easily in his heavily Democratic district. Yet he traveled around the metropolitan area and the state stumping for the party. He believed he could serve his district better if Democrats remained the majority party in the state legislature. He pointed out that Democrats were the supermajority in his district, and were thus likely to elect Democratic officeholders. A majority of Democrats in state office, he argued, helped his majority of Democrats back home. Advocate 1 often gave me the party line on issues. He claimed that the party deserved credit for the state's recent economic growth and resulting increase in state revenues—which were part of a nationwide trend. He attacked the Republicans on public-school issues, arguing that they sought to undercut the revenue base of schools with excessive tax cuts. He justified his approach by telling me, "I'm talking partisan, but I think it's important to our theme, our mission, and what we've accomplished."

Advocate 1 saw growing Republican strength in the legislature, and in his own metropolitan area, as antithetical to the best interests of public education and the working class. He thought those interests were crucial to his district. He saw Republican gains in the metropolitan area as an advancing battle line, and he fought to protect his flank. Wealthier suburban districts nearby had been electing Republicans recently, and Advocate 1 struggled to maintain a Democratic majority in what was once a one-party county. He told me: "The joke I always say is, I am the end of the line. Kind of like the battle of Gettysburg. If they get around me, we lose the entire war. I've got to hold the line. And I feel that way. I really do." To this end, he raised money for each of his campaigns, even though he anticipated easy reelection. He worked closely with neighboring Democrats and offered them financial support.

Obviously, election and reelection are crucial to the success of any legislator. Advocate 1 had a strong opponent when he first ran for an open seat. The Republicans nominated a World War II veteran with a long history of community involvement. Yet Advocate 1's party label helped him win the seat in his heavily Democratic district. Since then he had run unopposed. According to him, the Republicans kept a list of vulnerable Democrats. "I've seen their hit list . . . I'm not even on the list, because it's a Democratic district," he said. "I think it would take something very monumental for me . . . to be defeated."

How does a legislator become so safe after initially facing a formidable opponent? Advocate 1 thought that party labels were important. Yet he worked hard on other aspects of representation that helped keep his seat secure. Visibility helps name recognition. Thus his appearances in the district served a reelection purpose. Once, while in the district, we rushed to a meeting. We were running late, as Advocate 1 often did. We ran through a maze of hotel meeting rooms. I became disoriented as to which room we sought. I asked Advocate 1, "Have you ever gone into the wrong meeting?" He replied, "Oh, yes, but that's okay. It's always a chance to meet constituents."

Advocate 1's district had its fair share of struggles and frustrations. This kept him active, moving among his constituents. It also complicated the task of representation. The district encompassed portions of two suburban cities, Grove City and *Elmwood.* Advocate 1 identified most strongly with Grove City, a small bedroom community surrounded by annexed portions of the central city. Grove City is a community of working-class ranch houses, mostly built in the 1950s and 1960s on half- or quarter-acre lots. There are few expensive homes on large lots, and little land left to develop. According to Advocate 1, area growth had shifted to West Heights. More and more of his constituents were senior citizens who had paid off their mortgages and chose to stay. The community was not growing. Property values were flat. As noted, the growing proportion of senior citizens weakened support for local school taxes. Other struggles and frustrations also came up. Advocate 1 told the Elmwood chamber that the city must "thump [its] chest" to get its fair share from the state capitol. Though parts of Elmwood were in fact growing, the portion of it in Advocate 1's district was older, working-class, and aging—much like neighboring Grove City. Advocate 1 told both Elmwood and Grove City constituents that they needed effective representation in the statehouse to ensure that their interests did not get lost as growth shifted elsewhere. At times, Advocate 1's district struggled mightily.

Elmwood and the surrounding communities made headlines during my first field observations there. The news was not good. I looked on as Advocate 1 talked to constituents about that month's issue of *Rolling Stone.* Labeling Elmwood "Tweakville," the magazine discussed the popularity of homemade crystal methamphetamine ("meth") in the area.[3] According to the story, Advocate 1's district and neighboring communities had become the national center for production and use of the deadly homemade drug. Made with various recipes, it generally includes industrial solvents, ammonium hydroxide (an agri-

3. Peter Wilkinson, "America's Drug: Postcards from Tweakville," *Rolling Stone,* February 19, 1998, 50–68.

cultural fertilizer), and enormous quantities of cold medicine. In front of a chamber audience, and later at a schools forum, Advocate 1 denounced *Rolling Stone* for ignoring the work of local law enforcement against meth. Yet he conceded that the drug was an enormous problem.

At the end of the day, Advocate 1 and I socialized with his constituents. "Here in Grove City, we drink beer," Advocate 1 told me. "No, we don't," a child corrected him, "we take meth!" The child then took over the conversation, telling us how to recognize a meth house: "You look for people, in the middle of winter, no coats, standing on the porch, shaking."

The methamphetamine problem was an enormous embarrassment for Advocate 1, yet he chose to give more attention to the district's positive side, while ceding the policy work to the area's state senator. A former federal prosecutor, Senator 1 met the challenge with new legislation to stiffen penalties, regulate the bulk sale of certain materials used in making the drug, and fund drug treatment. The bill passed both houses unanimously and was signed by the governor. While he left it to Senator 1 to discuss the provisions of the legislation at home, Advocate 1 began the discussion by presenting himself as the local advocate who spoke out for the district. He encouraged constituents to discuss the issue with Senator 1 and local law enforcement, praised the police and sheriff's deputies for their work, and took *Rolling Stone* to task for its "unfair" portrayal.

Advocate 1 knew his district well. He grew up there and, like all the other legislators in this study, went home every weekend as well as after the end of the legislative session. His children went to local public schools. Yet he did not rely on these things alone to connect him with his constituents. He often went socializing, sometimes just stopping in a bar. He would "go in and have a couple of beers on a Friday night [and ask constituents], 'So, what's been going on?'" He prided himself on his presence in the district. He especially liked it when constituents said, "You're everywhere!"

It should be added that Advocate 1 was not alone: Ombuds 4 told me, "I know I'm about right when . . . about every tenth person I see says, 'Boy, you're everywhere, aren't you?'" Advocate 1's district was an inner-suburban one, and Ombuds 4's was small-town and rural. Both prided themselves on their visibility back home. Advocate 1 added that representatives who are not everywhere may need to look for a new line of work: "Once you're not showing up to all these different events, people will start seeing that. Then it's time that they realize, maybe [you] aren't interested in helping [them]." In general, both in-district advocates and ombudspersons are especially proud of their visibility back home.

Advocate 1 had a close relationship with the "old guard" back home, which resembled the primary constituency of the congressmen in Richard Fenno's study *Congressmen in Committees.* To Advocate 1, as to many of those congressmen, the old guard was not just a re-election constituency. It was also a source of information about local interests. One of the oldest of the old guard was a ninety-two-year-old former Grove City mayor. Advocate 1 regarded him as "a friend of the world" and an expert on the city's best interests. Deeply involved in the suburb's growth during previous decades, he understood the importance of local decisions in shaping that development. During the course of my study, this ex-mayor passed away. But other members of the old guard remained. Like Fenno's congressmen, Advocate 1 admitted that the old guard was made up of "people that have been involved in my campaign," but he added that they were "people that I would consider folks that I can consult with and get advice from as well: 'How would this affect the district?'" For example, he noted, "It's easy for me to call the superintendent" of Grove City schools for advice about how certain legislation would affect local education. Advocate 1 contacted these people and tried to find out what the district needed, instead of waiting for his constituents to raise issues and contact him, as an ombudsperson tends to do. Again, this home style usually suggests an advocate approach, with a strong emphasis on the district. Advocate 1's old guard also included "retired workers—blue-collar workers mostly," who typified his aging, working-class area.

I asked Advocate 1 if he ever felt a conflict between his conscience and his district. Such conflict is central to the Wahlke model. According to Wahlke and his coauthors, Burkeans vote their conscience, delegates vote the district, and politicos vote depending on the issue.[4] In answering my question, Advocate 1 highlighted the limitations of the Wahlke schema. He said he simply did not ever feel a conflict: "I

4. Wahlke et al., *Legislative System*, 267–86.

think you eventually evolve into becoming the conscience of your district in a large way. I grew up there. . . . Our kids are going to school there. . . . I think [I share] the values of my district." He also mentioned religion, pointing out that the community had many Catholics such as himself, along with a lot of Baptists. "I taught church there in the area," he noted. "I've not really encountered that type of moral conflict, where we're so diverse that it creates a conflict in how I'm going to vote." He later backed away from the term *conscience of the district,* adding, "I'm not the conscience of my district, I just understand my district." Yet his statements clearly show how a representative can "fit" his district and thus not encounter the type of moral conflict that underlies the Wahlke schema.

Ever the consummate politician, Advocate 1 was careful to tailor his comments to his audience. For example, mental health care and children's program advocates often complained that the state underfunded social services. At two separate meetings of such groups, I heard Advocate 1 attack the state's tight tax cap, which kept expenditures limited. Along with other Democratic representatives (there were no Republicans present at either meeting), he argued that the tax cap resulted in small tax refunds that were of little value to the individual taxpayer, while key social services went underfunded. Yet he pointed out to me that, like most people, his constituents enjoyed the extra break: "Everybody likes tax cuts." At meetings with other constituents, Advocate 1 did not mention the tax cap. The consummate politician reads his audience. He knows which issues to stress and which to avoid. Social-service workers are frustrated with limited state funds, while just plain folks like tax cuts.

A more challenging task came in the wake of a collective bargaining bill introduced by a colleague, Advocate 5. (This bill is discussed in the next chapter.) According to Advocate 1, his constituents favored collective bargaining for public employees by more than two to one: a supermajority (though Advocate 1 did not tell his audiences or me where he got these figures). Yet the local chamber and school board were opposed to the bill, arguing that it would raise costs. At each public meeting, Advocate 1 asked several times, "Have you read the bill?" He told skeptical constituents not only that the bill was popular in the district and the state, but also that it was not as dangerous as critics claimed. He pointed out, for example, that the bill included penalties for state workers who go on strike, while current law specified no such penalties. By asking if they'd read the bill, Advocate 1 hoped to turn the questions back to his audience. He sought to neutralize criticism while hanging tough as an advocate for labor unions, which he believed were popular in the district. The advocate must develop a strategy to cope with his critics. When constituents mailed anti-collective-bargaining letters to Advocate 1, he responded by mailing each critic a copy of the complete text of the bill.

Advocate 1 used his perquisites. Like his colleagues, he sent out a newsletter/survey to his constituents once a year, which helped build name recognition. Further, he did his share of casework. Advocate 1 stressed constituent service during our interview. He said that there were "a substantial amount of requests." He added that voters have come to expect constituent service—it is part of the job, not simply a favor for the folks at home. He told me, "They call the representative and trust that we get a response [for them]."

In addition to relying on his party label, visibility, perquisites, and casework, Advocate 1 kept his seat safe by raising plenty of money. He made it clear that he was prepared to take on any challenger. His connection with the metropolitan area's legal community helped him raise funds effectively. He also received support from local labor unions. The money he raised deterred potential challengers. In general, he did not leave his reelection to chance.

Advocate 1 thrived on the politician's role. He found himself adjusting his approach to representation in order to fit the various tasks with which he was confronted. Though his district was not growing, there was plenty at home to keep him busy—defense of the local schools, retirement issues, and drug problems, to name just a few. At home, Advocate 1 often took on the challenge of defending both of his chosen professions: attorney and legislator. When talking with constituents, he stressed how much work was involved in representing the district. He pointed out that he and other legislators often stayed up until late at night finishing tasks, then rose again at dawn for another day. "You never get away from it down here [in the capital]," he told me. He stressed the low pay of legislators, too. He referred to his basement apartment in the capital as "Squalor Arms," and loved to tell constituents about the poor accommodations. He claimed he had to wrap a blanket around himself to get from the bed to the shower, because the heat was so inadequate. Yet even with the low pay and poor accommodations, he seemed to thrive in the politician's job, appearing at home to raise support for education, the party, and other district interests at every meeting possible. As if to underscore the point that a legislator is always overbooked, he perpetually seemed to be running just a few minutes late. He presented himself as overworked and underpaid—and perfect for the job. He seemed to have found success and a safe seat as the consummate politician.

Advocate 2: The Conscience of the District

[M]y popularity in the district, and what I've done for the district over the years, . . . has a lot to do with [my safe reelection margins]. I could probably run for any office and get tremendous support from my district. I could run for mayor . . . and have 100 percent support from my district. I'm so well-known. I've never done anything wrong. I've got a good record.

—*Advocate 2*

Advocate 1 used the term *conscience of the district,* then backed away from it during our interview. But this term is actually better suited to Advocate 2. This legislator represented a racially mixed, heterogeneous district of retired, blue-collar whites and young, mostly African American families. Yet he did not worry about factions, and he seemed confident about reelection. Arguing that "term limits are going to take me out, and that's it," he stressed the huge Democratic majority that reelected him. Since general elections were not a concern, he could focus on the primary. But only once did he have to do that. Advocate 2 hadn't had a primary challenger since winning easily in 1994. His only opponent in 1998, during the time I was conducting my study, was a Libertarian candidate who had run against him two years ago. Advocate 2 told me he had won the 1996 race with 88 percent of the vote. Not surprisingly, he was confident.

Advocate 2 had lived in his district since the early 1960s. Though

he came from another part of the country and still had a distinct ac-
cent, he saw himself as a part of the community. He believed that his
neighbors knew and trusted him. He used his good reputation to socialize conflicts and struggled to bring as many people as possible to
meetings concerning the district. He hoped this would turn conflicts
to his advantage. Town hall gatherings were important to his home
style. He boasted that over three hundred people came to his first
scheduled public meeting regarding a local highway project. According to Advocate 2, this was the highest turnout at any legislative
meeting ever held in his district. By way of contrast, Advocate 6 told
me, "I found out that those town hall meetings are a waste of time"
because of low attendance. In the same vein, Advocate 4 attended a
few town halls only to discover that they were dominated by a handful of people with single-issue grievances or conspiracy theories.

Advocate 2 did not see himself struggling to articulate issues in the
district, as Advocate 1 did regarding local schools and methamphetamine, for example. Rather, Advocate 2 saw himself as the focal point
of a lot of trust and consensus in the district: "We have a district that
is pretty trustworthy, I think, because I've been in office either as
school board [member] or as a state rep since 1984. And we've lived
there since '62, so we're kind of pillars of the community. You know
I've been active in office. And even before I got in office I was active
in the community, so there's a lot of trust in me."

Advocate 2 saw his party as a key to reelection. I asked: "How does
the district look to you as a Democrat? Is there a partisan bent to it?
Are people partisan in their thinking, or not?" He replied, "It's all
blue-collar and it's all Democrat." He was the first representative I
interviewed who was comfortable identifying himself as a liberal. "It
wouldn't be wrong," he said, "to call me a strong liberal . . . mostly
liberal person. That's the way I vote. That's the way I present myself."

Labor unions appeared to be a major tie linking Advocate 2 and
his constituents to the Democratic party label. He was a strong supporter of collective bargaining and backed Advocate 5's collective
bargaining bill in 1999. In fact, he arrived at a Grove City schools forum with copies of the bill, which he handed out. When Advocate 2
first ran for school board, several years before my study, the board
president took him to task over his support for teachers' collective
bargaining. She predicted he would lose the election over the issue.

She also promised to "lock horns" with him over it if he did win the election. Advocate 2 won that race. Shortly afterward, the district established collective bargaining procedures for teachers.

His blue-collar constituents seemed supportive of Advocate 2's position on collective bargaining. His identification as a liberal urban Democrat was also evident in his opposition to the concealed carrying of handguns. He was a staunch opponent of the death penalty, and believed that his constituents were "willing to live with" this position. His credentials as a strong liberal were less noticeable in some of his other stands, however, particularly his pro-life views on abortion.

Advocate 2's district included parts of *Birchtree* and Grove City. Birchtree is part of the larger central city; Grove City is an autonomous suburb. Prior to his election as state representative, most of Advocate 2's involvement was in Birchtree, and he spent a great deal of time discussing Birchtree during our interview. Grove City got less attention. Unlike Burkean 1, Advocate 2 did not put special emphasis on parts of the district where he was less well known. He concentrated on the community where he was already known. Still, he did not ignore Grove City. He appeared at their school forums. His closest contact in the district was a teacher in the Grove City schools who kept tabs on local issues for him. This supporter appeared at ceremonies and meetings when Advocate 2 could not be there. Thus Advocate 2 kept up with both parts of the district, though his home community was clearly his focus. The 1998 election returns indicated that he won by a similar margin in both parts of the district, presumably due to his Democratic party label.

Legislative district lines did not coincide neatly with city or neighborhood boundaries, and there seemed to be a division of labor. Advocate 2 identified more strongly with Birchtree than did any other state representative, even though Advocate 4 and Ombuds 1 and 2 also represented portions of the community. Advocate 2 let Advocate 1 handle most major local government issues in Grove City, and did not get involved. This was in spite of the fact that part of Grove City was in Advocate 2's district and other parts of it were in other state reps' districts. Advocate 1 had most of Grove City, but not all of it. Further, Advocate 1's district also contained part of Elmwood. But because of their past involvement with the respective local governments and school boards, Advocates 1 and 2 observed this division of labor. Advocate 1 presented himself as Grove City's representative, while Advocate 2 played a similar role for Birchtree. Still, they frequently appeared together at Grove City school events.

One of Advocate 2's main challenges was to link constituents in a district that is racially mixed. Advocate 2, who is white, stressed his cross-racial appeal and outreach efforts: "Those [racial] barriers don't enter into my decision-making at all. And I've proven that when I was on school board. I was the first school board member who pushed for having Martin Luther King Day a holiday in our district. And other school districts around us weren't doing it."

At first, Advocate 2 pursued a color-blind strategy ("Those barriers don't enter into my decision-making"). But he did acknowledge the need to build bridges with the black community. He could not ignore the demographic changes at home. After the King holiday vote, he convinced an African American friend to run for school board. In a district still predominantly white, she did not believe she could win. But Advocate 2 endorsed her and she won, becoming the first African American on that school board. Advocate 2 knew that race was an issue. He knew that he had to acknowledge it and build a consensus in order to maintain support in a changing district. These concerns might not have been "barriers," but they entered into his decision-making. They influenced his home style.

Crucial to Advocate 2's home style were his legislative forums. He organized forums in the Birchtree school district that were modeled on similar forums he attended in Grove City. Advocate 2 enjoyed counting the people in attendance, and he encouraged me to do the same. I observed eighty to one hundred people at each Friday afternoon Birchtree forum. The two Grove City forums I attended drew somewhat smaller groups—perhaps fifty to seventy people. Since Birchtree was his home, Advocate 2 liked to point out that the forums there drew more people than the ones in Grove City. As far as he knew, he said, they drew more people than any other school district forums in the metropolitan area. In my travels, I did not observe any other school district that matched Birchtree for attendance at legislative forums. Advocate 2 took both community and personal pride in his constituents' involvement in decision-making. Note the sharp contrast here with Burkean 1, who argued that his constituents "just want to be left alone." In the course of my research, I saw Burkean 1 attend only one school forum. That gathering drew less than a dozen people, each one a teacher in the New Town district. Advocate 2's meetings, by contrast, drew a cross-section of parents, teachers, administrators, and other constituents.

Advocate 2 seemed confident and relaxed at one Birchtree meeting as he explained the status of his day care legislation. He told the crowd that "it's time to do some praying [that] some people will see fit to get this bill through. They don't have kids; they don't realize how important it is." He hoped that he and his constituents could persuade certain key legislators to stop opposing the bill. He assumed that his audience agreed with his position, and appealed for their prayers and support. Then he sat back comfortably for the rest of the meeting. He got no questions from the crowd. In sharp contrast, Senator 2 struggled to defend his views at the same meeting, particularly regarding the issues of charter schools and a private-school-tuition tax deduction. Senator 2 supported both of these ideas. The crowd was opposed. One audience member stated that these initiatives would "tear our school district apart." While Advocate 2 acted as if he was among friends, Senator 2 was on the defensive.

Advocate 2 claimed the "highest turnout ever" at a town hall meeting he organized to discuss the aforementioned highway project. According to him, over three hundred forty people attended. The state Department of Transportation had proposed closing access to two streets in the district—and one in Ombuds 1's district—as part of a highway renovation project. A retired engineer, Advocate 2 demanded that alternatives be designed. He even offered his own system to keep the ramps open. He then scheduled a hearing to get public input on the project, which led, he told me, to his winning a national award for highway policy. (The award was given by the Arizona Highway Department for best community involvement in highway planning; contestants came from all over the United States.)

Even the local school district got involved, organizing forums to protest DOT's plan. School officials worried that closing off access to local businesses would lead to a fall in school tax receipts. They invited representatives from the fire department, police department, and local ambulance service to voice concerns. Some of these participants worried that closing local exits would divert traffic and lengthen emergency-response times. The ambulance service spokesman, a former elected official from the area, contributed to the climate of unease. He warned that "if you can't get there on time, you might as well send a hearse."

The highway interchange that would be affected by the DOT's plan was one of the area's busiest. Some 220,000 cars passed through it each day, and that number was expected to climb to 300,000 in the next two decades. The highways served growing suburban areas on three sides of Advocate 2's district. Many commuters passed through the community on their way from one suburb to another. Because of the heavy traffic, it was not possible to close the interchange while a new one was built. Rather, construction would have to be completed in phases, taking care to reroute traffic during each phase.

Another problem was the poor design of the interchange itself. Built in the 1950s, it was a classic highway "spaghetti bowl": three highways and several city streets were linked, in a jumble of ramps, exits, and lane changes. One DOT engineer told me that a typical highway interchange has sixteen possible combinations of entry and exit. This one had sixty-four. Entrance and exit ramps were crowded together. Merging was hazardous, and accidents were frequent. The highways feeding into the interchange had been widened over the years to accommodate suburban growth and the resulting traffic, but the connecting ramps had not, and most were only one lane wide. This created a traffic bottleneck.

As it happened, economic growth and federal surplus provided the needed input for Advocate 2's highway changes. DOT started out with low public approval in the district. But under pressure from Advocate 2, the department changed its strategy to include numerous public meetings. DOT also worked with a local task force that suggested changes to the interchange. After many meetings, DOT submitted its plans to an engineering firm, which in turn designed a system using better-designed interchanges and frontage roads (or "collector-distributor" roads, in engineering jargon) to carry traffic from the highways to the local roads in Advocate 2's district. These side roads would allow for the closing of exit ramps without cutting off access to local businesses. In order to accomplish this, the working plan (as of 2001) called for the realignment of several local roads at state and federal taxpayers' expense. With federal help, the community was appeased. The new interchange promised to be safer, but expenses grew to between two and three times the original proposal's cost. Fortunately for Advocate 2's constituents, the time was right: a federal surplus had allowed a local congresswoman to bring home additional support from Washington. I attended a meeting where the congresswoman told DOT's director and a group of local mayors, "We've got a surplus up there, guys, and I'm going to get you some money whether you know what to do with it or not." In August 1999, DOT began construction on a relatively minor phase of the new interchange, promising more revisions to make the proposal even more neighborhood-friendly. More design changes were unveiled at a September town hall meeting. According to the city newspaper, over five hundred locals attended, breaking Advocate 2's previous record for attendance at a single meeting.

The interchange was not entirely contained within Advocate 2's district. Parts of it were in the districts of Advocate 5 and Ombuds 1 and 2 (legislative districts can be quite compact in an urban community—many are only a few square miles). Quite a few commuters who passed through the interchange lived even farther away—for example, in Burkean 1's district. Yet the other state representatives observed a division of labor on the issue. They let Advocate 2 take the lead. His engineering background and community support made him a natural leader on this subject. Ombuds 1 involved himself in the debate only briefly, early in the planning process, seeking to ensure that a key exit in his district was kept open. Advocate 5 did not involve himself in the controversy at all. Newly elected Ombuds 2 allowed Advocate 2 to educate him about the project. At one school district–sponsored gathering, I observed many state representatives sit without comment while listening to representatives of the DOT and constituents discuss (and sometimes argue) the changes. But while these representatives came and went silently, Advocate 2 stood outside the door before the meeting, greeting constituents and handing out flyers stating his position.

The other main issue in Advocate 2's district was the independence of the local schools. Though part of the central city, Birchtree had its own separate school district. Advocate 2 told me, "People in Birchtree do *not* want anything to do with the [inner-city] school district." For him, this was not a racial issue. Both school districts were predominantly African American. The minority population in Birchtree had grown to the point that enrollment in Advocate 2's school district was two-thirds minority. Birchtree struggled to avoid any involvement with court-ordered desegregation efforts. Advocate 2 stressed that it was a biracial coalition that wanted independence from the city school district. He noted the dangers that would lurk if the schools were merged: "[I]f that happens, you won't only have white flight, you'll have black and white flight. That's why the blacks came to our district. They didn't like [the city district] and they knew we had excellent schools, and they'll be leaving, too. I don't know who'll be left!"

In addition to articulating the issues, Advocate 2 paid attention to constituent service. He was particularly proud of the booklets that he distributed in the district, which listed frequently called phone numbers. He said that his constituents "love our little phone books" because they were easier to thumb through than the metropolitan telephone directory. Like the other representatives I interviewed, Advocate 2 also sent out an annual survey to solicit opinions about major issues on the agenda.

Along with his phone books and surveys, Advocate 2 focused on traditional constituent service—but with an interesting twist. He had many contacts in the federal government because of his position as chair of the house Veterans' Committee. Not only did he do constituent service work with the state government, he also contacted federal offices on behalf of the folks back home. He told me that constituents often called him before they called their congresswoman. This, he said, was because they knew and trusted him as a longtime "pillar of the community." Constituents felt comfortable coming to Advocate 2. He promised them that all it would take would be "one call" for him to address their problem. He further guaranteed that he'd have an answer within twenty-four hours.

Advocate 2 wrote a weekly column in a local newspaper that was distributed free—tossed into yards and placed in post offices and other public places. (In contrast, Ombuds 2's column was published in a newspaper that was sold by subscription or at newsstands.) Advocate 2 generally used his column to stress pro–labor union issues or neighborhood concerns. For example, one September 1999 column reminded constituents about the history of Labor Day, noting that the holiday was created in the nineteenth century under pressure from Samuel Gompers and other organized labor leaders. Advocate 2 encouraged constituents to celebrate the day in remembrance of labor union victories. Several other columns addressed his work on the highway interchange. Advocate 2 occasionally broadened his theme. Once he wrote to educate constituents about arts funding. Another column dealt with the challenge of commemorating Columbus Day in an increasingly diverse America (not to mention an increasingly diverse district).

In person and in print, Advocate 2 presented himself as sincere, easygoing, and compassionate. Yet during the course of our interview, he also showed himself to be a political strategist. When necessary, he could be aggressive in implementing strategy. But he was always careful to highlight the community interest that was served by his actions. The implication was that strategy in pursuit of power is not acceptable, but strategy in defense of the community is a necessary part of politics.

His first mention of strategy concerned the local school board's vote for the Martin Luther King Jr. holiday. Advocate 2 served on the school board when the vote was taken. None of the surrounding suburban school districts yet recognized King Day. According to Advocate 2, a majority of school board members opposed the new holiday. So how did Birchtree become the first area district to recognize it? Advocate 2 argued that his strategy made the difference. He invited African American community members to the board meeting and pressed for a vote in open session. This is how he recounted the story: "I think they were embarrassed, because it was [an] open meeting. And we had the finest Afro-American members of the community there, and they backed me up on it. And . . . they did voice opposition, and I think [the board] wanted to do it in executive session, closed door. And I said, 'No, not this, you can't do [it with] this issue, this is a public matter and it's got to be open.' And so, when they knew that they weren't going to be able to vote in secret, it changed their attitudes."

Advocate 2 practiced what William H. Riker called *heresthetics*—the art of simultaneously mastering the rules of a situation and being persuasive.[5] Like the protagonists of Riker's case studies, he strate-gized to change the voting procedure and the context of a meeting, thus altering the outcome. The King holiday prevailed in the face of initial opposition. This was not the only time Advocate 2 effectively strategized to change an outcome.

Another example of heresthetics occurred when Advocate 2 was challenged in the 1994 Democratic primary. Advocate 2 had been chosen in a special election, and was attempting to retain his seat in the next regular election cycle. His challenger had lived in a neigh-boring district for "all his adult life," according to Advocate 2, and had rented an apartment in the district in order to establish residen-cy. When Advocate 2 discovered this, he used strategy to his advan-tage:

> I said, "Well, either he moves into my district and becomes a bona fide member of the district, or I attack him on this issue." And he wouldn't move. I said, "Okay, then, you're going to have to suffer the consequences. People are going to know that you're not [really living here, that] you don't even have any intention. You have an empty apartment. You don't even have any furni-ture. And this is the apartment number, and I know when you . . . signed the lease and everything. So you're not fooling anyone, but unless you change that, I'm going to make this pub-lic." It was a local paper; it was an open letter to the editor, and they published it.

Here Advocate 2 effectively combined his use of strategy with a defense of the community's interests. He weakened his challenger by painting him as a carpetbagger, using the cost-free method of a let-ter to the editor. Yet Advocate 2 justified his actions not with self-interest, but with a reference to what was best for the community. Birchtree, he argued, deserved a representative who truly lived there and had ties in the community. According to Advocate 2's portrayal of the issue, he was not trying to defeat his challenger. Rather, he was trying to entice him to become a "bona fide" resident. It is worth not-ing that the challenger lived just blocks south of the southern bound-ary of the district, only about a mile from Advocate 2's own home.

5. William H. Riker, *The Art of Political Manipulation*, ix.

Both lived in the same school district. Nevertheless, Advocate 2 thought that the district would be disappointed by a candidate with an empty apartment as his local address. Advocate 2 later befriended his ex-challenger and endorsed his unsuccessful city council candidacy.

This type of aggressive approach to politics came up again when Advocate 2 faced his first general election. The Republican challenger was a local minister. He accused Advocate 2 of being insufficiently religious. The challenger took his message onto the local Christian television station. Citing equal-time rules, Advocate 2 demanded and received his own appearance on the station: "I called the station up and I said, 'You've interviewed my opponent but you've never asked me to be on the air. I think that's incorrect. I think I ought to have access—equal time.' I said . . . 'If you don't do it, I think I'll ask for an attorney to look into it, to either sue you or make you do it.' So they said, 'Oh, we just haven't gotten around to calling you! Sorry! You'll be on next week!' And I was!"

Advocate 2 went on the air and stressed his pro-life position, thus softening conservative Christian opposition to his liberal views on other issues. Here again, Advocate 2 used strategy. He never brought a lawsuit against the station, but he got on the air simply by suggesting the possibility of a lawsuit. He not only got his equal time, he also avoided the time and trouble of actually pursuing legal action. Again, he avoided attributing his actions to raw self-interest. This time he referenced an abstract principle, equal time, to justify his aggressive pursuit of air time.

A high level of constituent trust allowed Advocate 2 to act upon his conscience. His partisan advantage helped too. Advocate 2 took positions that were controversial in the district. However, this did not cut into his enormous reelection margins. Most notably, he was outspoken in his criticism of the death penalty. When I first met him, I was traveling with Advocate 1. At a lobbying luncheon, Advocate 2 took a moment to speak to the crowd about the injustice of executing the mentally retarded. A prisoner with the IQ of a young child was scheduled to be executed by Missouri in the next few days. In his remarks to the crowd, Advocate 2 called upon the governor to commute the execution. The execution was carried out on schedule.

The following year, Advocate 2 became even more heated in his opposition to the death penalty. He sponsored legislation that would temporarily stop executions while research was conducted to discover whether there were racial disparities in capital sentencing. The bill made it to the floor of the house, but was defeated overwhelmingly. Advocate 2, however, became a widely quoted critic of the death penalty. He did not temper his criticism of the governor on this issue, even though the governor was a fellow Democrat. He noted that the number of executions was increasing just as the governor was preparing to run for the U.S. Senate. The city's daily newspaper covered the story.

Here Advocate 2 put his conscience over his party. The governor's race for the Senate was one of the election cycle's most tightly fought and closely watched. Control of the U.S. Senate hung in the balance. Advocate 2 would not suspend his criticism of the death penalty for the governor, the party, or disgruntled constituents. The incumbent Republican senator criticized the governor for a commutation made at the request of the Pope during a visit to the state. Advocate 2 believed that this criticism just encouraged more executions. Thus he directed his harsh words at both the senator and the governor.

According to Advocate 2, his high regard at home allowed him to take this controversial stand. He did not believe there was an anti-death-penalty consensus in his district. In our interview, he described the sentiment back home: "It does depend on the issue. If we had a recent killing . . . where it's a violent crime, you know, a senseless thing, someone was murdered, [then] they want revenge. I want revenge, too, but I don't want to play God and say I'm going to take your life. They know that. They're willing to live with my position."

On a less contentious note, Advocate 2 dedicated a great deal of his time and other resources to legislation helping the blind. He did not have a particularly large concentration of blind people in his district; he only became aware of the issue when visiting a national state legislators' conference. Thereafter, he spent a good deal of time on a group of citizens who mostly lived outside the district. Once again, he relied on his reserve of trust back home. Of course, assistance to the blind is far less controversial than opposition to the death penalty. In 1998, I observed a staunchly conservative Republican representative praise Advocate 2. Speaking at a school district forum that they were both attending, she commended his work on behalf of the blind while acknowledging that they differed sharply on most other issues. Helping the blind was another way Advocate 2 buttressed his reputation as the conscience of the district.

In 1999, Advocate 2 spearheaded an effort to exempt government pensions from state income taxes. He said that his district's seniors were moving to states that did not tax pensions, and predicted economic development if his bill passed. In a district with plenty of seniors, the bill made political sense. In a neighboring district, however, Ombuds 2 told me that he could not support the bill, though Advocate 2 had become his friend and something of a mentor (despite their belonging to different parties). Ombuds 2 thought the bill was just too expensive and would drain the state treasury. Advocate 2 went on to stress the value of the bill to both seniors and veterans, and often touted it when meeting with constituents. He received strong support from veterans' organizations such as the Veterans of Foreign Wars, which was headquartered a few miles away in the same city. Still, the bill did not pass.

Advocate 2 had a large reserve of reelection votes due to a combination of his name recognition and his constituents' partisan leanings. He did the full complement of constituent service work. He made sure to be seen at local legislative forums. In addition, he reminded constituents that he refused all lobbyists' gifts. In sum, he did not take his huge margins for granted. He saw his presence in the district as part of the job, and criticized representatives who skipped legislative forums. But he did use his huge reelection margins as a sort of cushion. This cushion allowed him to take on controversial issues such as the death penalty—taking on a popular governor from his own party—and to address issues that did not have a large impact on the district, such as aid to the blind. He acted both as the voice of the constituents and as an opinion-shaping community leader. His constituents seemed much more involved than many others, as shown by the high turnout at his forums. As long as he continued to work at socializing conflicts, Advocate 2 believed he would be safe until removed by term limits.

During our interview, Advocate 2 said that he would not seek another office after his term limit. He later changed his mind, announcing his intent to run for state senate in 2002, when Senator 1 would be term-limited out. Advocate 2's aggressive style had helped build a foundation of name recognition that he believed would aid his senate campaign. In general, in-district advocates have progressive ambitions. Advocate 2 pursued a strategy that would be useful in a senate bid. His home style crossed boundaries. He involved himself in issues that affected surrounding areas. The highway interchange and school district were two such "widening" issues. Unfortunately for Advocate 2, redistricting later moved him out of that senate district, and he was unable to run for the seat.

The next section considers another legislator who socialized the conflict. Like Advocate 2, the inner-city advocate I studied broadened support from his district into neighboring areas.

Advocate 3: The Inner-City Advocate

> Moved back here after law school and just saw that, and felt that, people really had no voice. There was a general malaise, or non-participation in the electorate process. Here we are, a mass of people paying into the system through our taxes, involuntarily paying in through our taxes, with no voice, and no one really paying any attention to our concerns. The neighborhoods that I had known as a child crumbling and continuing to crumble. And I just felt that we needed to have somebody—I felt that then, and I feel that now—who would be responsive to those concerns. And I started looking around and asking around. Who would that be, and who could that be? Nobody responded, so I got in the race.
>
> —*Advocate 3*

Advocate 3's district was struggling. Driving across town to meet him one sunny Saturday, I saw how much poverty exists amidst plenty in a modern U.S. metropolitan area. The people I met in Advocate 3's district were friendly and welcoming. Like the folks in most other districts I visited, this working-class, racially mixed group seemed happy to be studied and wanted to help. Advocate 3 did, too. Still, I was struck by the deteriorating physical condition of the area in and around his district. Streets were crumbling. Young men hung out at street corners, looking like they had nowhere to go. I saw many abandoned homes and businesses. The gas stations, convenience stores, and other businesses that remained seemed to be in disrepair. Most storefronts featured bars on the windows or roll-down steel doors to deter crime. Homeless people panhandled on the streets.

Advocate 3's community was not entirely blighted. Some government buildings were in reasonably good shape, including a glittering new regional center of the U.S. Environmental Protection Agency. But with its open-air, energy-efficient design, the EPA center looked strange towering over a landscape of urban poverty. Advocate 3 entertained no illusions about his community's struggles. He saw himself as an advocate for a place that his state had forgotten—for neighborhoods that were ignored by the city-county government, and for a county that was often overlooked by the state government. No stranger to either publicity or controversy, Advocate 3 had placed himself in the middle of a poor community's struggle for recognition.

After giving him a quick overview of my study, I started our interview the same way I started all the others: I asked him to describe the district in his own words. He gave me the demographics: mostly African American, a white and "other" [mostly Hispanic] minority, many senior citizens and female-headed households, and low family incomes. Then he gave this sobering description: "We have had a problem, and continue to have a problem, with drugs. We have had, and continue to have, a problem with blight. We have had, and continue to have, a problem with local or civic response to some of these concerns, and that spills over into my role as a state legislator, because many people don't differentiate between an elected local official and an elected state official. So I find myself many times addressing issues that are really not within my purview, due to citizen response."

Addressing citizens' complaints was central to Advocate 3's home style. This included both casework and legislation affecting the community. Malcolm Jewell has observed that state legislators from lower-income districts tend to get more casework requests than those from higher-income districts.[6] Advocate 3 fit this pattern. He was not the only one who made casework promises; Advocate 2 promised constit-

6. Malcolm E. Jewell, "Legislative Casework: Serving the Constituents, One at a Time."

uents that he would respond to all casework requests within twenty-four hours. But Advocate 3 handled it differently. Unlike his predecessor, whom he had defeated in the Democratic primary some years ago, Advocate 3 was listed in the local telephone directory. He took constituent service requests at home. But that was not all: he had his calls forwarded to his cellular phone while he was away from home. He even took a constituent service call during our interview. I had to turn the tape recorder off when someone with concerns about a relative living in an assisted care facility called to ask about the state's role in overseeing nursing homes. Also during our interview, Advocate 3 had a visitor stop by the coffeeshop where we sat. She was a candidate for the local school board and wanted to discuss the upcoming election. Advocate 3 presented himself as being constantly in touch with constituents about one problem or another. He attributed his first election to the unresponsiveness of the incumbent, who had made the fatal mistake of losing touch with his constituents. Advocate 3 took him on and won. In this struggling district, losing touch was unacceptable. "I get, on average, a call a day" about constituent service, he told me (Ombuds 1, from a wealthier district, said the same). He added, "The quintessential commitment on my part is to stay in direct contact with the people that put me in."

Constituent service problems spilled over into Advocate 3's relationship with local government officials. He described this relationship as "rocky." The state had recently merged the city and county governments in his area in an attempt to streamline government and centralize authority. Advocate 3 argued that the new mayor-CEO's centralized power was indeed working—to the detriment of the community. The weakened county commissioners could overturn the mayor's decisions only by supermajority vote. According to Advocate 3, this stripped neighborhoods of their voices. Though the new system simplified the situation, constituents were still confused about the different layers and levels of government, and Advocate 3 often got calls about concerns that are supposed to be handled at the local, not state, level: crumbling sidewalks, broken streetlights, drug houses, and abandoned homes. He tried to be responsive and referred these problems on to the county commissioners, but he found they were frustrated by their lack of power due to their subordinate status within the new governmental structure.

Advocate 3's district included some of the poorest neighborhoods of a poor city, and he feared it was easy to overlook. He told me that after the state unified the city and county governments, he ran for mayor-CEO and lost by a substantial margin. But he easily won the precincts that were located in his statehouse district. He also won re-election easily, with over 80 percent of the vote. His district was over-whelmingly Democratic and primary challenges were common. Of course, name recognition was a major factor in his election margins. He attributed his good name recognition at home to his high visibil-ity, and that visibility, in turn, to the way he was there to meet a nev-er-ending stream of needs. Each day, Advocate 3 was asked to ad-dress yet another constituent request or need. He told me, "I never flat-out say no."

Advocate 3's home style would be virtually impossible to catego-rize with the schema designed by Wahlke, Eulau, Buchanan, and Fer-guson. He was a delegate, in the sense that he put heavy emphasis on listening to constituent concerns, being there when they called, and responding. But he was also a trustee, in the sense that he used his own judgment to respond to community concerns. He wrote legisla-tion, logrolled to get it passed, generated media publicity, did case-work, and opposed ideas he thought would harm the district. He saw himself as a community leader, and took it upon himself to formu-late alternatives. Wahlke's term *politico* does not describe him, be-cause politicos switch back and forth between delegate and trustee, depending on the issue. Advocate 3's home style blended the dele-gate and trustee roles and revolved around putting issues on the agen-da for constituents. He said, "My style of representation is that I may not be able to solve the concern, or the problem, but I will work with you towards finding that answer."

Advocate 3's community had many problems. Crime, blight, and poverty were all concerns. Jobs and health care were, too. Advocate 3 sat on a committee dealing with criminal law (Judiciary) and several committees dealing with social services, and had previously sat on the Governmental Organizations and Elections Committee, all of which were crucial to his district. Many of the legislators I followed could not trace a direct link between their committee service and home dis-trict. Advocate 3 could, and did. His constituents had needs, and he used his committee service, along with other strategies, to address them. In Governmental Organizations and Elections, he had been outspoken in criticizing the city-county government consolidation bill, but to no avail. In Judiciary, he successfully took on disparities in cocaine-possession sentencing. He also introduced a bill that required the state highway patrol to record the race of each person they stopped, which was intended to measure the extent of racial profiling. On the Social Services Committee, he helped oversee health care for the uninsured. Each of these met a district need.

Vacant housing became a major point of controversy, putting Advocate 3 at odds with the mayor-CEO and local landlords. Advocate 3 sought to renovate abandoned houses by encouraging low-income, working families to move in and do the maintenance. The city government sought to tear the houses down and redevelop the lots. The controversy swirled around abandoned houses that were in relatively good condition. According to Advocate 3, the city saw each one as a "nuisance" that attracted drug dealers and homeless people. He agreed but argued that the homes should be renovated, not destroyed. He introduced a bill in the house that would compel the city government to form a commission that would help match those that wanted to own homes with the most-salvageable houses. I sat in at a legislative forum while local bankers and landlords heatedly criticized the idea. The bankers argued that lower-income, would-be homeowners do not have the money to pay mortgages. The landlords argued that abandoned houses must be torn down promptly before drug dealers and other undesirables move into them. This issue inspired one of the two most contentious and drawn-out debates at the forum. It was clear by the end that neither side was going to convince the other. Yet the bill eventually passed the house.

The second, equally contentious debate concerned another local representative's proposed legislation. It would allow landlords to evict entire families if one family member was arrested for a drug offense. Everyone agreed that "partial evictions don't work." But Advocate 3 still opposed the bill, claiming that it violated due process. Most local businessmen supported it. In all my travels, this was by far the most heated chamber of commerce forum I saw. All of the others were sedate, and usually consensual. It should be noted that while opinions were strong and voices were raised at this meeting, the participants were civil to one another. They avoided foul language, and they chatted and shook hands afterwards. Still, this highlights the contentiousness that ensues when a community struggles with blight. Advocate 3 told me later that he built support by meeting with constituents, not business leaders. He had skipped an earlier chamber meeting to visit a neighborhood group instead, and he was late to this one, delayed by a meeting with constituents.

When I asked him what kind of casework requests he got, Advocate 3 mentioned many examples that I had heard before. But he also startled me by saying, "I do a lot of interfacing with the prison system." A number of his constituents had relatives in jail. They had concerns about parole hearings, transfers from one prison to another, health care in the prisons, and other problems. Ombuds 2 was the only other representative in my study who mentioned a casework request for a prisoner, but he presented it as an isolated incident. For Advocate 3, casework involving the prison system was rather common. Again, this highlights how difficult the issues can be in an inner-city district.

In addition to casework, Advocate 3 did community organizing. Over a month in advance, his secretary began sending me notices about an event Advocate 3 was organizing. To be held at a local high school, it was designed to discuss "Violence in the Media." Community leaders from both sides of the state line were invited, including elected city and county officials, judges, prosecutors, neighborhood leaders, and the ex-president of a local NAACP chapter. Then, weeks before the forum, two students murdered eleven classmates and a teacher in a high school outside Denver. Many schools in Advocate 3's metropolitan area responded by organizing task forces. These included police officers and school administrators, and they designed strategies to prevent such an incident.

The high school that hosted the event could not have been more different from the one where the massacre occurred. Columbine High School was overwhelmingly white, suburban, and wealthy. Inner-city *Roosevelt High School,* in contrast, was poor and racially mixed, with a majority of African Americans. Its students and teachers struggled to contain gang activity. At Advocate 3's forum, the speakers urged high school students to stay in school, say no to peer pressure, and look to positive role models within their families and communities. Local media covered the story. After the speakers, the students volunteered comments of their own. Most of them wanted to talk about the Columbine tragedy. They railed against the school authorities for overlooking obvious danger signs. They could not imagine how Columbine High School authorities could have condoned students' cliquishness and bizarre behavior. Officials at their own school aggressively ferreted out potential gang signs in students' dress and behavior. Students were often sent home to change clothes. While the cameras rolled, many of these inner-city students predicted that a tragedy like Columbine could not happen in their school, because they were so much more closely scrutinized for violent or gang-related behavior. The urban students could not believe that suburban school authorities were so naive. They discussed the need for greater parental involvement in their own lives. Echoing one of the invited speakers, a student said that "what it takes for a family is love." Several students suggested that blaming the media for violent images was an evasion of personal and family responsibility.

Setting up this forum did a lot for Advocate 3's visibility at home. His speech was prominently featured on the local news that night (with me unintentionally standing in the background). He had surrounded himself with leaders from the metropolitan area, men and women who were well known and respected, particularly within the black community. In addition, the students seemed appreciative of the opportunity to note the hard work their school did to contain violence. Some also had complaints and concerns. For example, one noted that local students had nowhere to go for socializing on evenings and weekends; the local mall was nearly empty, and other community institutions were far away or in disrepair. In sum, the forum gave Advocate 3 and his constituents a chance to highlight their community's struggles and spirit, and the television coverage sent the message across the metropolitan area.

After the forum, Advocate 3 chatted with teachers and students at a reception. The students discussed how things were going with their parents and older siblings. Advocate 3 knew some of their relatives personally. This kind of activity further helped build name recognition in the community. The students were not yet old enough to vote, but their parents and teachers could help keep Advocate 3 in office. Here again he showcased his theme of responsiveness, chatting with constituents about their families and their struggles. He told the teens about some of his pending legislation and his opposition to the death penalty.

Advocate 3 clearly believed that casework and name recognition are the best way to get reelected. He told me: "I keep these commitments. You know we do that, and this is why so many people get away with doing absolutely nothing in the legislature. They go down to [the capital], they probably go down to [other state capitals], they sit there and they don't do anything, and they get reelected time and time and time again because, as Tip O'Neill once said, 'All politics is local.' And I don't know what your future political aspirations might be, but I'll say this: the rapport that needs to be established and maintained is with the electorate."

Here he suggested that one can be reelected just by being visible and present in the district. Yet Advocate 3 did much more than that. His other actions fit his theme: he was an advocate for his struggling community. In addition to his presence at home, he introduced legislation, logrolled, and occasionally even received national publicity. These activities overlapped somewhat—logrolling was needed to get legislation passed, and some of Advocate 3's bills in turn brought him national attention. He pointed out that not all statehouse members introduce legislation of their own. According to him, many of them are content to simply take a stand on someone else's bill. Not him. He told me: "I can honestly say that I have introduced ten separate pieces of legislation that affect my district. And I'm an *advocate* for it. Will they pass? Maybe, maybe not. That's a secondary concern. The important thing is that we advocated, and that we push for it."

Here again Advocate 3 can be seen working as an advocate. Just as he showcased the struggles of his community on the local news, he also pushed to get recognition for them in the legislature. Outnumbered almost two-to-one by Republicans, he worked for an urban minority in an overwhelmingly suburban and rural state. He clearly understood that he would not get all his ideas passed into law. But the struggle and recognition seemed particularly important to him.

This is not to say that Advocate 3 lacked strategy. In fact, he told me that he traded votes to get bills passed. His abandoned-housing bill passed in trade for his vote on a hog-farming bill. He told me bluntly, "I don't care anything about hog farming or hog production . . . no hog farms in the district!" This makes an interesting parallel with Advocate 1's comments. Both of these urban-area representatives cited hog-farming issues to show that some legislation does not affect their district. But when it came to legislation for the inner city, Advocate 3 said, "it can't be done in a Republican state without building coalitions with Republicans."

Logrolling was not the only strategy that got this accomplished. For example, Advocate 3 did not have to trade votes in order to pass his cocaine-sentencing bill. Before his bill became law, sentences for crack-cocaine possession were longer than those for the same amount of powdered cocaine. It affected his district, because crack cocaine was a problem in the area. Why did the bill pass? He said, "It was not a partisan issue. It was a fairness issue." But that was not all. After the bill became law, Advocate 3 got calls from the offices of California Congresswoman Maxine Waters and Attorney General Janet Reno. Staffers from each office asked how he got the bill passed. They had been considering such a law at the national level. Advocate 3's response: "The credit goes to the fair-minded legislature of [this state] that passed this." Instead of a "trade" vote in this case, he offered praise and recognition for his colleagues who helped him pass the bill.

It should by now be clear that Advocate 3 thrived on publicity and recognition. Except for Advocate 2, who mentioned his national award for highway policy, none of the other legislators I interviewed made such explicit references to national publicity. Advocate 3 appeared at chamber forums in a well-fitting, blue pinstripe suit. Other legislators dressed casually. Advocate 3 acted as if he was ready and anxious to get attention—whether it be in the district, at the state level, or even the national level. One of his bills that was discussed on national TV was a proposal for tough new penalties for animal cruelty. He argued that such torture was often a precursor to violent crimes against human beings. His legislation was publicized on a nationally syndicated talk show and was also featured on a network newsmagazine. But, he pointed out, "The people that saw me on [the two national TV shows] can't vote for me," he said. This advocate could not afford to forget the voters back home. After the high school forum, he chatted with teachers and students about his animal-cruelty bill. He made sure that constituents who did not see the news still knew about the bill, the publicity it had received, and his work on its behalf.

The advocate's job also comes with frustration. Advocate 3 did not always win. He and I discussed his disappointment with the strong-mayor, city-county government structure. As mentioned, he felt that it was unresponsive to neighborhoods. He voted "no" on the bill to consolidate, which was sponsored in the house by Advocate 4. Advocate 3 believed that this bill was pushed into law by the delegation from the wealthier, neighboring county—the one which included Advocate 4's district. According to Advocate 3, the purpose was to get economic development projects passed into law more easily. He believed that these projects primarily benefited his suburban neighbors, while placing the costs on inner-city taxpayers. He was quite heated in criticizing the tax incentives given to the builders of an auto racing track at the edge of the county. He believed that the city-county government looked "a little bit silly" for giving out tax incentives and tearing down residents' homes for a project that primarily benefited hotels, banks, and land surveyors in a neighboring county. During our interview, he returned several times to the subject of the racetrack, "this boondoggle," as an example of unresponsive government.

Advocate 3 did not have kind words for the nearby suburban county's delegation. Like many legislators in the neighboring state, he seemed to vent his frustrations at that particular county. It worked hard to attract economic development, sometimes at the expense of its neighbors. When I asked him about his relationship with that county's delegation, he responded, "Oh, our rich sister!" Then there was a long pause. When he began to answer, he became more heated as he talked. He said: "They don't mind participating in what I call economic cannibalism by giving us the projects that aren't going to generate any income for this county . . . while they cream the plum positions. They cream the plum . . . they won't support fairness." Later he added: "They take the plum and leave us with the dregs . . . and they laugh all the way to the bank! So yeah, we've got some problems there!"

Advocate 3 argued that the political and economic power of this neighbor could overwhelm his own county. He was angry but knew he could do little about it. The neighbors had more wealth, their entire statehouse delegation save one was in the majority party, and they had a larger, growing population. Meanwhile, Advocate 3's area continued to struggle. He was particularly upset that there was no local vote on the city-county consolidation. For him, this was further evidence of the state's antagonism toward his county. Why not let the locals vote on what kind of government they want? He raised the issue but knew he had lost this round. He was searching for new issues to advocate for his neighborhoods.

This advocate legislator had future political plans. He was pleased with his incumbent state senator and did not plan to contest that seat while he was so safe in his own house district. But when that incumbent retired, he saw himself running for the state senate. He had mixed feelings about that. He thought it would be much more difficult to be an advocate when representing a district with more people. Like Burkean 2, he argued that the house is the more responsive institution. Burkean 2 called it the "people's house." Advocate 3 said, "I don't think I will enjoy being a senator as much as I enjoy being a house member." I asked him why, and he answered, "The senate is kind of like power. It's power absolute." Then he added: "The house is, I think, more responsive to the people, and I enjoy that. I enjoy the responsivity. I think [I would] be a little distanced, because it's a much larger district—it's three times the size of a house district—as a senator, and . . . I would probably be less accessible. I probably won't forward my home phone to my cell phone when I have a senate district [laughs]! It's sixty thousand people, you know."

While Advocate 3 suggested that it's harder to be an advocate in a larger district, he maintained that the most qualified people should run for senate. He said, "The senate is no place for on-the-job training." He told me about a senator from another district who was not experienced when he took office and was unable to keep up. Advocate 3 described him as "just a lost ball in high weeds" and added, "That's a lot of power going to waste that could benefit the district." This makes another interesting parallel, this time with small-town Burkean 2, who described a fellow legislator as "the biggest damn fool I have ever seen." Neither of them told me to whom they were referring, and I do not know if they were discussing the same person or not. Advocate 3 believed that his background would allow him to use the power of a state senator effectively, and that he might well move on to the senate when the time came. But he also knew that the larger district would make his advocate style more difficult to maintain.

In any case, Advocate 3 had already made quite a name for himself. He was a whirlwind of activity, meeting with constituents whose stream of needs never ended. He enjoyed the publicity and did not shy away from conflict. He noted that being an advocate makes the legislator's position a "full-time job," even though the state's legislature meets only for about five months each year, and the pay is low. There is much to do: people to meet, problems to resolve, alternatives to formulate, and support to seek. Given his youth and ambition, I thought it would surprise no one if this man ran for higher office.

Advocate 4: The Common Man Writ Large

Paradoxically, voters seem to want both the typical and the atypical in their elected representatives. In certain characteristics—religion, race, ethnic background—they compel the parties to select candidates in their own images. Yet they favor candidates with education, occupation, and general social status far above the average. They seek the successful, the respected man—the common man writ large, so to speak.

—*Frank J. Sorauf,* Party and Representation

You elect somebody . . . to represent you that is kind of a vision of yourself, or what you would like yourself to be. . . . [P]eople here aren't interested in someone that's too refined, you know, wears . . . Italian suits and so on, but they want . . . someone that conducts himself professionally, that is responsible, that can speak with business leaders. And above all, they want me not to do any harm.

    I don't know how you can divorce being a community leader from being an elected representative.

—*Advocate 4*

Advocate 4 typified Frank J. Sorauf's "common man writ large."[7] His commonness coexisted with progressive political ambition. Once a suburban city councilmember, then a state representative and com-

---

    7. Frank J. Sorauf, *Party and Representation: Legislative Politics in Pennsylvania,* 81.

mittee chair, Advocate 4 aspired to statewide elective office. During the course of my study, he began to openly discuss the possibility of running for state insurance commissioner. The GOP later sent him to "candidate school" in Washington, D.C. While traveling with him, I heard several constituents ask him for more information about his plans to run for statewide office. Yet he maintained a "just folks" style back in his comfortable suburb. A schoolteacher in his district, he wore slightly ill-fitting suits and had an unassuming air. His speaking style was not grandiose. He got right to the point and rarely raised his voice. He wrote and edited his own district newsletter; it often went out with a few overlooked typos. Advocate 4 was in the habit of inviting houseguests upstairs to his office. It was in a part of his home where remodeling work was begun years before, but never completed.

Advocate 4's home style was centered around the theme "do no harm." He presented himself as a representative who worked hard to stop the many proposals that threatened the district. These included ideas that were likely to divert tax revenue and undermine stability in the local schools. Advocate 4 offered a mixed picture of state government in his newsletter. He focused on justifying his own votes, not the institution. Still, he did not go out of his way to attack it, as did many of the congressmen studied by Fenno. One of his newsletters opened: "Dear Friends . . . Our three-day veto session will be at least five days. It could be longer. However, most issues have been resolved. Once again we have saved many things till last. I know I complain frequently but this is simply poor government."

Advocate 4's approach was a mix of praise, blame, and humor toward the legislature. (He told one group, "You're safe again. We [the legislators] are home!") His newsletter featured discussions of his views on key issues. On an economic development project he believed to be a boondoggle, he wrote: "The . . . project is still with us. Like a snake, it keeps rearing its head. I've voted against it so many times my finger is wearing out. I will vote no with my toes if necessary." However, he painted a more positive picture of state action to set up a trust fund for tobacco settlement money. He also praised his colleagues for passing a key highway bill and wrote kind words about a new law that required proof of insurance from people who applied for a driver's license. That law also mandated fifty hours of driver training for sixteen- and seventeen-year-olds who wanted a driver's license. In defending his votes, he prided himself on opposing most tax increases. Yet he voted for new highway taxes. In his newsletter, he wrote that "the alternative is to repair roads like the state of Missouri, which is not at all. I-70 to St. Louis is in terrible shape."

I overheard several constituents tell Advocate 4 that they liked his newsletters. He told me later that the secret was avoiding contentious issues. He put it this way: "Abortion? Gun control? It's not in there!" Thus he avoided conflicts that were particularly divisive, recurring, and unlikely to be resolved in the near future. But even on fights he lost, Advocate 4 was happy to tout his position if he believed his constituents supported him. On the aforementioned development project—tax abatements for a new amusement park—Advocate 4 was the only statehouse member from the county to oppose it. Yet he believed his constituents were with him. They were distrustful of the newer, developing parts of the county, where the project had been proposed. Advocate 4 told me that his constituents sometimes felt forgotten by the county. According to him, the county expended a great deal of its resources promoting and subsidizing new development, while neglecting older suburbs. He worried that the amusement park project would make the problem worse.

While we walked past bare walls and floors to get to his office, Advocate 4 pointed to his half-finished home improvement project as an example of the district's stability. He said that he was so slow to finish because he had no intention of moving. Nor did many of his constituents plan to leave. He told me: "When I first got into the legislature in 1992, a little under 25 percent of [the district's] residents were fifty-nine years of age or older. And of those people, over 70 percent . . . had lived here more than twenty years. This is an extremely stable community."

Why the stability? Advocate 4 had no trouble answering this question: "Oh, that's easy. The property values track the stability, the quality of life, and in this county . . . property values I believe have everything to do with the perceived quality of the school district." His inner-suburban community was just a few miles away from the troubled city schools across the state line. Beginning in the 1950s, residents of the city fled to Advocate 4's county. This part of the metropolitan area was one of the first to experience suburban growth. Much of the flight was due to the struggling city schools; migrants were drawn by the perceived quality of schools in Advocate 4's community. Growth has since moved on to outer portions of the county. Even so, Advocate 4 felt that his district had a stable future due to its good schools. The local newspaper noted that property values throughout the county continued to appreciate—even on older, smaller suburban homes such as the ones in Advocate 4's district.

This stable, inner-suburban district preferred moderates to outspoken liberals or conservatives. It featured strong, two-party competition. Like most representatives I followed, Advocate 4 believed that he fit the district. In fact, he believed that most legislators fit their districts: "I think a lot of people in [the capital] end up representing the kind of districts [that are] like them, and I have moderates pretty much all around me in this area, and I'm a moderate myself." His was one of the only Democratic-leaning districts in his wealthy county. A Republican, Advocate 4 had secured his seat by stressing his alliance with the state GOP's moderate faction. He had watched the election returns in his district and noted that conservative Republicans, particularly those allied with the religious right, were consistently defeated when matched up against moderates from either party.

But it was not enough to be a moderate. Advocate 4 believed that local issues were crucial to reelection. He focused on schools and small businesses. He understood that the schools were the primary reason that people chose to live in his community. Since he taught in the district, school needs were never far from his mind. Though a Republican, he had strong support from the National Education Association's state affiliate. His in-home office decorations included NEA awards and thank-you certificates, and he attended NEA meetings regularly. He played a dual role, participating in decision-making as a teacher and NEA member, and also giving legislative updates at NEA meetings. Advocate 4 was not alone in this. A neighboring representative who I'll call Rep 2 is the only Democrat in the county's statehouse delegation. A teacher in the same school system, she also appears at NEA meetings and plays a similar dual role.

Partisanship was not stressed at all at the NEA meeting I observed. Advocate 4, who described himself as "clearly a moderate," was in complete agreement with Rep 2 on every issue discussed. They sat together, working with each other to divide up the job of presenting the statehouse update. Rep 2 went first. She spent her time discussing how much money the district should expect from the base funding formula for that year, and compared it to last year's level of state aid. Then Advocate 4 took the floor. He focused on three emotional, contentious concerns. He opened by saying, "[Rep 2] did a great job telling you what we did this session. Now let me tell you what we didn't do." The first two issues he mentioned put him and Rep 2 at odds with the state GOP's conservative wing. They opposed a proposal for private-school tuition vouchers, and they opposed concealed-carry handgun permits. Rep 2 started to applaud when Advocate 4 denounced the latter proposal. Others joined in. Rep 2 told the teachers that there was a metropolitan/rural split on concealed-carry: "No legislator west of [the capital] voted with us on this," she said. Advocate 4 said, "We stood strong against concealed-carry and we prevailed," drawing more applause. The teachers also applauded his anti-voucher stand. Finally, Advocate 4 chided the legislature for not extending insurance benefits to all schoolteachers, a move that the NEA supported. I followed up with Advocate 4 afterward. He told me, "Rep 2 gave me the easy issues," and said that it was not difficult to be popular with this group when speaking against vouchers and concealed-carry. During our interview, Advocate 4 had said that it was "laughable" to propose private-school tuition vouchers in a stable, successful, suburban school district. However, that was exactly what conservatives had done. Particularly on these contentious issues, Advocate 4 and Rep 2 chatted as friends and worked hard to support one another. Advocate 4 even told Rep 2, "You're a wonderful citizen" during the meeting.

Of the six Republicans interviewed for this study, only two were members of the NEA, and Advocate 4 was the only one of these to proudly and openly tout that fact. He believed that his position as a teacher fit the district, that his support for the NEA was a part of supporting the status quo in the local schools. He believed that the status quo was what kept the population and property values stable, even as new home construction moved past the community.

The quality of local schools was a theme to which Advocate 4 returned again and again. But what can a state representative really do to help schools? According to Advocate 4, he had two basic responsibilities toward the school district: to ensure adequate funding from the state, and to act as a community leader to quell disputes at home. Of the latter, he told me that such local feuds—"personal agendas," he called them—consistently happened in the district. As an example, he cited a flare-up that occurred when the local Gay-Lesbian Alliance placed some books in the public school libraries. This triggered a reaction: "Folks that are, uh, gayphobic came out of the woodwork and indicated that if those books weren't removed, they were going to sue. And the Gay-Lesbian Alliance turned around and said, if they are removed, they were going to sue. People called me up on both sides, and I said, 'Take it out on the street. Get it out of the schools.'" In the end, the schools retained the books but agreed not to accept any more from the Alliance.

This example highlights the way in which a state legislator's work at home may have no direct relation to his decisions in the capital. Advocate 4's part in the dispute did not involve any pending legislation, committee work, or house leadership roles. Rather, it put him in the position of community leader. As is shown by one of the quotations at the beginning of this section, Advocate 4 sees being a community leader and being a state representative as two intertwined responsibilities that cannot be divorced. The common man writ large is sometimes called upon to resolve disputes that have no connection to his work in the state capital. Advocate 4 happily filled that role, in the belief that his incumbency, background, and name recognition made him the right person to do it.

According to Advocate 4, surrounding districts had interests that were similar to those of his own district. This again illustrates how "fuzzy" district boundaries can be in the mind of a state representative. Advocate 4's district was compact—"one of the smallest in the state, only three miles square." The school district spread across several other statehouse districts besides his own and Rep 2's. Person-to-person campaigning was both possible and important. Advocate 4 regularly attended chamber of commerce meetings and other functions. He focused on local schools and businesses. As chair of the Insurance Committee, his attendance at chamber meetings was considered particularly important. Insurance issues are very important to local business. This small-business focus exemplifies the boundary-crossing that an effective, metropolitan state legislator must negotiate back home. I asked Advocate 4 for information about the small-business owners that he consulted. Did they live in his district? He said:

> They live around here. Not every business owner lives in the district . . . [N]ot every person that owns a small business [and] that lives in the district has their small business within the district. Most of them have them very close. The concerns are the same. So, . . . because the district is so small, it is not uncommon to have people who have been there a long time move out, and still be within the area. . . . [I]t is not uncommon to have people move in and out. Or, it is not uncommon to have their children move in when they move out.

• • •

Advocate 4 was first elected against a one-term Democratic incumbent. When the current districts were drawn, Democrats controlled the house (though not the senate). However, Democratic control is a relative rarity in this state. According to Advocate 4, the district was redrawn to help Democrats by grouping together many of the most heavily Democratic precincts in what is otherwise a Republican county. But in the process, the Democrats also made it a better district for Advocate 4. He told me:

> They reapportioned the . . . district to exclude the former twelve-term incumbent, eliminating *Maple Heights*. And in doing so, they also improved the district for [the incumbent] by lessening the number of Republicans and raising the Democrats 2 percent. But what they didn't do is they didn't factor in *me*. At the time I was serving on the *Cherry Township* city council. And they eliminated Maple Heights, but they added in four precincts of Cherry Township. So, of the eighteen precincts, there were five [in which I had been on the ballot before:] the four [in Cherry Township] plus my own . . . I was the "incumbent" in the election . . . I was the one that had always stood for election before, and not him . . . The second thing they did is on the other side of the district, where the heaviest concentration of Democrats were, in the precincts they had left in, that was exactly the place that I had been raised. And so, in what we call the yellow-

dog Democrat district, I won . . . in *Walnut Grove,* the most Democrat precinct in the area. And that win came as a surprise to the Democrats too.

Advocate 4 believed that strong name recognition was much more important than party labels here. His service on the city council had helped him build name recognition. So did his years of growing up in the community. The new district was perfect for him. This view strongly contrasts with those of Advocates 2 and 5, who work toward name recognition but also believe that their party label is enormously useful in securing reelection. According to Advocate 4, the Democrats made a fatal mistake in what became his district: they relied on party voting instead of personal name recognition. As he put it, "they didn't factor in *me.*"

Overall, Advocate 4 believed, the statehouse Democrats used poor strategy. Not only did they fail to factor Advocate 4 into the district equation, they also passed school funding legislation that "hurt their own rookie" (the incumbent). Advocate 4 told me that the Democrats came up with a new base funding formula that was more redistributive than the previous one. It would aid inner-city and rural districts, but give less money back to Advocate 4's stable, middle-class suburban community. The incumbent Democrat voted against the bill, but it passed anyway. Campaigning door-to-door, Advocate 4 argued that the bill would not have passed had Republicans controlled the statehouse. He believed that this strategy was crucial to his very narrow victory in that election. Subsequently, he was reelected by safer margins. In a rematch against the defeated incumbent, Advocate 4 won by a larger margin than before. Interestingly, the new base funding formula has not been repealed or replaced, even though Republicans now lead the statehouse and governor's office. Advocate 4 decided that the new formula did not harm his district. Still, he believed that the needs of his district and the county are more effectively represented by Republicans, who favor a more proportional, less redistributive approach to school district funding.

This study was more than half-finished when Advocate 4 joined on. I did not have as much time to observe him as I did with most of the other legislators that participated. Yet even in this short time, it became clear that Advocate 4 served his stable suburban district as the common man writ large: presenting an unassuming air while struggling to advocate local interests and shore up his credentials as a moderate. He spoke his mind, and got quite a lot of publicity throughout the metropolitan area when he criticized the amusement park project. Ideologically, he did not waver between his party's moderate and conservative wings: he took an unequivocal position in favor of the moderates. This mix of pragmatic ideology, home-district issues, and name recognition served Advocate 4 well. He had upset an incumbent, and had been solidly reelected several times since. It remained to be seen whether this advocate strategy would help him win and hold onto statewide office.

Conclusion

Like the Burkeans discussed in the previous chapter, in-district advocates must meet the four tasks that Malcolm Jewell described. Their *communication with constituents* takes the form of town halls and other meetings—sometimes with enormous turnout—and media appearances. The theme of such communication is generally that they know the district has needs, they understand those needs, and they are working hard to get those needs on the agenda. They also seek to place new issues on the public agenda. In-district advocates are very active in their communities and they work hard to be visible. They interact with constituents, presenting themselves as community leaders and stressing their district-centered focus. This spills into neighboring communities that share municipal or school-district boundaries. It also spills into communities that share resources such as highway interchanges. In general, advocates seem quite comfortable in the spotlight and in the district.

For in-district advocates, *policy responsiveness* comes in the form of legislation and other actions that respond to the district's needs. This can mean promoting new projects, such as the revised highway interchange favored by Advocate 2 after months of town hall meetings. But it can also mean opposition to threatening projects. In Advocate 4's case, responsiveness came in the form of standing against proposals that threatened the community, such as the amusement park tax abatement, private-school vouchers, and concealed-carry handgun permits. While ombudspersons, as we shall see, are responsive in the sense of letting issues bubble up, in-district advocates work to be the first to respond, thus taking the lead and socializing the conflict. In-district advocates generally present themselves as leaders in responding to forces, projects, and proposals that threaten the community.

In-district advocates place more emphasis than Burkeans do on *allocation of resources for the district*. The four legislators discussed in this chapter believed that their districts must work hard to get their fair share from the state. They believed that resources were likely to go elsewhere unless they were effective advocates who kept district needs on the agenda. Advocate 3 sponsored a lot of legislation that was important to his district, and, to a lesser extent, the others did too. But these in-district advocates' accomplishments did not always take the form of legislation in the statehouse. Advocate 1 spent a lot of time stumping for his school district's financial needs (bonds and tax levies). Advocate 2 led the effort to negotiate a new highway interchange by working directly with DOT. Advocate 4 was particularly proud to be fighting *against* legislation that threatened the community.

Casework requests seemed to be more common in the mixed or changing districts served by these advocates. Thus *constituent service* was important to them. Advocate 3 got a lot of calls and believed that casework was crucial to his reelection. Advocate 2's "little phone books" helped constituents stay in touch when they needed something. In general, though, these advocates were not comfortable with casework alone. It did not generally result in the type of publicity that they sought. They saw casework as part of the job. But they also sought out opportunities that brought more publicity and protected their reputations as community leaders.

All four of these advocates were outspoken about their progressive political ambitions. The in-district advocates in this study were clearly the ones most ambitious for higher office. The in-district-advocate approach involves neighboring communities, and is therefore an especially popular strategy for those seeking a state senate seat. These legislators were ambitious, comfortable in front of crowds and cameras, and visible back home. Their home styles were centered on protecting and advocating for changing, struggling, or threatened communities.

5

Advocates beyond the District

Like in-district advocates, advocates beyond the district like to socialize conflicts. They put issues on the agenda. Yet Advocates 5 and 6 had a less district-centered focus than the four in-district advocates. Advocates beyond the district often use strong reelection majorities back home as a secure base. After being reelected by substantial margins more than once, these two legislators took a low-key approach to reelection, sending out flyers a few days before the campaign. Advocate 5, whose party was the statehouse majority party, raised campaign funds for reelection, but then gave most of it away to Democrats who were in more closely contested races. In contrast, Advocate 6, a Republican, said, "[I] kept my nose out of everybody else's race." Her party was in the minority, both in the statehouse and in the major city that encompassed most of her district. Her less partisan approach helped her earn support from many prominent Democrats.

These advocates broadened their focus to include issues that extended beyond their district, and even beyond adjoining districts. Advocate 5 was immersed in education issues and public employee concerns. He did go home and meet with constituents, but he did not bring up district-specific issues. Rather, he worked to win constituent support for his education agenda and his party's overall agenda. He also stressed his pro-union labor record. He took strong stands on issues that affected the entire state, and he believed these stands were particularly popular in his blue-collar, urban constituency. His district was overwhelmingly Democratic. Even Republicans who were popular statewide could not win in this district. Thus it should come as no surprise that Advocate 5 pushed his party agenda aggressively in the statehouse. He emphasized his support for that agenda when among constituents, often putting in a good word for the governor and other party leaders. Advocate 5 made an important announcement during this study: he said he would not seek reelection. And unlike Advocate 6, he did not seek another office. Yet his career was well served by his advocate approach to organized labor. After he finished his last house session, his union organizer job became a full-time one, instead of part-time (more accurately, part-year) as it was. This brought more prestige and better pay, and the job fit nicely with the pro-union work he had done in the statehouse.

Advocate 6's approach was somewhat different. She focused on the entire city and metropolitan area when she went home. Many of her constituents were commuters who worked downtown, outside the district. In turn, many of the businesses in her district employed people who lived in other parts of the city and the metropolitan area. Advocate 6 won an at-large city council seat during the course of this study, and resigned from the statehouse. Anxious to be closer to her grandchildren but unwilling to leave public life, she had been pondering the council run for some time. Putting together the district's interests and her own ambitions led her to emphasize the good of the whole city. For example, without better local roads connecting her district with the rest of the city, she worried that growth in her community would stop. But at home, she presented her actions in terms of the city's overall good, not just that of the district. Thus I label her the "civic booster." Her advocate's approach helped her move from statehouse to city hall. With term limits looming, she was able to stay in public office and continue to be active in the city's public life.

Both of these representatives sponsored important legislation, and both presented themselves back home as advocates who set the agenda and get things done. They responded to their constituents not with district-specific service, but with an emphasis on broader city- or statewide causes they believed were popular in the district. In Advocate 5's case, that meant stressing labor and education. Advocate 6 focused on the city's economic development. This chapter shows two advocates approaching issues that go beyond the district, yet returning home to tell constituents what they have been doing.

Advocate 5: The Progressive

Studies have shown that people have to hear something seven
times before they really remember . . . seven times before it
soaks in and they remember it. And . . . I'm not just in competition with [my opponent]. I'm in competition with Tide [and]
McDonald's. Right? Every message . . . and I usually lose.

—*Advocate 5*

"Come here, I want you to meet somebody," Advocate 5 said during
our first encounter. "I want you to meet my opponent." And so an in-
troduction was made. I greeted Fred and Fred's wife (Advocate 5 always referred to his challenger by his first name only, which I have
changed here), then rode around with Advocate 5 in his car on campaign-related errands. The election was only weeks away, and Advocate 5 was confident. He'd run against Fred twice already, and each
time he had won more than 65 percent of the vote. The district was
urban, blue-collar, and Democratic. During our interview, he reminded me repeatedly that he was "so safe." He was confident enough
to send volunteers away, telling them to go help Democrats in more
competitive races nearby. His confidence was well placed. He won
reelection easily, again capturing more than 65 percent of the vote.
However, all this confidence coexisted uneasily with a sense of frustration.

Advocate 5 got upset with a political system that he believed was
out of touch with the voters. As the quotation above suggests, Advocate 5 believed that his constituents, and most others as well, know
and care very little about politics. I once asked him to describe his
constituents, and he answered: "They're basically nonpolitical, but
the three minutes a month they think about politics, I'd call them
pissed-off malcontents. They think they're not getting a fair deal
from government, and they see the big boys winning: the bankers and
the brokers and those kind of people . . . One of my emphases in the
legislature is to represent the people who don't have a lobbyist . . . to
try to give the little guy a fair break, and . . . to the extent that they
think about me, which is two minutes every other year, I think that
I have a reputation of doing that."

He made a similar point the day we met, on the way to visit with his friend, who was then running for state auditor (she won). He told me, "She's about to pull her hair out." I asked, "Why? Just because of the pressure of campaigning generally?" He said: "It's all money. She's just on the phone dialing for dollars all the time, and nobody knows her. What is the state auditor? Nobody knows. What do they do? And she's got to somehow break through the static of people's lives, in between thinking about the last episode of *Friends* and what they're going to have for dinner, and they've got to think 'state auditor' for a second."

I call Advocate 5 "the progressive" because of his emphasis on issues and his left-of-center leanings. During our interview, he chose the label himself. He preferred *progressive* to *liberal*. "Even back when liberal was cool," he said, "I didn't like that term." But what did it mean to be a progressive in his district? According to him, his constituents were "not conservative or liberal," but angry with an out-of-touch government. By emphasizing the issues he cared about most, Advocate 5 believed he could connect with these constituents. He worked hard at representing those who he believed were cynical. At times, he listened to the local school boards and others articulate the needs of the diverse neighborhoods he represented. But other times, he rested comfortably on his strong partisan majority back home and focused on the issues he thought were important. At the same time, he tried to bring working-class cynics back into the political system. It could be an uphill battle.

In presenting his own approach to nearly every problem, Advocate 5 found a way to articulate the issues. For example, he represented portions of three school districts. One was the inner-city school district, beset by white flight, low student achievement, political patronage, and costly court-ordered desegregation. The other two were neighborhood districts. These were located within the city limits, but were entirely separate from the inner-city school district. The people of the two neighborhood districts had long been known for their intense opposition to any involvement with the inner-city district. The people of the two smaller neighborhood districts got along with each other but distrusted their urban neighbor. They feared the city district might one day try to annex them or draw them into court-ordered desegregation. As I noted in the previous chapter, Advocate 2, who represented part of one of these districts, mentioned this rift to me, even suggesting that virtually all families—white, black, middle-class, and working-class—would flee his district if there were any involvement with the inner-city school district: "I don't know who'll be left!" In his interview, Advocate 5 admitted that he and his wife had moved to their current home because it was located in a neighborhood school district, noting that it was "time for the kids to go to school. We had some serious concerns about the [city] schools." But while Advocate 2 sided squarely with the neighborhood and inner-suburban school districts, Advocate 5 represented a district that included both neighborhood and inner-city schools. With all this potential conflict, how does a state representative cope? Here's Advocate 5's approach: "All the education reform stuff we've done, I have just always looked at what makes sense and what's right for my three districts and I've done it. And [the city] has benefited sometimes, and they've lost sometimes. It's not a big deal. I'm a real pro-school person: one of the main education legislators. So I get along with all of them."

Advocate 5 approached potential conflict between school districts by broadening the issue. The issue, as he saw it, was not city schools versus neighborhood schools. Rather, it was his own status as a "main education legislator." He could also draw on his outside job as an organizer for a teacher's union. This gave him contacts among teachers and organized labor and aided him enormously in his heavily unionized, blue-collar community. Not all legislators have Advocate 5's confidence in the unions. Ombuds 4, for example, believed that most of his constituents supported his stance against Advocate 5's collective bargaining bill. But this was not a worry for Advocate 5, who knew that two of his three school districts already allowed collective bargaining. His working-class constituents were eager to support a pro-union Democrat. Thus he shifted the issue away from the rifts that divided his local school districts, and placed his emphasis instead on his own "pro-education" status. This illustrates why I classified Advocate 5 as an advocate beyond the district. His home style on this issue contrasted sharply with that of Advocates 1 and 2, both of whom stressed their advocacy on behalf of *local* schools when at home. Advocate 5 preferred a statewide orientation at home. He presented himself not as a community leader, but as an issue-based policymaker.

Advocate 5's teacher-union background had an enormous effect on his legislative priorities. During the 1999 legislative session, he sponsored the collective bargaining bill, one of the most controversial bills in the statehouse. The bill's backers sought to allow collective bargaining for public employees, subject to certain restrictions. Those to be covered included state and local workers, as well as employees in public school districts. The popular Democratic governor called for the bill's passage in his State of the State address. This drew a sharply divided response among legislators. Democrats gave the governor a standing ovation. Republicans sat silently. The bill exposed the state's political cleavages in sharp relief: urban Democrats strongly supported the bill, all the Republicans except one senator opposed it, and rural Democrats wavered. In the end, the bill did not pass the house.

For Advocate 5, politics is done right when it is issue-focused. Whenever someone tried to move a political debate away from the issues, he would get angry. I observed a chamber of commerce forum that was attended by Advocate 5 and Ombuds 1. Ombuds 1 was attacked by a political opponent for not having filed a campaign finance disclosure form on time, and Ombuds 1 shot back, "I've been found guilty of nothing." Talking with me afterward, Advocate 5 expressed frustration with Ombuds 1's opponent: "This stuff about having your report in late . . . I don't know, I agree with [Ombuds 1]. In a forum like that, that was totally inappropriate. You should be talking to people [that] are there because they want to know a little bit about what you think, specifically about small-business issues."

Advocate 5's relationship with his own opponent stood in stark contrast with the above example. At the same forum, Fred spoke of the need for quick responses to constituent mail, and about tort reform. "To me," said Advocate 5 afterward, "that's all fair. That's on the issue level. He's saying that I'm not doing things that he thinks I should do." Advocate 5 did not address his challenger's remarks during his own short talk at the forum. However, he did tell me that he already worked hard to respond to constituent service needs.

Still talking about Fred, Advocate 5 said, "Now, to be honest with you, the . . . reason that I . . . have the luxury of being so friendly with him is, my district is so Democratic that he's not really a threat." Thus, with some ambivalence, Advocate 5 regarded his issue-based campaign as a luxury, granted by a strong partisan majority. Ombuds

1 agreed that issue campaigns were more likely to be conducted in safe districts, suggesting that his own challengers were "always nasty" because "this is a swing district." This seems to corroborate Advocate 5's view that issue campaigns are a luxury—although one not available in Ombuds 1's district. However, Ombuds 2 had a completely different view, claiming that he and his challenger were able to remain friendly and issue-focused even in a high-turnout, close election.

Advocate 5 regarded the Democratic party label primarily as a shortcut that helped voters identify his views on the issues. After a long discussion about name recognition, I asked, "What if [your name] didn't say 'Democrat' next to it?" Advocate 5 laughed and replied: "I would probably be in trouble! I certainly would have been in trouble my first time. Now, my fourth election, I guess I'm conceited enough to think I've broken through and they'd even recognize my name without the party label. But that party label helps a lot."

Advocate 5 depended on the party label, not the party organization. Of the latter, he said: "It's almost a nonentity as a structure for me, okay? All the party is, they call and say, 'Can you give us money?' Because I'm a safe person. They're not like they used to be. But the party . . . is helping some candidates."

For Advocate 5, the party label stood for issues and ideology, not organization. He became frustrated with Democrats who didn't share his approach: "When I said the Republicans are big business, the Democrats are working people, I actually believe that historically. Now, unfortunately, Democrats have kind of gotten to where we've blurred that, to our detriment, I think. And you've got plenty of people who call themselves Democrats who don't act like that. But I still think it's important."

Parties and ideology may correlate, but they should not be confounded. Advocate 5 saw his constituents as Democrats. He suspected that they were more progressive than those in other parts of the state. But according to him, they did not necessarily identify themselves as liberal. In particular, he did not think that social issues were central to his constituents' politics. They focused on local issues. He told me, "They're not nearly as focused on gun control and abor-

tion and the kind of hot-button liberal-conservative issues as we are."
He added: "These people aren't liberal or conservative. They just want
a chance. They want a good life. They want the [highway inter-
change] fixed. When they turn the electricity on, they want it to work
alright. Stuff like that." Still, Advocate 5 did not spend much of his
time at home discussing specific local issues. Rather, he was usually
an advocate for statewide causes.

I asked him about the neighborhoods that made up his district. He
saw it as a diverse community, and said that each neighborhood had
its own character. But, except for a narrow corridor of old-money, urban mansions, he saw virtually all the neighborhoods as Democratic
ones. According to him, his constituents were mostly "hard-core,
working-class Democrats." While knocking on doors before elections, he said, he was particularly enthused about the reception he got
in a heavily African American, lower-income neighborhood. It
should be noted that, like Advocate 2, Advocate 5 is a white representative of a racially mixed district. But unlike Advocate 2, Advocate 5 put very little emphasis on explicitly addressing racial issues in
the district. Rather, he stressed his party label. Regarding that lower-income neighborhood, he told me:

> It's the poorest part of my district, the most racially mixed, and
> those people are all Democrats. They understand on a real vis-
> ceral economic level what the parties mean.
>   It's real fun to knock on their door, because I'll say, "Hi,
> I'm [Advocate 5], I'm the Democrat for state representative."
> [They'll respond,] "Democrat [snaps fingers], you've got me, al-
> right!" That's all I have to say. Even when I wasn't known, when
> I was a brand-new candidate, as soon as they hear that Demo-
> crat word [they say], "You've got my vote! You want to put a yard
> sign out here?"

Knocking on doors was one way Advocate 5 learned about the partisan leanings of his district. He didn't have much time for this first
lesson—he moved to the district only fifteen months before he was
elected! A native of another state, he had moved to this city years earlier, but had been living in a different part of town. State law requires
state representatives to live in the districts they represent for one year
before their election, and Advocate 5 barely made it. Shortly after

moving, he was recruited to run by the retiring incumbent, local unions, and groups on the pro-choice side of the abortion-rights controversy. At first he said no. But then his wife encouraged him to take a second look—"sometimes to her regret!" he said. With strong pro-choice and union support, Advocate 5 ran and won. Like many of the other representatives I studied, he found knocking on doors to be an indispensable tool in the election. Unlike those others, however, he did not have years beforehand in which to establish himself as a community leader and serve in local offices. This contrasts particularly sharply with the in-district advocates described in the previous chapter. Advocates 1 and 2 served on school boards first, Advocate 4 served on the city council, and Advocate 3 ran for several other offices before finally winning a seat as state representative.

In addition to knocking on doors, Advocate 5 also learned about his district's partisan leanings by hiring a campaign consultant. The consultant ran the "dead Democrat numbers," which estimate how a Democratic candidate would fare in the district if he died one month before the election. These numbers are run by taking an election that was the worst-case scenario for Democrats—that is, when a Republican won in a landslide—and figuring out what percentage of votes the district cast for the defeated candidate. The election that Advocate 5's consultant used was one in which a popular, incumbent Republican U.S. senator overwhelmed his Democratic challenger. Even then, the challenger won a majority of votes in Advocate 5's district. After running the dead Democrat numbers, Advocate 5's consultant asked, "What am I doing here?" and moved on to more competitive races.

A winning candidate needs campaign funding as well as partisan support. For Advocate 5, this came from his biannual fundraiser. The host was a friend of his, a lobbyist for a health maintenance organization. Advocate 5 raised much of his money from unions—both from political action committees and individual contributors who were union members. Yet he did not believe that these contributors were buying votes, only access. Making light of the voters' cynicism, he said to me: "People think there's some direct bribery going on. Like [contributors will] say, 'Hey, how 'bout that bill over there! Give ya a check?' [But that's] never even been hinted at. . . . It may have happened at one time, but it's way too sophisticated for that now. But it's the lobbyist's job to be my pal so that when he does come to me on an issue that his client cares about, I'm talking to a friend at that point. I'm not talking to a lobbyist. So they try to be friendly, invite you out to dinner, that kind of stuff. And they give you checks."

Once again, he spoke of his frustration with the general public's disinterest and cynicism regarding politics. Then he turned the questioning on me, asking why I chose to study state legislators. I said, "I went into political science because I think politics is fun." "Isn't it interesting?" he agreed, but added, "I can't convince people of that, though. [They say,] 'Oh, boring, I hate it!'"

His sometime frustration did not deter Advocate 5 from his issue-based focus. At the chamber forum mentioned above, he used all of his time to talk about one issue. This was in keeping with his progressive theme. Unlike Ombuds 1's challenger, Advocate 5 did not raise negative campaign-related issues about his opponent. Nor did he point to his own record of public service, as some legislators might. Rather, he addressed an issue that was of special interest to the small-businesspeople in attendance: health insurance reform. He began by thanking the chamber for giving him a rare forum to discuss issues, then moved on to his topic:

> The big guys in federal office get this opportunity a lot. This is my first forum this election. This organization is the only one here that has these forums. I want to talk about one issue: health care—access and affordability for small business. Let them buy into the state employee fund. The problem is, there's not enough competition for small groups. This plan [in proposed legislation] would allow, not mandate, that we open up the state system to small business. I, as a state employee, get insurance at a reasonable rate. Small business should too.

This is one of several times I watched Advocate 5 use forums as an opportunity to discuss issues in-depth and thank his hosts for allowing him the opportunity. This was his issue-based, progressive style. Again, his focus was not district-specific.

I watched him further develop his progressive theme at two Birchtree School District forums, about a year apart. At the first, in 1998, he discussed desegregation legislation for the state's two inner-city school districts and how it would affect the state funding available for other districts, including Birchtree. At the 1999 meeting, he again addressed the question of school funding formulas, this time putting in a plug for the Democratic governor. A few years earlier, the governor had successfully championed legislation to increase education monies and restructure state school funding.[1] By 1999, the governor had declared his candidacy for the U.S. Senate, and his campaign was under way. A loyal Democrat, Advocate 5 put in a good word: he noted that the governor had increased funding for local schools, including those in Birchtree.

Advocate 5 faced some opposition at public meetings. At one chamber of commerce meeting, a "legislative action sheet" was distributed that listed the chamber's stands on, and priorities for, pending bills. Advocate 5 complained that the collective bargaining bill was listed on the sheet as "Item #1 under 'strongly oppose,'" adding, "I'm the sponsor of that bill!" Addressing issues and policy concerns, he noted that the bill set tougher penalties for public employees who strike. He also mentioned that a neighboring state had collective bargaining provisions, yet had not experienced either high costs or employee unrest. It is doubtful that Advocate 5 converted the chamber to supporting his bill. However, he created a more congenial atmosphere, and their opposition softened. They thanked him and his colleagues (all Democrats) for other legislative efforts that the chamber supported. After the presentations, I listened in as Advocate 5 chatted with chamber members. Some of them said that, personally, they did not think collective bargaining would be a major problem.

Far away, in Ombuds 4's district, Advocate 5 was not present to make his case for his bill. There, the local chamber's opposition was more heated and less forgiving. In his hometown, Advocate 5 was treated as an old friend with whom the chamber had an honest disagreement. Across the state, Ombuds 4 and the small-town chamber spoke of the same bill in ominous tones. They feared "arm-twisting" by Democrats trying to pass it, "bloodbaths" in schools where unions went head-to-head over who would represent the teachers, and closings of small local school districts that could not afford the costs.

1. Gregory Casey and James W. Endersby, "Funding for Education in the 1990s: A Case Study," 266–71.

Where he was present and known, Advocate 5 was able at least to temper business's strong opposition to his bill. Still, it was too little, too late. As noted, the bill ultimately did not pass.

I have said that Advocate 5 was a progressive, not only because he stressed issues, but because of his left-of-center leanings. His discussions were replete with references to the differences between the "big guys," who tend to support Republicans, and the working people, whom he believed supported him. His campaign literature emphasized this theme. Before the 1998 midterm election, he sent out a brochure to his most reliably Democratic precincts. He was not optimistic about voter turnout, telling me, "It's going to be real low." Still, he tried to get Democrats to the polls. (This was partly a favor for Senator 1, whose district encompassed Advocate 5's house district and who was in a reelection race against a tough Republican challenger.) This is how he described his mailer: "On the front, it says something like, 'Insurance Companies. Bankers. Lobbyists. Tobacco Companies. Big Business.' Something like that, and . . . that's all it says. Open it up, and it says, 'If you don't vote, they win.' And then there's some text from me. 'That's why [Advocate 5] wants you to vote.' And I'm . . . mailing it only to . . . the precincts that have over a 65 percent Democratic performance. In the last three elections, those districts on average voted 65 percent Democrat or above."

Advocate 5 saw himself as a representative for those who did not have a lobbyist of their own. Often, lobbying groups that do not have their own offices in the capital will use the offices of sympathetic state representatives. For example, Advocate 2 let lobbyists for the blind use his office resources. Advocate 5's office-sharing reflected his theme of favoring workers over the big guys. Among the groups that worked out of his office were a welfare-rights organization, credit unions (which seek to expand their range of banking services, and are often opposed by big banks), labor groups, community groups, and environmental groups. Banks and big businesses did not work nearly so closely with him. He told the following story: "The bank lobbyist, he's a nice guy. He actually used my office one day, used my computer. I took a picture of him and I have it on my wall. And . . . I keep ragging him, telling him I'm going to tell the bankers that he was in my office. 'No,' [the banker replied], 'I'll lose my job!'"

For Advocate 5, being a progressive meant, in part, articulating the issues to the folks that don't have a lobbyist. He tried to bring people into the political system as Democrats and his supporters. He reached out to people who had been made cynical, he believed, by a political system that favored the big guys. Still, he sometimes perceived his reelection interests as being at odds with what was best for the political system. On several occasions, he seemed to share his constituents' cynicism. As we drove around the city on that first day, our first stop was to pick up some campaign brochures at a local printer. When we got back in the car, I asked, "What money paid for those brochures in the trunk?" Laughing, he replied, "Dirty campaign contributions!" Later in our drive, he expressed himself less whimsically. As we passed the offices of a local public television station, he noted that their cameras had been present at an earlier forum. However, he said, after the state senate candidates had spoken, the crew shut off their cameras and left. The only other media present was a suburban newspaper, one not distributed in Advocate 5's district. I asked him if he was disappointed—if he had hoped for more coverage. He replied, "No coverage helps me!" I asked why that was. He replied: "In this race . . . I'm the incumbent who got 68 percent last time. Fred is challenging me. The less media, the better . . . for my selfish purposes. Now, I think our democracy's dying on the vine, and I'm glad [the city newspaper] did one article on us anyway."

Advocate 5 made clear his ambivalence about the political system in which he worked. For "selfish purposes," he would be pleased to have no media coverage at all. But this view was in tension with his opinion that "our democracy's dying on the vine." Later, he found some comfort in the single article about his election, in the major daily newspaper's metropolitan section. Still, he was not truly content with the political system, perhaps not even with his own role in it. His own selfish interests in reelection did not square with the democracy he wanted to promote. His progressive theme and drive toward reelection created a tension that he had to negotiate. Sometimes frustration and a little disappointment were the order of the day. Even so, Advocate 5 kept working to draw the cynics back into the political system and to represent those who did not have a lobbyist.

Advocate 6: The Civic Booster

If you don't get that money for your district, or for your general area, that money's going to be spent, and it's going to go somewhere. And it'll probably go to [another city], or somewhere, but it won't go to [your city], or to your district. So you're not doing anybody a favor by sitting on your hands and saying, "Oh, no, I'm not going to approve that!"

—Advocate 6

There's damn few Republicans that we old *Saline Countians* would vote for, but so many people say they'd vote for Advocate 6 because she's done so much for us.

—One of Advocate 6's constituents

Advocate 6 wanted money. She sought resources for her hometown. She skillfully used her fifteen years in the statehouse—more than twice the average house member's tenure in her state—to get onto appropriations committees, oversee the spending of taxpayer dollars, and, most of all, to develop, develop, develop. She was unabashedly pro-growth and pro-hometown. Every time I saw her meet with constituents, she stressed her record of "bringing home the bacon." Her pro-growth philosophy seemed appropriate to the district she served, a fast-growing suburban community, most of which was annexed to the central city. She prided herself on being one of the first women to serve on any of the state's appropriations committees. She was competitive, sometimes taking on the state's other major metropolitan area in the safe presence of her constituents. Advocate 6 was busy, outgoing, and well connected with business. During the course of my study, she won an at-large seat on the city council and resigned her statehouse seat. Anticipating a term limit in the house, she had found a chance to bring her civic boosterism home and help spend some of the resources she'd been sending from the capital. She immediately rose to the council's leadership due to her background, the esteem she was held in, and her connections. She was well known, well liked, and knowledgeable. In short, Advocate 6 was a model civic booster.

Cities and their boosters face certain limits, and Advocate 6 seemed well aware of these constraints. Paul E. Peterson argues that local officials must pursue developmental policies in order to be effective.[2] These are the policies that lure in jobs and growth, thus expanding the local tax base. Such policies include the building of new highways and offering tax incentives for businesses to move into the city (or at least not move out). Developmental policies may also include regulatory reform, again designed to promote business and lure it into the city's borders. Advocate 6 made developmental policies the very centerpiece of her self-presentation. At every meeting, on each campaign stop, and in most news stories about her, the pro-growth theme showed through. She always seemed organized and on-message. She was thus particularly effective at helping the city pursue its developmental imperative.

Like Burkean 1, Advocate 6 represented a well-to-do suburban area. And like Burkean 1, she sometimes made decisions on her own and then justified them to constituents. Regarding her approach, she told me, "I always feel . . . that if I learn all I can about the issue, [then] when I vote, . . . I'm voting from an educated position. I've learned all I can, both pro and con. Then I think, that's how the people of the district would vote after they learn about it and know about it."

Though Advocate 6's style sometimes resembled the Burkean approach, she was more aggressive than the two Burkeans in this study when it came to building support and putting issues on the agenda. She worked hard to make sure her constituents knew what she'd done in the statehouse to bring resources to the city. She was as an advocate beyond the district. Unlike a Burkean, though, Advocate 6 strongly favored home district interests over the "whole-state" orientation. She put local interests at the center of her justifications for decisions. While she had been relatively secure in her reelection, her plans to seek another office pushed her to expand her base of support.

Advocate 6's approach changed over her years in office. She started by trying to solicit feedback from constituents before taking action. But as the years went by, she developed more and more confidence in her own judgment. She cultivated better name recognition and safer

2. Paul E. Peterson, *City Limits*, 41–43.

reelection margins. Thus she evolved into more of an advocate as she gained expertise and recognition at home.

Since she sought constituent support for her decisions, Advocate 6 had to find ways to reach them. She was particularly proud of her mail surveys. Like Burkean 1, she found the open-ended constituent comments on those surveys to be useful in finding out what was going on at home. She got her share of casework requests, but referred most of these to her legislative assistant, thus creating a division of labor that allowed her to devote more time to promoting the city. She spoke to many different groups. I asked her which groups those were, and she said: "Whoever calls you. It may be a neighborhood group, a trucking group, an industry group, a homeowners group. It's just whatever, everything that society is made up [of]. That's about what you meet with. Yeah, we do a lot in the schools." I asked what the people who organized those meetings wanted from her. She said, "Usually a speech in regard to what is happening, what I see coming up in the legislative session, or clarification of a bill that was passed, or several bills that . . . passed."

I observed Advocate 6 make many such appearances in the city. She was always on the go, and when I told her of my plans to follow her around at home, she said, "Boy, are you going to be busy . . . I just don't know how you're going to keep up with all of this!" Advocate 6 was once a homemaker and community volunteer, but with her children grown and husband deceased, she dedicated herself full-time to the legislator's job. She did not limit her appearances to the district (this was in part due to her city council race). Yet she told me that some approaches to meeting the public were more effective than others. She said: "I started out trying to have town hall meetings. That was a joke! You get about six people there that just want to complain. I mean, that was it. It didn't matter. I tried doing them all over the district, and it didn't make any difference. . . . I found out those town hall meetings are a waste of everybody's time, a waste of the coffee!"

This comment contrasts particularly sharply with those of some other legislators in this study, most notably Advocate 2. In Advocate 2's changing district, town halls were the centerpiece of his home style, and over five hundred people attended the meeting dealing with the controversial highway interchange. But in Advocate 6's more secure district, only the "complainers" bothered to attend. Thus she came to rely on giving speeches and reading the annual mail-in survey more carefully in order to keep in touch with her constituents.

As a Republican in a heavily Democratic city, Advocate 6 had struggled to win hearts and minds ever since her first election. Toward the end of her tenure in the statehouse, she had gotten used to running unopposed. But back when she first ran for the open house seat, it was an uphill battle. She had strong name recognition as a community leader in women's auxiliary groups and local fund-raisers. She was active in the parochial schools that her children attended. She was the wife of a prominent local dentist. Still, these credentials had to contest with a countervailing factor: the district's overwhelming preference for Democrats. According to Advocate 6, the district had been gerrymandered for the Democrats. She ran anyway, winning by 786 votes. Democrats challenged her votes, arguing that some voters cast ballots in the wrong state legislative district. But Advocate 6 prevailed. In ensuing years she had a number of high-quality challengers, but her reelection margins grew. She ran unopposed in her last statehouse election. Later, she won her city council race with 57 percent of the citywide vote.

Advocate 6 had to deal with the tensions her party label created. On one hand, she liked being a Republican, arguing that the Republican party is the one that "doesn't want to grow government." She strongly favored limiting government regulation of business. She was honored with invitations to dine with a popular state Republican leader when he served as governor. She also had several chances to host President Reagan when he visited her hometown. Still, however comfortable she was with the Republican label, Advocate 6 knew she was outnumbered. She negotiated this tension by working closely with Democrats in the legislature and departing from the party line on some issues. But most of all she stressed the city, instead of the party, as her constituency and base of support. She was not above being a little competitive. For example, she worked with other representatives to win five million dollars in state aid for restoring a World War I veterans' memorial near downtown. (It was not in her district.) At the check-presentation ceremony, Advocate 6 told onlookers and local media: "They said, 'Five million dollars for [our hometown]—where's [the other city's] money?' I told them, '[That city] gets the money anyway.' Legislators planted our feet firm, and said, 'We're going to keep our dollars.' I hope you're as excited as I am. This [memorial] is more than [the other city] ever had!"

None of the other legislators at the ceremony stressed this type of competitiveness. Some of them did reinforce Advocate 6's other themes, though. One said: "The team from [our city] all worked together. It doesn't matter what party you're from. We all represent [this city]." These comments seemed directed specifically at Advocate 6; there were no other Republican legislators at the ceremony. According to Ombuds 3, who also worked on the project, Advocate 6 was the only Republican who was so involved. As a matter of fact, few Republicans were invited when the city's Democratic delegation set the local agenda, but Advocate 6 was one of those few, according to Ombuds 3 and others. This was not the only time Democratic colleagues praised Advocate 6. The theme of their praise was, "She helps our city." In her run for city council, Advocate 6 got endorsements from virtually all of the metropolitan area's house and senate delegation—mostly Democrats. These included the powerful senate majority leader and the president pro tem. Of course, there was also a self-interest involved for Democrats. After her landslide election to the nonpartisan council seat, Advocate 6 was required to resign her house seat, and Democrats spent a great deal of money in the ensuing special election. But it was to no avail; Republicans held onto the seat with a political newcomer in a very narrow victory that recalled Advocate 6's own surprise victory fifteen years before.

Advocate 6 avoided stressing partisanship at home, telling me that during elections, "[I] kept my nose out of everybody else's race, and kept on working, taking care of constituents." This contrasts sharply with many of the majority Democrats I interviewed, some of whom also had safe seats. The Democrats often got involved in more competitive races. For example, Advocate 5 sent money and campaign volunteers to Ombuds 2's opponent, hoping to pick up that seat for the Democrats, and Advocate 2 helped a Democrat knock on doors in a completely different part of the state.

Advocate 6 was pleased to see recent Republican gains in the legislature. Still, she knew her party was outnumbered at home. She had to work effectively with Democrats to stay powerful and promote development, so she took a bipartisan approach. Because she was so safe in her later statehouse years, the party did not send her much help. However, she said, "I think they would [help] if I had a tough race and I had to call on them immediately." She praised local Republican women's clubs for offering to stuff envelopes and get out mass mailings. She said that while the party "wrote her off" during her run for the open statehouse seat, since the district was so Democratic, the Republican women's clubs turned out to support her. That proved invaluable, and she had relied on their support ever since.

Advocate 6 worked hard to gain acceptance as a Republican, stressing her anti-regulation credentials as an asset for jobs and growth. She was the past president of a pro-business group of legislators and private sector leaders that worked to coordinate regulations among the different states. Their goal was to reduce the cost of interstate commerce. Advocate 6 received a bust of Thomas Jefferson from the group, with an engraved plaque commemorating her service. She proudly displayed it in her capitol office, telling visitors that the group offered one more way to make contacts and bring jobs to the city. Advocate 6 had even led trade missions to Mexico, El Salvador, Brazil, Guatemala, and South Africa, where she "brought back information [and] took information there, where businesses have been able to develop contacts in those other countries for export and import." According to Advocate 6, her free-trade credentials also helped the city grow. Thus she attempted to shift her party label from a negative to a positive. The message was that, though Republicans may be outnumbered in her hometown, having a few of them around could help promote business.

Advocate 6 missed the old days, when she dined with a Republican governor and hosted a Republican president. But she was aggressive in cultivating her relationship with Democrats and with the city leaders. Advocate 6 and a candidate for mayor endorsed each other in their respective bids for office during the same election. Both won. It did not seem to matter that the mayor said her party leaning was Democratic, while Advocate 6's was GOP (all candidates for city office run without party labels). The new mayor was instrumental in finding leadership positions for Advocate 6 once the new council took office. She appointed Advocate 6 to head the council's powerful Legislative Rules and Ethics Committee. Advocate 6 seemed a natural choice for that job because of her statehouse tenure and her past presidency of both the business group and a multistate association of women legislators.

There was a clear, obvious link between Advocate 6's committee service in the statehouse and her pro-development orientation to the city. As a longtime incumbent, she served for years on several "money" committees: Budget, Appropriations, Commerce, and Banking. She was one of a new breed of female state legislators; in the states, women were more likely to serve on appropriations or finance committees in 1992 than in 1972.[3] Advocate 6 told me that as one of the first women to serve, her presence on these committees helped break open the "cigar-smoking, backroom-dealing" old boys' network. This gave her an opportunity to promote new ideas—and her hometown. Of course, like virtually all legislators, Advocate 6 told me, she wanted what was best for her state. But her top priority was bringing home the bacon.

Her district was mostly a newer area of the city. Constituents there felt neglected by city hall. Advocate 6 had put particular effort into highway funding and other state development policies. Such funding was especially beneficial to her area. Bridges were particularly important because they linked her part of the city with downtown, across the river. Not only did Advocate 6 work to get state funding for bridge widening, she also lobbied the federal and city government for matching funds. She told me, "We need a little money from the feds, a little money from the state, and a little push from the city." Now that she was a councilwoman, she could work to push from city hall instead of allocating from the state capitol. In her race for city council, her pro-development theme remained much the same.

I was struck by how thematic and organized Advocate 6 was each time I observed her. Some of this may have been due to her city council race. Even her choice of clothes reflected the hometown-first theme: at her inauguration into the council, she wore an outfit with the city's skyline depicted on it. Her office in the state capitol also seemed on-message. In addition to the Jefferson bust, she displayed a rack of "collector cards" with her photo on the front. Designed like

3. Kathleen Dolan and Lynne E. Ford, "Change and Continuity among Women State Legislators: Evidence from Three Decades," 144. Seventeen percent of the female legislators in Dolan and Ford's sample served on budget and appropriations committees in 1972; that percentage rose to 29 percent by 1992.

a baseball card, the back of each card listed her accomplishments. These included "serving on the vital committees," which were listed, and "drafted, supported & passed legislation for more jobs, growth for industry and small business, support and funding for law enforcement, state and local parks [and] cleaner environment." During her bid for council, too, Advocate 6 emphasized her pro-development record. She suggested that her suburban district's growth could be replicated throughout the city if taxes were restrained and the right policies pursued. Across the river from her district, she told a downtown business association how proud she was to see them redeveloping empty older buildings into loft apartments by using Tax Increment Financing (TIF). She argued that developmental policies should be pursued even further into downtown, telling them, "I dream of [being like] Seattle. Twenty years ago, we were like Detroit!" Of course, she also offered her own support for this development. Her opponents for council were both closely tied to the Hispanic community. They tried to balance their comments on development with neighborhood and minority issues. But for Advocate 6, growth was clearly the theme that tied the whole city together. She asked the crowd, "How many of you think you're not paying enough in taxes?" After the forum was over, she reminded her supporters, "I was the only one that said, 'Enough taxes!'" Always on-theme, she stressed that lower taxes and TIF could bring new growth throughout the city.

Advocate 6's statehouse district embodied her pro-growth theme. It was a new, fast-growing community of office parks, malls, and subdivisions located on a freeway corridor between the city's downtown and the distant local airport. In the state's other major metropolitan area, virtually all suburban areas were separate municipalities. But much of Advocate 6's district had been annexed to the central city. There were also a few suburbs that had been incorporated when the city launched its incorporation drive in 1960. Many of those suburbs were now surrounded by the city on all sides. Advocate 6's district and the surrounding areas were the reason that the city had begun to show population growth again after years of gradual decline. The fast-growing community was suburban in all but name. Local schools had been kept separate from the urban school district. The district was a model of what annexation can do to expand a city's tax base and prevent it from becoming "like Detroit." According to Advocate 6, the district's population had grown from about 32,000 to roughly 46,000 since the last redistricting seven years before. The community's growing, suburban face reflected the allocations she had brought home, particularly for highways and bridges. New, upscale housing was being constructed there, which brought in more upper-income Republicans. It is possible that these new constituents were one reason that Advocate 6's margins grew while she was in office—though her progrowth strategy and name recognition seemed to have helped, too.

Growth can bring tensions at home. While waiting for Advocate 6 to give a speech, one constituent (the same one quoted at the beginning of this section) told me, "We don't like our new neighbors. We think they're snotty." This woman felt that the older, working-class residents of the district were being politically displaced by their wealthier, more Republican neighbors. She also said that the whole suburban area felt ignored by the central city (a theme Advocate 6 and other constituents also stressed). Finally, she added that the community was "lily white." It had little racial diversity, in sharp contrast with the urban area across the river. Many of Advocate 6's older constituents did not even refer to themselves as residents of the city, preferring to tell outsiders that they were "Saline Countians." Some never accepted the annexation as fact. Advocate 6 worked aggressively to promote her district and the city at the same time, in hopes of bridging that gap.

Population shifts within the city seem to have contributed to Advocate 6's successful career as a representative and her city council election. Council districts had been configured to link communities on either side of the river. Otherwise, those in Advocate 6's area feared, their influence would be limited to just one or two councilpersons, who could always be outvoted. The new council district linked Advocate 6's growing suburban area with much of the city's Hispanic community across the river. The city council is made up of both in-district and at-large councilpersons. Candidates for the latter positions compete in a primary in-district, then the two top finishers face a citywide runoff. (Advocate 3 compared this system favorably to his own city's strong-mayor unified government). In the primary, Advocate 6 faced two Hispanics with ties to local labor unions. One of these challengers, a former councilman once ousted on corruption charges, survived to make the runoff against Advocate

6. The citywide election was widely viewed as a contest between the older urban core of the city and the newer annexed areas. Because they were both well connected in local politics, Advocate 6 and her challenger each raised a great deal of money for the race, though from different sources. Advocate 6 solicited business donations, while her challenger got local union backing. The local black political organization endorsed Advocate 6's opponent, but most of the Democratic state representatives from black-majority districts endorsed Advocate 6. Her opponent suggested that Advocate 6 did not understand the needs of the city's minority community. She ignored racial issues and stayed focused on her pro-growth, hometown-first theme. Some commentators in the local newspapers saw Advocate 6's victory as a political coming-of-age for the pro-development, annexed areas of the city—particularly her own community. However, it is still too early to gauge the long-term consequences of such changes.

Civic boosterism is a busy job. It was remarkable to see Advocate 6's enthusiasm for her late-starting political career. She did not enter the political arena until her children were grown, but then made a career out of elected office and civic boosterism. All this work took a toll: Advocate 6 told a local reporter that one reason she moved to city council was because she wanted to spend more time with her grandchildren, who live in the metropolitan area. It remained to be seen how Advocate 6's influence would develop in the city council. But she had made a successful career as a representative by closely identifying herself with her city. She had sent money home and bragged about it. Advocate 6 changed jobs, but she stuck with the hometown-first approach that had served her so well. When her city sought money for growth, the civic booster would be there to push for it.

Conclusion

Jewell's four tasks are just as important to advocates beyond the district as they are to the other types in this study. Advocates beyond the district take their own strategic approach to these challenges. Their *communication with constituents* centers around the advocacy of a citywide or statewide agenda. They believe this will be popular back home. They often travel home and meet in or near the district, but they are less likely than in-district advocates to discuss district-specific needs. Instead they promote broader causes and take stands on broader issues that are popular back home. Advocate 5 did not get involved in the intense rivalry between the inner-city school district and the two neighborhood school districts he represented. Rather, he presented himself as a "pro-education legislator," working for better schools throughout the state, and stayed out of the local controversy that could divide his district. Advocate 6 believed that her growing suburban community stood to benefit from the economic development of the city as a whole.

For advocates beyond the district, *policy responsiveness* means making progress on citywide or statewide issues. Again they believe that their districts will support them in this. Advocate 5 believed his blue-collar, urban, Democratic constituents were especially supportive of both collective bargaining and greater state funding for public education. Thus, he responded to those issues instead of spending a lot of time on district-specific projects. For Advocate 6, the city's economic development was the single most important thing that affected her district. This development could not be cordoned off district by district. She thus took the lead in advocating the city's policy needs, even when they extended well beyond her own community. This served her political ambitions for a seat in city hall.

Allocation of resources for the district is handled a little differently by advocates beyond the district, as opposed to in-district advocates. Advocates 5 and 6 believed that their districts would benefit directly from the legislation they promoted. Advocate 5 believed that more pro-union legislation would help organized labor, which had a lot of members in his district. He further believed that area school districts stood to benefit from his education bills. Advocate 6 argued that her community was one of the city's fastest growing and would thus reap the benefits as the city grew. For example, growth in the city's downtown would bring in more commuters, many of whom would live in her district. In general, these two advocates focused on allocating resources in ways that benefited their constituencies. At home, they did not present their projects in terms of specific benefits to the district and immediately surrounding communities, as was often the case with the in-district advocates.

Constituent service was not particularly stressed by Advocates 5 and 6, either in interviews with me or in meetings at home. Both of them said that they did casework. Advocate 5 said he prided himself on quick response to casework requests. Advocate 6 boasted that, with one of the most experienced legislative assistants in the capital, she could help get constituent work done. But with less of a district-centered focus, these two advocates did not make casework central to their home styles, as did the ombudspersons. When Advocate 5's challenger suggested that his response to casework was slow, Advocate 5 just ignored the charge.

Advocates beyond the district often stay out of controversies that divide portions of their districts; they take an issue-centered approach and work actively to get constituent support for their projects. Advocates 5 and 6 were always reelected comfortably, and did not worry much about the next campaign. They believed that they fit their districts. They argued that their pro-labor and pro-growth approaches, respectively, were the best ways to respond to their districts' interests. Their home styles centered around promoting their own legislation and other activities that put statewide and citywide issues on the agenda. This approach served both legislators' career aspirations: as we have seen, Advocate 5 moved from the statehouse to a job as a full-time union organizer, and Advocate 6 easily won her at-large city council seat.

6

Ombudspersons

Ombudspersons are listeners. Like advocates, they focus on issues that raise concerns in the district. Yet the two groups take different approaches. While advocates aggressively socialize the conflict, ombudspersons generally wait until someone else has put an issue on the agenda. Responsiveness is their theme. They let issues bubble up, but stay involved in resolving controversy. For example, while Advocate 1 said he liked to "thump my chest" to bring attention to the district, Ombuds 3 and 4 presented themselves as levelheaded peacemakers who could settle controversies back home. Ombuds 1 worked closely with local leaders in his district, while Ombuds 2 attended every meeting he possibly could when he was at home. Ombuds 3 responded quickly when a state university proposed to acquire and destroy several of her constituents' homes. Yet she was not the one that raised the issue. Instead, it was neighborhood activists who organized the protests and meetings. Ombuds 3 then responded, by attending the meetings and working to negotiate a compromise between university administrators and neighborhood activists. Likewise, Ombuds 4 did not take credit—did not want credit—for starting the debate in his district about indoor hog farms. Rather, he presented himself as an ombudsman who could respond to this problem. It was placed on the agenda by others.

The metropolitan-area ombudspersons—Ombuds 1, 2, and 3— all represented districts with above-average incomes, high education levels, and high voter turnout. They each told me that their constituents back home were active and involved, and that this made their job easier. Their constituents relayed concerns and issues to their elected officials, instead of waiting for the officials to take the lead. Thus the ombudsperson approach seemed to fit these districts. In contrast, Ombuds 4 argued that his rural community needed an ombudsperson in the statehouse to do what might be done by elected officials at other levels of government in a metropolitan area: focus on district needs and casework, and be responsive when issues arise.

The adjoining districts of Ombuds 1 and 2 were mostly suburban and comfortably middle-class. Ombuds 1 and 2 both took the ombudsperson approach in spite of their quite different personalities. While Ombuds 1 always seemed busy, and sometimes aloof, Ombuds 2 was patient and grandfatherly. Ombuds 1 did not believe it essential to attend many meetings back home. He argued that the district's interests were relatively clear: protect funding for the local schools and facilitate effective governance for the local municipalities.

In contrast, Ombuds 2 made the extra effort to attend district meetings with constituents. A former chamber president, he regularly attended that group's legislative forums. He also appeared at school district functions and meetings of veterans' organizations. He kept in close touch with a local suburban newspaper editor who published his weekly column.

None of the ombudspersons I studied planned town hall meetings and media appearances to socialize controversial conflicts, as did some of the advocates. When they responded to local controversy, they often presented themselves as voices of reason who were there to settle people down and moderate an overheated debate. For example, homeowners in Ombuds 3's district feared that the nearby state university campus would continue to threaten their houses. They were prepared to go to extremes in order to prevent this, calling for a vote of the people every time there was an eminent domain proposal. But Ombuds 3 argued that her constituents would be going too far if they required the state to get their approval for each use of eminent domain. Meeting with university administrators, she claimed that eminent domain can actually be a good thing, and that the state university system must simply be restrained from abusing it. She cosponsored several bills to restrain the uses of eminent domain by state universities, bills that would require open meetings to be held before any state university purchased homes.

Much like Ombuds 3, Ombuds 4 sought a middle ground to resolve disputes. This approach characterized his response to the waste leaks at confinement hog farms. He did not put the issue on the agenda, and felt that those that did—the "hog radicals"—went too far in order to keep out the factory farms. Both Ombuds 3 and 4 presented themselves as offering balanced responses to issues that were raised by others in their district.

All four of these ombudspersons generally let issues "bubble up" before getting involved. All but Ombuds 3 placed a heavy emphasis on casework as part of a broader reelection strategy. Their personalities varied significantly, but they all stressed listening and responding as the core of their approach.

Ombuds 1: Doing His Job, Voting the District

> I work on [one] ward no more than I do any other one, because the whole way I run my career as a legislator has been voting my district. And that's why I vote the way I do. It's not always with the party; most of the time it is. And that's why they keep electing me.
>
> —*Ombuds 1*

Ombuds 1 liked to keep it simple. He voted his district, he did his job. This strategy sustained him even though he was in a "swing district" (his words) where Republicans nearly balanced out his fellow Democrats. Every election, Ombuds 1 had a general election challenger. And every election, he stuck to what worked. His overriding theme with constituents was that he put the district's interests over any other priority.

Serving as a state representative need not be complicated or confusing, according to Ombuds 1. But it is a lot of work, particularly when serving as a committee chair and working a busy outside job. He acknowledged this and said it was a real struggle to balance his legislator's job with his other one, selling automated teller machines. Yet for all the work, Ombuds 1 kept his answers and approach straightforward. District interests stayed front and center. In many pieces of legislation, he did not need to concern himself directly with the district, because his constituents' interests were not particularly affected. Yet sometimes he faced issues of immediate concern at home, particularly tax increases. At those times, Ombuds 1 voted the district and assumed that other representatives would do the same. He did not fault anyone for voting differently than he did. Rather, he traced it to the differences between districts. He felt he had to focus on taxes. This focus and the general lack of crises back home both reflected the unusually high levels of income and education in his district, he said.

With their high socioeconomic status and tendency to have fewer immediate concerns, Ombuds 1's constituents were much like those of Burkean 1. Yet while their districts were similar in this respect, Burkean 1 and Ombuds 1 differed in how they perceived their well-off districts. Burkean 1 said that because his district was "upper-middle-income," his constituents had "less problems." But Ombuds 1 focused on the high education levels of his constituents, rather than just on their higher incomes. He argued that his constituents were particularly well informed and knowledgeable, and that this made his job easier. Many times during our interview, Ombuds 1 told me that "the voters are smart." He also pointed with pride to his district's high voter turnout: over 60 percent of registered voters for midterm elections, and an astonishing 88 percent in presidential elections. I asked, "How does it feel representing a district of people who are so well informed? Does it change the nature of the job?" Ombuds 1 answered: "No. In fact, it probably makes it easier because . . . I can explain [issues] to the people. If they're wanting to know, and they're willing to know, and they're willing to go to the polls, it makes my job easier, because when I send them things, they read it, they understand it, they get involved."

This answer is significant for a couple of reasons. First, in responding "no" to my second question, Ombuds 1 suggested that he would take the same approach to representation if he were in another district. He repeated this point a few times during our interview. Second, he praised his constituents and noted that it was easier to "just do my job" when they were active and interested.

Ombuds 1 and 2 represented neighboring districts. Both acknowledged that some issues were not of immediate concern or interest back home. They had to rely on their own judgment to reach decisions on such matters. But when district interests were affected in some way, each worked hard to "vote the district" (in Ombuds 1's oft-used phrase). Further, they each stressed the importance of voting for the district over the party in these situations.

This is not to say that Ombuds 1 and 2 were identical in approach. As described in the next section, freshman Ombuds 2 worked hard to find out what was on the mind of his constituents so that he could respond effectively. Ombuds 1, by contrast, having defeated an incumbent and then being reelected four times, believed he already knew what his constituents expected him to do. He was more confident, clearly in a different stage of his legislative career than Ombuds 2. Further, he had to balance his political career with his outside job, while Ombuds 2 was retired and dedicated himself to being a full-time legislator. In my visits to their home districts, I noticed that Ombuds 2 was able to attend many more meetings than Ombuds 1. I attributed this partly to Ombuds 1's other work responsibilities, which consumed most of his Fridays. Both these representatives took "voting the district" quite seriously, but their approaches and careers differed considerably.

One thing was clear: the difference between them was not due to a difference in their districts. In fact, no other two districts I studied had so many similarities. Not only did these districts adjoin each other, but both were an upper-working-class/upper-middle-class mix. Ombuds 1 and 2 split the inner suburb of *South Poplar*. Each also had an annexed portion of the central city, featuring many new housing starts. These newer subdivisions featured homes valued at $200,000 and up (considered high property values in this metropolitan area). Ombuds 1 and 2 represented parts of the same three school districts, and each faced an electorate that was divided between the parties. Ombuds 2 saw his own district as Democrat-leaning, but, he said, "a Republican can win it, because they vote for the person, not the party." Ombuds 1 saw his district as evenly split, with moderate swing voters deciding elections. In these districts, no incumbent was safe. It appeared likely that the combination of electoral insecurity, together with well-off, well-educated, and involved constituents, facilitated the ombudsperson strategy. (Ombuds 3 also described her constituents as highly educated and financially well-off, with a particularly large group of involved, educated, voting people who involved themselves in the issues.) Many people in both districts owned their homes, and most parents sent their children to local public schools. Both districts had consistent, above-average turnout on election days. Throughout this study, I could not help but notice that while the districts of Ombuds 1 and 2 were similar, the personalities and career stages of these two representatives differed remarkably. Also, Ombuds 1 was a Democrat while Ombuds 2 was a Republican. Thus the fact that each followed an ombudsperson strategy was particularly striking. The evidence shows that district characteristics can shape home style strategy.

Ombuds 1 seemed to agree with this conclusion. During our interview, he referred several times to the differences between himself, on the one hand, and Advocate 5 and Ombuds 3, on the other. He noted that these other two, in neighboring districts, had liberal voting records on social issues and had voted with the governor on a controversial school tax increase. Ombuds 1 believed that their votes were in large part due to their safely Democratic districts, while his own "moderate-to-conservative" tendencies reflected a wealthier district with "a different approach." Again, his focus was on the district, not the representative's own personality or views.

During the course of my research, Ombuds 1 made news for two of his proposals. Both fit the ombudsperson strategy nicely, because in each case, he suggested a vote of the people to resolve a conflict. The first proposal concerned a controversy over the slow response times of the city's ambulance service. The major local daily ran a story that suggested that an ambulance service employee had falsified data to cover up the problem. The local firefighters' union—itself no stranger to controversy—suggested that the city fire department take over the ambulance service. Ombuds 1's response came in the form of an amendment, to a larger bill, that would allow for a vote of the people to decide who controlled the city's ambulance service. The move attracted criticism from city hall and local newspapers. The amendment passed the house, but did not make it all the way to becoming law. But Ombuds 1 had tried to resolve this conflict by passing it along to the voters: an ombudsperson's approach.

The second proposal was to shrink the size of the Missouri House. Ombuds 1 suggested that it be reduced to one hundred seats. He was quoted in the city newspaper as saying that the current size made it difficult to get things done efficiently. He did not believe the house would place such a proposal on the ballot, so he suggested that citizens use the initiative-and-referendum process to make the change. As of the writing of this study, it was not clear how successful Ombuds 1's proposal was going to be. But again, he took up the theme consistent with an ombudsperson's approach: let the voters decide the issue themselves.

The only exception Ombuds 1 saw to district-driven representation was the abortion-rights issue. He believed that districts tend to elect people in the local majority on certain issues, and that his pro-life leaning probably reflected that of a majority of his constituents. But he did not believe that legislators changed their views on this question to fit the district. He told me:

> Generally speaking, people in [the capital] are on . . . whatever side they are for personal beliefs. I don't think—and there may be one or two out there—but I don't think there's a senator or a rep out there who is a die-hard pro-choicer but votes pro-life because it's good for the district. That's the one issue. I'm not saying it doesn't go on, but . . . I think Advocate 5 is sincere as he can be that he's pro-choice. And that if he runs for higher office, or down the road, he would always be pro-choice. And I think I would always be pro-life, and Ombuds 3 would be pro-choice.

This highlights two points. First, it underscores the difficulty of reaching a compromise on this seemingly unresolvable issue. On every other issue, Ombuds 1 believed, legislators can vote their districts and accept the outcome—every issue, that is, except abortion rights. As he said, "that's the one issue." Second, though it's nonsensical to suggest that the exception proves the rule, this exception does put the rest of Ombuds 1's votes in sharper relief. This is the only issue he mentioned to me in which he could see his own personal views as the primary basis of his decisions. If he had discovered the district actually had a pro-choice leaning, he would not have changed his vote. But only on this issue did he take a strong personal stand that could set him apart from the district.

The centrality of district interests to Ombuds 1 was illustrated by his vote on a major education bill. When the governor spearheaded an effort to restructure education funding, a tax increase was planned to pay for it, in the form of a bill that would limit the deductibility of federal tax from state taxes. This deduction was unlimited, but the education bill would cap it at $10,000. Because he represented a high-income district, Ombuds 1 had many constituents who would be affected by such a change and would owe more taxes. Further, his school districts would get, in his words, "little, if any, new money" from the bill. Thus he saw his decision as an easy one. He voted "no." This decision was made in spite of the fact that he was pressured for a "yes" vote by both the speaker and the governor. He told me that his vote got him in trouble with party leaders. He said he did not think the bill had been bad for the state as a whole—only for his district.

When I asked him in our interview if he ever had to take a stand that was not popular, his response was a great example of his district-centered focus:

> Well, it's not popular with who? I mean, I voted against the tax increase, which got me in all sorts of hot water with the party. And that didn't bother me a bit. I did it. I say it didn't bother me a bit, I would have rather not upset my party, but I knew damn good and well, when I ran for reelection in two years, people [were going to say,] "You did the right thing by voting no." And they did, because they knew, or I made sure they knew, the reason I voted no. You know, I voted for the gas tax. I've voted for a tax increase before. But this one was wrong, and it was wrong because it didn't help my district, which is my first obligation. If you look at the good of the state, it looks like [the bill has] done a pretty good job, and I will never vote to dismantle it. Once the word has been, we're going to pass it, . . . now we've got to let it work. But I would vote against it tomorrow if the same tax package was involved.

Why did Ombuds 1 stress district interests so heavily? The overriding reason was reelection. Not only did he always have a challenger, but the challengers were, he said, "always nasty." His strategy was to go door-to-door and focus on his record. He also hired a campaign consultant who handled many day-to-day details for him. This way, he could focus on his other job and go door-knocking. In the most recent election cycle, he had gotten some money from the party. However, it was Ombuds 1 and his consultant, not the party, who oversaw his mass mailings and door-to-door activities. The location of our interview underscored the contested nature of the seat: Ombuds 1 was the only one of the twelve legislators in my study who had our interview take place in his campaign headquarters. In fact, some of the state representatives in less closely contested races did not even have campaign headquarters, only post office boxes for campaign mail. Ombuds 1 ran his campaign out of a building in downtown South Poplar that used to be a hardware store. He shared this space with several other candidates for state and local office.

Ombuds 1 did not often appear at in-district events. This is not to say he never went to meetings back home. In fact, he told me, "I don't know how many Eagle Scout ceremonies I've been to!" I saw him at two events during the course of my research. One was the chamber forum at which Ombuds 1 exchanged heated remarks with his opponent (the confrontation I later discussed with Advocate 5, who was also there). When his opponent accused him of filing campaign finance disclosure forms late, Ombuds 1 responded:

> I've been found guilty of nothing. My opponent didn't report part of his money on *his* disclosure. But I'm not going to talk about that. I'm going to talk about issues, what I've been doing in the legislature: I've returned $60,000 to the state treasury in expenses. That's a state record. I sponsored the Community Redevelopment Act, the Safe Schools Act, . . . local control, juvenile crime, a bill for [conversion of a nearby decommissioned Air Force base to civilian use], a transportation district bill, and an economic development bill. I have a 98 percent attendance record and a 96 percent voting record. I supported the bill to lift the food sales tax. [Turning to opponent:] Let's talk about issues. Where do you stand? I'd like to talk about issues.

In this exchange, Ombuds 1 exhibited his way of stressing his incumbency as an asset that helped the district. He told me later that he tried to avoid "nasty" clashes, but that his opponents usually attacked him. He thought the reason for this was that he and his opponents were all "moderate-to-conservative on the issues." Like Anthony Downs, he suggested that the candidates of each party converged at the center of the local electorate.[1] In this context, why

1. Anthony Downs, *An Economic Theory of Democracy,* 36–50.

switch from the incumbent, who is better known? Thus, Ombuds 1's opponents attempted to distinguish themselves by attacking him on non-issue-related matters. He successfully countered them by stressing his incumbency and service to the district.

I saw Ombuds 1 at one other meeting: one of the forums on the highway interchange. Advocate 2 had organized the forum, and was the only legislator to hand out flyers stating his position at the event. None of the other state legislators who were present spoke up. Ombuds 1 withdrew from the controversy after DOT promised to keep open a key exit in his district.

In spite of his presence at these two gatherings, Ombuds 1 was less likely than other legislators to attend local meetings. He attended none of the Birchtree school forums that I visited, even though his district included part of that school district. He did not appear at any of the other meetings on the highway interchange (by way of explanation, he mentioned to me that most of the controversy was in Advocate 2's district, not his). Ombuds 2 told me that Ombuds 1 once attended local chamber meetings, but stopped after a chamber official kept attacking him over his voting record. According to Ombuds 2, that official was the incumbent whom Ombuds 1 had defeated for his house seat; she was angry and wanted her old job back. As a result of her attacks, Ombuds 1 stopped attending chamber meetings on a regular basis. Two years after Ombuds 1 won his seat, there was a rematch with the ousted Republican. Ombuds 1 won again. By the time of my study, several election cycles had passed since then. For two years, I went to nearly every one of the meetings held during legislative sessions, and did not see Ombuds 1 at any of them. The defeated incumbent had also stopped her regular attendance at chamber meetings, but now that things had calmed down, Ombuds 2 was encouraging Ombuds 1 to come back and attend chamber meetings again.

If voting the district was one of Ombuds 1's major themes, the other was, "just doing my job." His approach to each election cycle was the "standard campaign": running on his record and knocking on doors. He did not think his challengers could beat this, so he avoided making major changes to his style. According to him, his challengers had outspent him, attacked his record, and sent out mail making wild accusations just days before the election, not giving him time to respond. Some flyers featured accusations of missed committee meetings—but he didn't even serve on the committee in question! All was to no avail, however: the results were usually about the same. Ombuds 1 won the Democratic wards, lost the Republican ones, and won overall by about a ten-point margin. In short, if your campaign strategy isn't broken, why fix it? Ombuds 1 said he would not "monkey with something that seems to be working." He thought it was unnecessary for some candidates to spend $100,000 on legislative races. He suggested that once one has an approach that works, "it's just not that big a deal" to run a campaign. When I questioned him about it further, he added, "You were asking about an inner circle, and strategy, and all that, and I don't have anything like that." Again, the point was this: he just did what worked, year in and year out. Of course he had a strategy, but he did not spend any time rethinking it each election cycle. I asked him if he had any changes planned for the upcoming election. He said: "I will campaign and I will continue to communicate. But no, there's not going to be any changes."

It might be supposed that this theme was the result of incumbency advantage. But the "just doing my job" concept was not limited to a reelection strategy. Ombuds 1 also took this approach to his service in the state capital, and said that he had done so ever since first taking elected office. I asked him: "Think back a little bit to when you were, say, in your first two years as a state rep. Did you find that the job was a lot like what you were expecting, or did you find a lot of surprises?" He said:

> Didn't know what I was expecting, but didn't find a lot of surprises. I mean, it was like any other job. And I know [how] that sounds, of course. That was a ways back. But I mean I didn't find it to be any more overwhelming than starting any other new job. So, no. I would say no, I wasn't that overwhelmed. I'm not easy to overwhelm anyway. No, not at all. I mean, you know, I had friends in state government already, I had friends who were state representatives, so I kind of knew what went on there. So, the answer, without giving it a lot of deep thought, is no, there is nothing that overwhelmed me.

I observed Ombuds 1 only a few times in his home district. Following Richard Fenno, I have tried to integrate as much material as possible from my two years of "shadowing" state legislators, but I had fewer opportunities to do that with Ombuds 1. However, this is not to say that Ombuds 1 lacked his own approach to his home district. Synthesizing data from our interview, newspaper coverage of Ombuds 1, my limited observations, and discussions with neighboring representatives, his approach comes into clear focus. Ombuds 1 came home with the following themes: he knew the district sentiment on key issues, worked with local leaders, ran on his record, stuck with what worked, and did his job. The following section, about Ombuds 2, offers further insight into the similarities and differences between these two ombudsmen.

Ombuds 2: The Good Citizen

History and background count. My dad was a state representative in Arkansas, and I spent time in the state capital. I learned to seek solutions. I have served my country and my community. I was in the Air Force twenty-one years. I've lived fourteen years in the district. I'm in the Lions Club. Several business and church groups have endorsed me. I hope you'll vote for me.

With freedom comes responsibility.

—*Ombuds 2, speaking to voters and on the house floor*

No one seemed to have an unkind word about Ombuds 2. His gentle, grandfatherly ways, sincere smile, and southern drawl gave him a charm that made him enormously popular among those that knew him. Few, if any, of his detractors criticized his personality or his way of presenting himself. While other legislators, such as Advocate 1, could be brash and aggressive in pursuing their political goals, Ombuds 2 was deferent to those with seniority. Having completed only one session of the legislature, he had already established himself as a community ombudsman.

His was a diverse and changing district. Ombuds 2 began his campaign by listening eagerly to constituents on issues they cared about most. These issues generally centered around the local schools. But Ombuds 2 also acted on his own judgment, which revolved around the view that everyone in a democracy has a responsibility to participate in government. He argued that government runs best when overseen by citizens of "good moral fiber."

Ombuds 2's home style was actually something of a blend. He seemed to have a strong, personal inclination toward a Burkean approach. But electoral realities pushed him to be an ombudsperson. He won office by a hair's breadth. He believed that he had to attend every meeting possible, aggressively respond to casework requests, and serve district interests in order to have any chance of being reelected. On issues not of direct concern back home, or those with mixed cues from the district, he did take a Burkean approach. But his home style centered on responsiveness to district concerns that were raised by others. He saw the latter as being the key to reelection.

Ombuds 2 was the only participant in this study who was elected to an open seat during the course of my research. I met him at the same candidate forum where Ombuds 1 exchanged heated remarks with his opponent. I then began following his campaign. The day after his election, I called and secured his participation in the study. Personality may have been a key factor in Ombuds 2's surprise victory. He was recruited to run for the seat when the incumbent Republican representative retired. The conventional wisdom was that this increasingly blue-collar, urban/inner-suburban district was becoming more and more Democratic. Many thought that the outgoing incumbent would be the last Republican to represent the area. Ombuds 2 told me that the district voted solidly Democratic in national elections. His Democratic challenger was a high-quality candidate in every sense of the word: community involvement, a good base of campaign contributions, and name recognition. But Ombuds 2 also had these attributes. He was able to pull off an upset, defeating his opponent by less than 1 percent of votes cast in a relatively high-turnout midterm election. How did he do it?

According to Ombuds 2, the Democratic candidate "was a good opponent, but I outworked him." Ombuds 2 started early with his door-to-door campaigning, targeting the part of the district where he was least known. The Democrat appeared at candidate forums and the like, but he did not go door-to-door. Ombuds 2 believed this made the crucial difference, along with his pro-life stand. He saw the district as one dominated by pro-life Catholic Democrats, and he was

able to sway just enough of them to his column by stressing his position on that issue. Once in office, Ombuds 2 was not entirely comfortable with the divisive abortion fight. He generally did not stress
it, arguing that "it shouldn't be an issue."

In addition to door-knocking, Ombuds 2 used a different fund-raising strategy than his opponent. While the Democrat raised money
mostly from attorneys outside the district, Ombuds 2 got many more
small contributions from would-be constituents. Again, he thought
this worked in his favor. He was able to cement the loyalty of these voters while asking for their small donations. It also involved more effort.
This shows how Ombuds 2 "outworked" his "good opponent."

The race was a model: two high-quality candidates, both of whom
ran on issues and background. Ombuds 2 was recent past president
of a local chamber of commerce. His opponent, an attorney, had done
years of work for a local school board at the opposite end of the district. Following the campaign both in person and in the newspaper,
I observed no name-calling or mudslinging at all. Ombuds 2 was particularly proud of this. During our interview, he praised his opponent
and stressed that their only differences were over tort reform and
abortion rights.

Ombuds 2's upset victory surprised many observers, but none more
than the state's Democratic governor. After the election, he took Ombuds 2 aside and asked, "How'd you do that?" The governor was not
the only one caught off-guard. Advocate 5, for example, had assumed
that the Democratic candidate would win the seat and pick up a gain
for the party. Ombuds 2 told me, "The party helped immensely." He
relied more heavily on the state party organization than most other
candidates I interviewed. By way of contrast, it has already been noted that Advocate 5 said of his party, "It's almost a nonentity as a structure for me." Burkean 1 said, "I'm not a party person." The Missouri
GOP sent Ombuds 2 a campaign consultant who advised him to remove all Republican labels from his campaign literature, stress his
pro-life position with the Catholic community, and, most important
of all, go door-to-door. With his instantly likable personality, Ombuds 2 made many friends while knocking on doors:

> Old hats in the political arena all agree . . . everything I got from
> anyone who'd been in politics before is, you can't beat knocking

on doors. So I did concentrate on that and did that a lot. I probably knocked on about six thousand doors. That's a lot! . . . and I had to do that a lot in the summer, in July and August when it was hot. And personally, I'm a sweater. I mean, I always have been and I [can't] change that, but when I'm out in the sun and walking and working, I perspire. And so I took a towel and would wipe my forehead before I'd go to doors, but sometimes people would open the door and say, "Sir, do you need a drink?"

Ombuds 2 depended on organization and personal reputation, not party label, to get elected. Again, there is a sharp contrast with some others in this study—particularly Advocate 5, who relied more on party label than on anything else. Ombuds 2 knew his seat was not safe. During our interview, he speculated that the higher turnout in presidential elections would bring a higher proportion of Democrats to the polls in 2000. As of August 1999, one candidate had already filed for the Democratic nomination to challenge Ombuds 2. She appeared to be a high-quality candidate: a young attorney with the county prosecutor's office, active with the local chamber of commerce. She told me that she planned to take Ombuds 2 to task for his vote against Advocate 5's collective bargaining bill.

I label Ombuds 2 "the good citizen" because of the way he referred to civic duty in connection with all tough decisions. From his mud-free, model campaign to his weekly newspaper columns, Ombuds 2 always presented himself as an involved citizen of "good moral fiber." His primary focus was on the district, but if district cues were mixed or absent, his decision-making showed a Burkean influence. However, his district focus was too strong for him to be labeled as a Burkean.

The good citizen theme was particularly clear in his vote on the collective bargaining bill. In 1998, he was the only Republican endorsed for Missouri statehouse by the National Education Association (NEA). He was intensely cross-pressured on the bill. Republicans pulled him toward a "nay" vote. The NEA pushed for a "yea." District cues were also mixed, with school boards pushing for a "nay" vote, and local teacher's unions, reminding Ombuds 2 about the NEA's endorsement, pushing for a "yea." All the surrounding representatives from his county were strong pro-union Democrats who voted "yea." Indeed, the bill's sponsor represented a district which not only bordered Ombuds 2's, but was similar in terms of politics and demographics. So, how did Ombuds 2 decide?

Ever the good citizen, Ombuds 2's decision was based on his own sense of principle. While guest-speaking to my class, he argued that public service is a duty and a responsibility of all citizens. This higher calling is more important than increased pay or benefits, he said. According to Ombuds 2, all citizens have a duty to serve the public, regardless of personal profit. For this reason (and in spite of his NEA endorsement), he was not entirely comfortable with public employee unionization or collective bargaining. His position drew many critics and a strong challenger for the next election cycle. As always, Ombuds 2 seemed sincere in his pronouncements. But his decision showed the limits of an ombudsperson's approach: district cues were too mixed to push him clearly in one direction or another.

Ombuds 2's sense of civic duty also played a key role in his opposition to one representative's motorcycle-helmet amendment. If added to a larger transportation bill amendment, it would repeal Missouri's helmet law for motorcyclists over eighteen years old who travel without passengers. On the house floor, its sponsor defended the bill on the grounds of personal freedom. Ombuds 2 rose in opposition. "With freedom," he said, "comes responsibility." He then drew an analogy, suggesting that if the state was to safeguard personal autonomy at all costs, Missouri should give back all of its tobacco settlement money. His remarks made the city's daily newspaper.

Public responsibility was Ombuds 2's theme in public life. In his suburban newspaper column, which featured short discussions of pending legislation, he often repeated this theme. In a column he wrote about a veto session, but which is also applicable to his votes in regular session, he said: "I have researched the vetoed bills and read each one. I plan to base my votes for or against each veto based on its merits. I believe this is the way the job should be done." Again he showed a Burkean leaning, while at the same time believing that responsiveness was the key to reelection. When a major trailer park was proposed for his community, Ombuds 2 researched the issue and listened to opinions on all sides. Most of his constituents were opposed, particularly school district officials. They feared an influx of new schoolchildren without corresponding increases in property tax receipts. Ombuds 2 responded by opposing the rezoning request. He

used his newspaper column to discuss his opposition, mostly referring to the concerns of local and school officials. His stance prevailed;
there would be no trailer park.

The district Ombuds 2 represented was diverse and changing, and
the principal issues he saw revolved around the public schools. According to him, two of the three school districts he represented were
working-class, while one was wealthier. All were suburban or city
neighborhood districts, not part of the inner-city school district.
Ombuds 2 noted that those in the wealthier district were "particularly sensitive" about issues such as property values and new development. Going door-to-door, he learned why: this district received
more property taxes per capita, and thus got less state funding from
the state's somewhat progressive schools formula. The wealthier schools
relied more heavily on property tax revenues; the other two school
districts got significantly more state money. In spite of these differences, all three school districts were struggling to maintain test scores
and accreditation in the face of racial and demographic changes
among the students. Parents from the inner city were moving their
children to these schools, and the new students were sometimes un-
prepared. Ombuds 2 noted that over the twentieth century, the community had gone from rural to suburban and now seemed to be
changing again, becoming more and more urban in terms of its racial
mix and social issues. The wealthier portions of the district were more
competitive between the two parties, Ombuds 2 noted, while a few
working-class precincts had "never voted Republican."

Since the schools were so central, Ombuds 2 emphasized these issues. He appeared regularly at the schools' legislative forums. Further,
he convened a group of local superintendents to discuss local issues
and help him make policy decisions about education. Thus his learning process went through many stages: from learning about the importance of schools by knocking on doors, to his election, to his responsiveness to his constituents' concerns. This demonstrates how
much information a newly elected representative must process and
act upon quickly, both before and after the election.

Ombuds 2 loved to praise his opposition. For him, politics was an
arena of principled disagreement over important issues. There was no
room for personal attacks or mudslinging. It has already been noted

that he praised his 1998 challenger. But he also had kind words for others with whom he disagreed. Advocate 5 worked hard to get Ombuds 2's Democratic opponent elected, then offered the collective bargaining bill that put Ombuds 2 in such a quandary. Still, there were no hard feelings. In fact, Ombuds 2 told me that Advocate 5 "did a good job" of putting the bill together, and that it was hard to vote against it. Ombuds 2 was completely comfortable appearing as the only Republican at many forums. He was kind to his opposition and never forgot to smile. He avoided stressing partisan, divisive issues. Further, he did not generally take strong positions on such issues. For example, during the course of my study, Missourians voted on whether to license the concealed carrying of handguns. Advocate 2 and Ombuds 3 both raised the issue during my interviews with them, stating an emphatic opposition. Burkean 1 was outspoken in his support for the measure, attacking the governor for his opposition and telling public gatherings that concealed-carry would likely reduce crime. Traveling with Ombuds 2 as the election approached, I didn't hear him say a word about it. The referendum was narrowly defeated due to high turnout and a strong "no" vote in suburban areas. Afterward, I asked Ombuds 2 how he had voted. "Oh, I don't know," he told me. "I voted for it, but my wife voted against it!"

Ombuds 2's good-citizen style and nonconfrontational ways were not only part of his personality, they were also good political strategy in a district where his fellow partisans were outnumbered. As noted, he did not even stress his party label. When I first met him as a candidate, he told me, "I'm running on the Republican ticket," rather than "I am a Republican." He added, "I really could run on either ticket." For Ombuds 2, politics was about citizenship, not partisanship. In fact, he didn't choose a party affiliation until shortly before declaring his candidacy. But he chose the GOP, because he thought they were the most likely to reform house procedures to make them less partisan. In particular, he wanted to see reform in the assignment of committee chairs and capital offices, noting that Democratic freshmen had better offices than the minority floor leader. He also lamented the fact that Republican-authored bills did not pass the house. To get a bill past its first reading, Republicans had to either attach it to another bill as an amendment or get a Democrat to sponsor the bill instead (Ombuds 3 also mentioned this). Ombuds 2 wanted to see a "citizen house" instead of a "partisan house," with the majority setting the priorities for the state. Then, any house member could sponsor a bill pertaining to those priorities, regardless of party.

Though Ombuds 2 saw a GOP majority as the best hope for house reform, some of his constituents disagreed. I went with him to chat with the editor of the local suburban newspaper that carried his column. This editor was generally a strong Democrat, but he had taken a liking to Ombuds 2 and decided to publish his column. He did not agree with Ombuds 2's advocacy of a "citizen house." When Ombuds 2 complained about the house Democrats' partisanship, the editor shot back that "the Republicans would do the same thing!" Ombuds 2 acknowledged that his ideas "may be pie in the sky," but he seemed sincere, as always, about wanting reform. Further, he stressed that most Democrats are good citizens too: "I do believe that people in the Democratic Party as well as the Republican Party . . . want to improve Missouri. And there's a lot of common ground. . . . I can't really fault my colleagues across the aisle, because, really, they're trying to help Missouri too. And I really believe that. I don't just say that to sound good. I really think they have that at heart, and I've talked to enough of them that I'm convinced that's true."

While out knocking on doors, Ombuds 2 met many other good citizens. He learned a lot about their opinions and priorities. They chatted with him and made friends, convincing him that there were a number of solid citizens in the community. This made him feel good about the district, even though it meant more work for him. He told me:

> Well, I was probably surprised at the number of people that wanted you to talk at different things. You know, I really gather[ed] that . . . there is an element of people, not all people, but . . . a good element of voting people in the district that are really pretty interested in knowing their elected officials. I also discovered that there's an element that's not, you know, that don't really seem to have a lot of interest. But that's really not surprising, and I don't think that's any different than it ever has been at any time throughout our history. But that was probably the biggest surprise. And [I was] pleased. I was pleasantly surprised that there were more people than I expected who were interested and did want to know their elected officials, and were appreciative of meeting and talking with me because I was running.

Ombuds 2 referred to these interested constituents as "the back-bone of society" and "good, solid citizens." He did not make distinctions by income. In his mind, anyone rich or poor could be a solid citizen. The most active constituents he met were those with children in the local public schools. However, he did note a number of factors that might have contributed to the high voter turnout and citizen involvement in his district. First, parts of his district were upper-income: one of the three school districts he represented had among the highest property assessments in the state. Second, his three suburban school districts drew families from the neighboring inner-city district. This increased the proportion of families with children in the public schools, and with parents who were often involved in state politics, at least where schools were concerned. Finally, the most active citizens were the ones with the most "stability" (Ombuds 2's word). That is, those who moved a lot were less likely to be active. "A good portion of the working class," Ombuds 2 told me, "is really sort of mobile." He told me the story of a colleague who went out knocking on doors two years after his first election, only to discover that many of the houses he had gone to before now had new occupants. "That mobility can be a problem, if you don't keep up with it," Ombuds 2 said. He did not see mobile citizens as being so active in the community, but in keeping with his style, he avoided criticizing them too harshly.

In addition to rank-and-file constituents, Ombuds 2 met still other good citizens along the campaign trail. Of his opponent, he said, "He was well qualified and a nice guy. I liked him." Ombuds 2 saw his predecessor as another good citizen. The Republican whose seat he took did not endorse Ombuds 2 in the general election, even though she had recruited him to run. The Democratic candidate was a friend of hers and her past campaign treasurer, so she stayed neutral. But once again, there were no hard feelings. Ombuds 2 told me, "I accepted that, because . . . it was the right thing for her to do, I think." Shortly after his election, he told a local chamber of commerce that he had "big shoes to fill" because his predecessor had done so much.

He was cautious when discussing those who might not be such good citizens. He was dissatisfied with the quality of some GOP statehouse candidates, telling me that "the quality of people that show up and run isn't always that red-hot." He thought that Republican candidates should apprentice by shadowing current representatives for at least one session before the election. He said that the party must recruit good citizens: "I [am] thinking in terms of credibility with voters, people with high integrity [and] a solid reputation with communities. . . . There are some people who run for office, some I've seen, that I'm glad they didn't get in."

During his first session in office, Ombuds 2 faced few situations that offended his sense of good citizenship. He mostly defended the General Assembly's actions at public gatherings in the district, and praised his colleagues in both parties for addressing pressing issues. However, one incident left him angry and disappointed. Late in the session, a law professor at a local university published a controversial op-ed piece in the city newspaper. The professor suggested that the two area state legislatures were producing poor-quality legislation due to a shortage of lawyers in public office. The contention was rather strange, for two reasons. First, though they do not make up a majority of legislators in Missouri, Kansas, or most other states, lawyers remain the single most heavily overrepresented profession among state legislators.[2] Second, bills in the Missouri General Assembly are usually drafted by a committee of attorneys at the request of the legislators. The legislators do not generally write the language of the bills. Ombuds 2 pointed this out in a letter to the editor, published a few days after the editorial in the same newspaper.

Missouri legislators reacted to the professor's editorial with sarcasm and anger. One representative retaliated with a voice-vote amendment to punish the university where the professor taught. The amendment would cut appropriations to the university by over $2 million and redirect the money to legislative research. All the representatives acknowledged that the amendment was for symbolic purposes only, and that the senate would put the money back. (This is exactly what happened.) Still, the house overwhelmingly passed the amendment by voice vote. Several state representatives told me that there was a lot of laughter afterward. In effect, the house had pulled a prank on the university.

Ombuds 2 was appalled. He felt the passage of the amendment re-

2. Hamm and Moncrief, "Legislative Politics in the States," 164–66.

flected an immature, even childlike approach to serious public policy issues. He understood that the senate would put the money back,
but for him this did not make the amendment acceptable. For the rest
of the legislative session and the following summer, he raised the issue with constituents. He worried over freedom of speech and took
the house to task for the amendment. Not surprisingly, the brunt of
his criticism fell on the shoulders of the representative who sponsored
the amendment.

At each gathering I observed, Ombuds 2 ran through a similar se-
quence of events. First he would praise the legislature for the worthwhile bills it had passed, and note that the constituents had tax cuts
on the way. Next he would remind constituents that Missouri had yet
to deal with its needs for highway funding. And finally, he would
mention a few things that were done poorly that year, and tell the story of the voice vote. In public, Ombuds 2 maintained his composure
and gentle persona when criticizing the house over this. But when I
asked him about it one-on-one, he became more heated, writing me
a long, detailed E-mail message explaining his position. He had actually considered calling for a roll call on the amendment before the
vote was taken. He did not do that, though, because he decided that
the amendment was so silly that it had no chance of passing. When
the vote was taken, Ombuds 2 wrote, he "drew a deep breath and prepared to yell 'no,' but the yeas were so overwhelming that the opposition just wilted." He said that the vote embarrassed the house, and
that the sponsor "looked like a spoiled child." His sense of good citizenship was deeply offended and he was not shy about telling his
constituents and me about it.

Ombuds 2's approach to this issue contrasted sharply with that of
several other representatives, each of whom downplayed the issue. After the voice vote was taken and became front-page news, I wrote
Advocates 1, 2, and 5, as well as Ombuds 2, to ask for an explanation. Advocate 1, an attorney, sent a short reply noting that he voted
"no" on the funding cut and that the house's action showed yet again
that society does not appreciate the contributions of lawyers to lawmaking. Advocate 2 wrote that the amendment's sponsor, a law student at the university, had written it as "just an attempt . . . to embarrass his law professor." And Advocate 5, after noting that people like
the amendment's sponsor "do not care about issues like academic

freedom," reassured me not to worry because the senate would restore the money. Advocates 1, 2, and 5 all saw the issue as a minor annoyance with no lasting public policy significance. None of them brought it up in legislative forums. Ombuds 2 did not take this approach. For him, his vocal opposition to the amendment was a part of good citizenship. He took the role of a scold, pointing out the house's irresponsibility and taking the sponsor to task for acting like a spoiled child. When he could, the good citizen praised his colleagues. But when he had to, he scolded them in full view of his constituents.

With no other job competing for his time, Ombuds 2 worked particularly hard to be an ombudsman. He tried to collect constituent opinion as much as he could and to be responsive. His ombudsman's approach appeared to derive from the fact that his was not a secure seat. He had to be responsive or risk losing the next election. Like other legislators, Ombuds 2 sent a mail-in survey to constituents. But he also collected constituents' E-mail addresses so that he could survey their opinions more frequently and cost-effectively. A few other legislators I followed mentioned E-mail, but some saw it as a mixed blessing. For example, Advocate 1 found E-mail to be useful but frustrating: at one forum, he reminded constituents that he did not respond to anonymous E-mail messages. But Ombuds 2 endured the frustrations and worked hard to find out what his constituents thought. Sending out surveys and using E-mail to stretch his perquisite budget was prudent. As George Serra has found, perquisite use is beneficial to reelection even among constituents who do not identify with the incumbent legislator's party.[3] At the statehouse level, Ombuds 2's was just such a district.

During his first year in office, Ombuds 2 learned of many constituent service requests, and he worked closely with his legislative assistant to address them. He found that he had to work year-round to address these requests, even though the legislative session lasts only from January to May. This strategy seemed wise. In her study of Congress, Diana Evans Yiannakis found that constituent service is more effective at gaining the votes of those who identify with the other par-

3. George Serra, "What's in It for Me? The Impact of Congressional Casework on Incumbency Evaluation," 413.

ty.[4] Given that he had many such constituents, Ombuds 2 was hoping for similar results in the statehouse.

Meeting constituent service requests is a learning experience. Ombuds 2 discovered some of the pitfalls when a constituent wrote him regarding her son, who was in prison. She had some concerns about the fairness of his parole hearing. Ombuds 2 promised her that he'd get some answers from the parole board regarding the parole process. He followed through on his promise, got the information, and sent it along. Then, he got a surprise: the son had handed Ombuds 2's name and address out among his fellow prisoners, many of whom also wanted answers from the parole board about their own cases. Ombuds 2 was deluged with requests. Unlike the first, none were from his constituents. He decided he did not have the time or energy to respond to any of the other requests, and they went unanswered.

The good citizen did a lot of on-the-job learning. For example, while knocking on doors, he heard several of his soon-to-be constituents complain about a section of the local newspaper. It seemed that the newspaper published announcements of all births in area hospitals. It got this information from the hospitals, and parents were not consulted before publication. People asked Ombuds 2 to file a bill that would allow parents to have this information withheld from the newspaper. A good ombudsman, he promised to do so. Upon his election, his quest to file such a bill was a key learning experience for him. First, he was made aware of the aforementioned committee of attorneys that drafts legislation. Then, when he requested that the committee draft a bill on this topic, he was advised that this was unwise. The committee told him that any such bill would almost surely be challenged by the local newspapers as a free speech issue. Ombuds 2 withdrew his request, but he had learned two valuable lessons. The first was about how bills are drafted. The second was about the unworkability of his campaign promise. Several times afterward, I watched Ombuds 2 explain the bill-drafting process to constituents. However, he did not take it upon himself to mention that he could not follow up on his campaign promise.

The good citizen was a hard worker. As a retiree, he had no other

4. Diana Evans Yiannakis, "The Grateful Electorate: Casework and Congressional Elections," 576.

job to distract him from his work in the house. He listened carefully to constituents, published his weekly newspaper column, and met as many constituents as possible. He was deeply loyal to his home district, having chosen to move there fifteen years earlier because of its location, job opportunities, and "small-town feel." At a personal level, Ombuds 2 had Burkean leanings. But he argued that he had to serve as an ombudsman in order to hold onto his seat. This diverse district had elected a good citizen who professed good intentions and kept alert to public opinion back home.

Ombuds 3: Listening and Responding

Most of the people in my district are happy that I'm doing this and that they're not. I hear it all the time at parties. All my friends [say], "We're so glad you're doing this and we're not!"

I would never have thought of [flood insurance legislation] on my own had not [a] flood occurred, and had not constituents called me and said, "We have a problem." So, I mean, a lot of issues boil up that way from the constituents. I have a whole series that involve [a state university] in my district. I have three bills that are coming forth that have to do with reducing problems there that, had that not been in my district and had that not been my constituency, I probably would not have thought to bring it up. It doesn't mean that I wouldn't have supported it, perhaps. But it kind of follows a [pattern]. If it's in your district, it's kind of your deal.

—Ombuds 3

Ombuds 3 listened. When new issues arose, she worked hard to be responsive. She had built a successful early incumbency by supporting district issues. She listened to the constituents as issues "boiled up." Responsiveness was her theme at home. Her upper-income, highly educated constituents made fewer casework demands than those in many inner-city or rural districts. Still, they had strong feelings about protecting the quality of life in their scenic, gentrified urban neighborhoods. Further, they communicated frequently with each other and with various elected officials. Ombuds 3 told one gathering, "The citizens in this city are amazingly well connected. Instead of being seven people away from anyone else, around here it's more like two people. Everybody knows somebody."

When controversy arose, Ombuds 3 did not shy away. Though only in office for three sessions at the time of my study, she already had a long record of introducing legislation to serve district interests. She worked especially hard to defend the budget share of the state university campus in her district. But she took the side of the neighborhoods when that same campus proposed tearing down historic homes for a parking lot and soccer field. Joined by Advocate 5, her friend Rep 3, and Senator 1, she insisted on accountability from the university system and pressured them to withdraw the teardown proposal. Confronting a different local concern, she and Rep 3 passed legislation setting up charter schools in the inner-city school districts, so that their constituents (and others in surrounding communities) would have options beyond the troubled urban school system. This idea also came from constituents. Always issue-oriented, Ombuds 3's style revolved around listening to her constituents and responding with appropriate legislation.

Of all the legislators I studied, Ombuds 3 and 4 were the only ones with a major state university campus in their district. This gave the state a strong presence in the community. Campuses are often the focal point of local concerns and controversy. At the same time, Ombuds 3's district lacked a major state interest that many others had: freeways. There were no interstate highways in her district, and as far as Ombuds 3 was concerned, it could stay that way. She celebrated the quality of life in her urban area by attending neighborhood parades. She saw her district as one blessed with a particularly high quality of life, serving as a model for other communities. She said:

> The . . . city planners will tell you that it revolves around the town square and *Redbud,* that there's a sense of community there and that people like living in that kind of an area. It's considered safe, very middle . . . to upper class. And that sense of community is important to them. I mean, there's a new thing going on [in the suburbs], a new housing development, and they're modeling it after Redbud because they like that mixed-use development. Everything's very close. We're eight minutes from downtown. You know, I'm not worried about freeways, highways, or

anything. We can get wherever we want. I mean, if one road is closed, we just go to another one, because it's all on a grid system. Everything we want is right there, with the exception of Wal-Mart.

Ombuds 3's district was different from many others in the metropolitan area. It was urban, not suburban. The community was based around city streets instead of freeways. Residents did not need to fight blight or struggle for economic development. Many notable locals lived in the district, including the city's mayor, the publisher of the major daily newspaper, and the county executive. Ombuds 3's constituents wanted to keep their quality of life as it was. This lesson was learned by the local state university when it issued its plan to tear down homes. The constituents were appalled and went to the newspapers immediately. (Perhaps it was foolish for the university to threaten the neighborhood where the publisher of the city's newspaper lived!) Ombuds 3 denounced the university's plans. The story was the subject of front-page headlines for weeks. Yard signs sprouted around the university, protesting, "[The University] Kills Our Homes!" More than any other issue, this one called upon Ombuds 3 to be responsive, and she was. Representing adjoining districts, Ombuds 3 and Rep 3 introduced bills to require public universities to open their records to public scrutiny and hold hearings when they purchased property. Ombuds 3 appeared at community forums with Senator 1, and together they worked hard to pacify the crowds and protest the university's actions. The university leaders drastically scaled back their expansion plans, then shelved them. The chancellor was released from her job and replaced. I sat in on a meeting where the new interim chancellor appealed for forgiveness and support from a skeptical Ombuds 3 and Senator 1. Before taking the olive branch, they let the new chancellor know how disappointed they were with his predecessor. They told him they felt "caught between the institution and the neighborhoods," and Ombuds 3 added, "I'm really tired of this." Senator 1 said he had attended a forum with over five hundred people from the neighborhoods, many of whom were very angry. The new university leader said he understood and would work hard to address their concerns. Ombuds 3's constituents were placated—but they also vowed to watch the university closely in the future. The yard

signs and bumper stickers remained visible for many months afterwards. One legislator even spotted a "Kills Our Homes" sign hundreds of miles away, in a different part of the state.

This was by far the most heated controversy I watched Ombuds 3
confront. Local politics in her area were mostly quite calm. Her well-
to-do constituents often took care of casework problems on their
own, or approached the city or federal government. Thus Ombuds 3
spent less time on casework, with a few exceptions. She told me:

> There are always a couple of people that you hear from all the
> time about something. Some of the older people in the district
> have become pen pals. They write all the time, you write them
> back, and they write you, and you write them back, and on and
> on. And they're mostly great and it's no big deal. Other than
> that, I think it's more [on] an issue-by-issue basis. I get a lot now
> about [university] stuff, but that's because it's a hot topic in my
> area. Other than that, . . . I do not get much constituent, per se,
> what to a lot of people is constituent work.

Here the theme is issues, not casework. This helps explain why
Ombuds 3 sponsored so much legislation dealing with the district.
Her constituents sought policy changes from the state, not particu-
larized favors from their representative. They protectively guarded
their historic homes. Sometimes they felt threatened by the university or by natural disasters such as flooding. Ombuds 3 listened and
responded. Little wonder that she "fit the district" (her words) and
was elected and reelected easily against weak Republican challengers.
She stressed her role in sponsoring legislation, telling a chamber
meeting that "there are just quite a few bills I'm working on," including those dealing with the university and flood insurance. Per the
latter, she sponsored a bill that would require the state to notify residents in flood-prone areas that insurance was available.

I have discussed how Ombuds 3 responded to constituents. Yet she
also saw it as her role to moderate their demands and pacify their concerns. In spite of her outrage with the university's proposal, she rejected some constituents' suggestions on how to fix the problem.
Most notably, some asked for legislation that would require a public
vote every time a state entity proposed to use eminent domain. I lis-

tened to Ombuds 3 reassure the university's interim chancellor that such a law would be overkill. She believed that this proposal would often have the effect of making state action impossible. Because the neighborhoods were so protective of their homes, she argued, few if any eminent domain proposals would pass a vote of the people. This would stop some worthwhile projects. For example, the university had recently acquired an aging apartment building and was refurbishing it for use as on-campus student housing. Ombuds 3 regarded this as a good investment and a nice way to fix up and improve the building, which was also in her district. But if this proposal had gone to a public vote, she thought, constituents would have instinctively voted "no." They had come to completely distrust the university's intentions. She promised the interim chancellor that if he would keep the teardown proposal off the agenda, she would quietly work against any proposal for a public vote on eminent domain acquisitions. She also noted that if the university did not cooperate by withdrawing the offending proposal, the constituents and other legislators would be much more likely to call for popular voting on eminent domain. In other words, she suggested that the university's best interests would be served by cooperating with her, in exchange for her filtering out some of her constituents' more extreme ideas. With Rep 3, she sponsored legislation calling for open records and public meetings whenever a state university sought to acquire property in a neighborhood. Colloquially speaking, Ombuds 3 played "good cop," while the angrier neighborhood activists (though not present at the meeting with the interim chancellor) took the "bad cop" role.

In this exchange, Ombuds 3 complicated the ombudsperson role by filtering constituent demands through her own judgment. She often assumed this filtering role to refine constituent demands even while aggressively responding to them. This is how she summed it up to a chamber meeting: "[The university] and their neighbors had a little falling out. What we got was a good decision. Neither side is completely happy. In legislation, that's a good sign."

There may have been fewer casework requests for Ombuds 3, but she still got some surprises. I was with her when she dropped by an abused children's center in her district. She had been given some handmade dolls to present to the children. She was not anticipating casework requests, but in an impromptu meeting, the directors pled with her to negotiate a better contract for them with the state. Their private donations were "maxed out," they said, and without higher re-imbursements and more flexibility in which children they could ad-mit, they would have to close their doors. They were well organized, and even gave Ombuds 3 handouts detailing their financial plight. She said she would do what she could. She was on the Social Ser-vices Appropriations Committee, and the budget was in the process of being drawn up, so it was a good time to address this concern. She promised to arrange a meeting with the center's directors, state social service personnel, Senator 1, and herself. Though presenting the dolls was her original purpose in coming, she found herself performing constituent service—and not for an individual, but for an entire agency. Again, her theme was listening and responding—even when caught by surprise.

The "good listener" theme also persuaded Ombuds 3 and her friend Rep 3 to do something about the troubled public schools in their districts. According to Ombuds 3, her constituents did not send their children to the city's public schools, and were quite frustrated. She was aware of these problems, having lived in the district since 1969. She learned still more as her constituents demanded reform. Regarding the recent history of the school district, she told me:

> I think it started in 1974 when there was a teachers' strike in [the city], and it went on, and on, and on, and on, and on. And, at that point in time, you had a white flight anyway, fleeing the city, and you had people who just got absolutely disgusted with the school district. And since 1974, one thing or another in that school district has been wrong. . . . It's a jobs program, they don't care about kids, and that is institutional. The number of administrators they have is humongous, maybe the largest per-centage in the world, the galaxy, I don't know. It seems like it. And that doesn't get any better. They've been through . . . nine-teen superintendents. Isn't that amazing? So, you know, it is just a pattern.

Constituents of Ombuds 3 and Rep 3 loved their homes and neighborhoods. But they either chose private schools or ended up moving across the state line to nearby suburbs (for example, to Advocate 4's district, which was just several blocks away in another state). They began to demand more options. Two constituents, one in Ombuds 3's district and one in Rep 3's, approached them with a proposal for charter schools. The proposal drew on experiments used in other states; in Ombuds 3's words, "We didn't have to reinvent the wheel." The legislators responded, adding an amendment to an education bill that allowed for charter schools in the state's two inner-city school districts. (Ombuds 3's constituents had been far more aggressive than residents of the other major city when it came to chartering schools.)

Ombuds 3's experiences with constituents on this issue reinforced her earlier comments about the district. These constituents were educated, well organized, and had a proposal ready before they approached the legislators. Meeting their request required legislation rather than casework. In order to get the legislation passed, Ombuds 3 and Rep 3 had to be vigilant. The education bill came back from the senate with the chartering provision removed. Ombuds 3 and Rep 3 made sure that the amendment was reinserted in conference. There was quite a bit of resistance from the inner-suburban districts. At a Birchtree schools forum, I watched several constituents lobby their legislators to vote "no" on the charters amendment. They feared it would eventually lead to charter schools in the suburban districts and "tear our district apart." Still, the amendment prevailed.

Several schools were chartered in the adjoining districts of Ombuds 3 and Rep 3. The minority communities as well as the white communities responded. According to the city newspaper, the racial mix of charter school students roughly mirrored that of the other city schools. When the state threatened to revoke the school district's accreditation, for reasons unrelated to charter schools, Ombuds 3 defended her decision. She was quoted in the newspaper as saying: "There is only so long you can put this off. Quite frankly, I have been concerned that the district has spent a lot of time talking about the damage charter schools have done when the reality is that [its own] academic deficiencies are much more serious."

The close friendship of Ombuds 3 and Rep 3 was very much a part of each one's home style. They often worked together on matters of importance to their districts. Their adjoining districts were quite similar, though Rep 3's had somewhat fewer homeowners, a larger gay and lesbian population, and more Democrats. But each district was urban, gentrified, and middle-to-upper-income, and both representatives described their constituents as socially moderate or liberal. Ombuds 3 said the people in her district elected her in part because "I'm certainly not right-wing. I think it's easy to figure out what that is. Even the Republicans in my district are not right-wing, very few. Very few would support concealed weapons, you know, or prayer in the schools. I probably am on the liberal side on social issues, probably a fiscal moderate."

With both districts dominated by social liberals with similar concerns, Ombuds 3 and Rep 3 found it easy to work together. Rep 3 sat in on my interview with Ombuds 3, adding comments about his own district. He noted that Republicans were very weak in his district—in fact, the Reform and Green candidates often outpolled the GOP. Advocate 5 had told me that Rep 3's district was "probably one of the most liberal, if not in the state . . . then certainly in [the city]." Advocate 5 often joined these two for dinner, and they worked together on city concerns. As a "triumvirate" (Ombuds 3's word), the three Democrats represented a contiguous area encompassing the city's moderate-to-upper-income wards. They often appeared together at chamber meetings and other in-district events. As we have seen, Advocate 5 and Rep 3 worked with Ombuds 3 to fight the university teardown proposal, even though the affected neighborhoods were entirely contained within Ombuds 3's district. They joked and teased one another at forums. Advocate 5 entertained a chamber audience by saying, "Let me warn you, if you watch me, [Rep 3], and [Ombuds 3] in the house, you will think we hate each other, but we bicker because we love each other."

I have shown several times throughout this study how metropolitan legislators work together at home instead of following the strategy preferred by Fenno's congressmen, which might be described as a "lone wolf" approach. But how expansive is this inclusiveness? I asked the triumvirate if they ever invited suburban representatives from near their city to join them at working dinners and the like. Rep 3 answered first, telling me, "We try to forget them!" But Ombuds 3 interjected that some suburbanites were pleasant enough. She noted that Ombuds 2's predecessor, in addition to Advocate 6 and one other suburban house member, were often invited along. She anticipated that after they got to know him, Ombuds 2 would probably be asked to come along, too. But her working relationship with others was more distant, she said, because "there's some philosophical stuff there." I asked her to clarify, and she added, "Well, quite a few of the suburban Republicans are very far right, and that is just not my bent." Neither she nor Rep 3 mentioned the outer-urban/inner-suburban Democrats such as Advocates 1 and 2. But it was clear that these representatives' districts clashed with those of Ombuds 3 and Rep 3 at times (over charter schools, for example). Ombuds 3 and Rep 3 also said nothing about the inner-city representatives whose poorer districts were not far away. Nor did they discuss any cooperation across the state line. They identified strongly with their part of the city, and their immediate circle did not usually extend into other areas. Thus, they worked closely with their immediate neighbors. As borne out by most of the public appearances I saw, those from districts that are adjacent or nearby are more likely to work together than those whose districts are spaced far apart. Ombuds 3's comment above suggests that differences in partisanship or ideology, as well as district interests, may play a role in these decisions. At the chamber forum, all present were Democrats. The only legislator who didn't represent a nearby district was Senator 3, who was in town anyway for another meeting. (He had recently announced his candidacy for statewide office.) All others present represented contiguous districts. Senator 1's larger district encompassed those of Advocate 5 and Ombuds 3, among others.

Ombuds 3 had been easily elected two times in a row. She faced the same opponent each time, a Republican opponent who had run for many offices, always stressing foreign policy, "which people in my district have a little trouble connecting with the state of Missouri," Ombuds 3 said. Still, Ombuds 3 had a reelection strategy. It was centered on fund-raising. She did not ask for party help at all, taking things into her own hands instead. She called friends and contacts around the city (not just in the district). Ombuds 3 believed that her longtime residence in the city gave her more contacts and a fund-raising advantage. She did not discuss other reelection concerns in detail with me, apparently because she deemed fund-raising the hardest part, and because she had been reelected easily against her weak opponent. I asked her why Republicans did not choose a stronger challenger. She speculated that they would "if they could find one." She did not deem reelection to be a serious worry. In the quotation that opens this section, she indicated that most of her constituents did not envy her job, which featured low pay and hard work. Nor did they seek to replace her. For her part, Ombuds 3 claimed no future political plans after the house. "After that," she told me, "it's golf and the beach!"

Ombuds 3's constituents liked to elect women. In fact, women had held this statehouse seat for over twenty years. The city's first-ever woman mayor, who was in office at the time of my study, lived in the district. The local U.S. congresswoman once represented Rep 3's nearby community in the statehouse. The current mayor won most wards of Ombuds 3's district easily, as did the congresswoman in each of her reelection bids. Hamm and Moncrief note that women are still underrepresented in most state legislatures, particularly outside the western United States.[5] This pattern of underrepresentation includes Missouri and Kansas. It is not clear why some districts are so comfortable electing women, but it seems reasonable to hypothesize that once a woman "breaks the ice" by being the first one elected, other women have an easier time winning in the future. Advocate 6 told me that she was one of the women who first broke the "old boys' network" in the legislature. Perhaps this ice-breaking also explains the pattern in Ombuds 3's district. The two women in this study both represented upper- to middle-income, urban or suburban districts. However, there are not enough cases here to draw any inferences about a larger population of legislators and districts. Still, there seemed to be something about Ombuds 3's district that made the residents especially comfortable with women in office. The ice-breaking hypothesis seems plausible and deserves further study with more cases.

Ombuds 3's constituents seemed generally content with their quality of life. However, such an attitude might make them particularly defensive about the district if future controversies arise. In her first three sessions, Ombuds 3 spent a lot of time listening. She sponsored several pieces of legislation in response to many of her constituents'

5. Hamm and Moncrief, "Legislative Politics in the States," 163.

concerns. Her reduced casework demands gave her more time to focus on legislation affecting the district. With some "flare-ups" coming almost overnight, it was impossible to predict what controversies would be brought to her attention in the future. But it could safely be assumed that whatever the issue, Ombuds 3 would be listening and responding.

Ombuds 4: The Rural Ombudsman

The thing that distinguishes a rural representative from an urban one? I can go to just about everybody in [the urban area] and ask them who their representative is. You know, if they're not politically totally plugged in, . . . they're not sure. There's no doubt in anybody's mind in [the rural] area who their representative is. We're very visible. We're very accessible, and still not . . . looked at with respect by many, and [are looked at with] scorn and disdain by others, but we're kind of the ombudsmen . . . for a lot of . . . problems that come up, and people just don't know what to do about the bureaucracy or the . . . frustration with it, so they call us.

—*Ombuds 4*

The rural representative's job is not easy. Ombuds 4 put over 100,000 miles on his truck in only a few years by commuting between his farm, the population center of his district, and the state capital. He was constantly being asked to attend one event or another, and he obliged. He told me: "I show up. If it's a bean dinner, if it's . . . the Eagle Scout induction, whatever it is, I try to be there. I don't . . . catch everything, but I know I'm about right when . . . about every tenth person I see says, 'Boy, you're everywhere, aren't you?'" Ombuds 4 faced special challenges in his rural community. Even *Lone Oak,* the population center of his district, was located two hours away from the nearest interstate highway. Widening two-lane highways to four lanes was a major concern. In the still-more-rural communities outside Lone Oak, Ombuds 4 found growing concentrations of senior citizens, law enforcement sometimes overwhelmed by crystal methamphetamine production (and asking for more state aid), and a major shift from open-pasture to confinement-feeding (indoor) hog farms. This last problem brought new environmental challenges.

Many urban and suburban house members agree with Ombuds 4 that the rural representative has greater name recognition than the metropolitan legislator. It was Ombuds 3 who encouraged me to expand this study to include rural representatives; I responded by including Burkean 2 and Ombuds 4. Speaking of rural legislators' greater name recognition, Advocate 4 told me: "Oh, man! They can't go anywhere! Not only the representatives, but their kids are representatives' kids. Their wives are representatives' wives." Ombuds 4 was just such a rural ombudsperson. He had to be careful when he went shopping; a constituent might run into him and want to have a long conversation right there in the store, and a short shopping trip could end up taking hours. Among the metropolitan legislators, only Advocate 6 mentioned a similar problem to me.

Like Burkean 2, Ombuds 4 lived in the "wrong place" within his district, from a political perspective. About 80 percent of the district's population lived in Lone Oak, but he did not. Instead, he lived about forty miles away, on a farm near the edge of the district. Again paralleling Burkean 2, he found that every year, his challengers came from the population center, a small city that served as a farm-to-market center and college town. Living in a different part of the district created extra challenges. Ombuds 4 relied on a handful of old political friends in Lone Oak to keep him up to date on what was going on, especially when he had been out of town or busy on his farm. Their houses were frequent stopping points when he was in Lone Oak to attend meetings. He stopped in to ask what was happening in local politics, what was important, and what was not. His most trusted ally in Lone Oak had recently passed away, leaving him looking for new intimates with whom to consult. He also stopped to chat with a group of older gentlemen at a local café. Wearing bib overalls and farm caps, this group reminisced about old times and talked about the news. They had been meeting for years and were sure to have strong opinions on issues past and present. Ombuds 4 tried to stop in every Friday. When I traveled with him, he asked me to sit at a separate table and eavesdrop instead of coming in to the café with him and being introduced. He feared that the group would grow quiet if they knew a stranger was listening in on their conversation. Ombuds 4 mostly just listened while the old-timers talked.

Of all the representatives studied here, Ombuds 4 was the most likely to appear alone. That is, he was the only one who usually followed the "lone wolf" strategy of Fenno's congressmen. He rarely appeared with other legislators at home-district forums. Instead, the others in attendance would be city officials, chamber of commerce members, and administrators from *Southern State University*, the medium-sized state campus in Lone Oak. Ombuds 4 lived in a different senatorial district from the one that encompassed Lone Oak; the latter was represented by a Democratic state senator. Ombuds 4, a Republican, rarely appeared with that senator. Nor did he find himself working at home with house members from neighboring districts. His neighboring districts were much farther away than were those of a metropolitan legislator such as Advocate 4, for example, whose district was only about three square miles in area. Ombuds 4's, in contrast, covered several counties. It has already been shown that metropolitan legislators frequently appeared together at chamber forums, school district meetings, and the like. While he also attended such meetings, Ombuds 4 was often the only state legislator present.

Not only did Ombuds 4 find himself going it alone more often than his metropolitan counterparts, he also had access to different types of media. This might have helped account for his greater name recognition. Radio is not usually a practical outlet for a metropolitan legislator. For example, in Kansas City, a single broadcast interview or commercial can potentially reach the metropolitan area's 1.6 million people in two states, plus the residents of surrounding rural areas that are close enough to receive the broadcast. But the vast majority of these potential listeners do not live in the district of any given state representative.[6] This makes radio advertising cost-ineffective in a metropolitan area (though some metropolitan state senate candidates did use radio spots during the course of this study). For the same reason—most listeners do not live in any given representative's district—urban radio talk show hosts rarely ask a state legislator to be a

6. Gary F. Moncrief, Peverill Squire, and Malcolm E. Jewell, *Who Runs for the Legislature?* 76.

featured guest. Burkean 1 and Rep 1's appearance on a religious Sunday morning radio show was a rare exception.

For the rural legislator, the cost-benefit decisions surrounding radio are quite different. The urban legislators I interviewed were well aware that their rural counterparts ran radio commercials during campaign season. In fact, while the legislature was in session, Ombuds 4 did a radio show every week with a host from the station. The host asked friendly, open-ended questions ("What can we expect coming up in the legislature next month?") and Ombuds 4 answered. He told listeners what had happened in the legislature that week and what to expect in the near future. The station gave airtime to incumbents but not challengers. The idea was to discuss current and upcoming legislation, not to campaign for reelection. Yet the shows helped Ombuds 4 gain name recognition, contributing to his incumbency advantage, and they were cost-free. Senator 3, whose district included Lone Oak but not Ombuds 4's farm, did a similar weekly show at the station.

Appearing on his own can lead a legislator to take a more individualistic stance in defending his record and to downplay any defense of state political institutions. While I traveled with him, Ombuds 4 rarely mentioned his rural colleagues in the statehouse or senate. Instead, he spent a good deal of time discussing his own take on the state's deep metropolitan/rural split. On his radio broadcast, he denounced the city's two urban school districts for their enormous desegregation expenses, which were paid partly from state monies. The show's host added that frustration with desegregation expenses was a long-standing sore spot in the rural parts of the state. Indeed, it predated Ombuds 4's election to office. Many rural residents insisted that they did not get their fair share of school money due to the drain caused by the desegregation lawsuits. Ombuds 4 suggested that he was struggling to get a fair share for his rural community against the resistance of metropolitan legislators.

Schools were not the only issue that prompted Ombuds 4 to mention the metropolitan/rural divide. He also alluded to the state's divided politics during a "listening post" session at the Lone Oak Chamber of Commerce. When a constituent brought up Advocate 5's collective bargaining bill, Ombuds 4 took time out to denounce several unions that had spent substantial monies to support his op-

ponents. He told his constituents that these city-based union organizations collected dues from urban workers, then spent the money
interfering in outstate campaigns such as his own. He claimed that
most of the rank-and-file, which lived in the metropolitan areas, was
unaware of what was going on with their money. He made it clear
that he was unhappy with the union organizations and their supporters in the legislature, most of whom were urban or inner-suburban Democrats. Here Ombuds 4 directed his criticism not at the people of the metropolitan areas, but at the politicians there.

Rural frustration with an increasingly metropolitan-dominated
legislature was one of Ombuds 4's major themes. His strong opinions
on the subject prompted him to "totally reverse" himself (his words)
on the issue of term limits. He had supported the state's term-limits
initiative when it was on the ballot. Later, he became deeply concerned that rural representatives would lose power. No longer would
they be able to use seniority to counter their shrinking numbers in
the legislature. According to Ombuds 4, the rural communities had
been able to keep their voice over the years by reelecting incumbents
for many terms, thus allowing them to rise to leadership positions in
both the houses. When these longtime rural incumbents were gone,
their communities were likely to lose some influence. Thus Ombuds
4 became a critic of the state's eight-year term limits. He argued that
they should either be abolished or replaced with twelve-year limits.
Such actions would require approval by the voters. Ombuds 4 did not
know if there was any public sentiment for this action. At any rate,
when he was at home, he presented himself as a legislator who struggled to maintain a rural voice in a state whose population was two-
thirds metropolitan.

I chose the term *rural ombudsman* to emphasize the importance
Ombuds 4 placed on constituent service and listening to constituents.
He often focused on district-specific issues. The rural legislator cannot divide his labor with lawmakers whose districts are only a few
miles away, as is the case with urban and suburban representatives.
Patricia K. Freeman and Lilliard E. Richardson Jr. have observed that
rural state legislators do more casework.[7] Ombuds 4 attributed his
higher volume of casework requests principally to name recognition.

7. Freeman and Richardson, "Exploring Variation in Casework," 48.

Through radio and "lone wolf" appearances, he had made himself known to quite a few constituents, who called him when difficulties arose with the state. He further pointed out that metropolitan residents are more likely to call city government to deal with problems such as roads and sewers. But in a rural community, the counties or even the state must take responsibility for many of these activities (particularly outside a population center such as Lone Oak). Further, none of the counties in his district had home-rule charters. They were more dependent on the state and more affected by its actions.

In our discussion, Ombuds 4 linked casework with economic development. Regarding the latter, he found that rural local governments, when compared with urban areas, do not have as many specialized offices staffed by ombudspersons who can work with state legislators. Likewise, he did not have neighboring representatives close by with whom he could divide the work of developmental policy. He told me: "[I spend] a much higher percentage of my time tied up in constituent work [and] economic development type things. Whereas in the city, you'd have . . . an economic development person." For example, he got calls about raw sewage running into grader ditches in unincorporated areas. In a city, similar concerns would be more likely to go to local officials. But in a rural community, the state representative has the highest name recognition of any elected official. There is often no specific local government office to deal with such problems. Thus, Ombuds 4 got the calls. He had to either get the state to intervene or refer constituents to appropriate local officials—if there *were* appropriate local officials to deal with the problem in their small, rural counties.

The ombudsperson must work to solve problems while referring other concerns to local government. But that is not all. Ombuds 4 also worked to represent district concerns to federal officials. He spent a great deal of time working with the local congressman's office, arranging to have the Department of Veterans Affairs open an outpatient medical clinic in Lone Oak. Constituents first approached Ombuds 4, not the congressman, with their concern. Veterans were making the two-hour trek to *Spruceville*, where the nearest VA hospital was located. Many of these veterans were elderly and did not want to face the long drives. Further, the highway connecting Lone Oak and Spruceville was mostly two-lane, and fatal accidents were common. Local veterans argued strenuously that there must be an outpatient clinic in Lone Oak to save them these long trips. Ombuds 4 was convinced and spent several years working with both the state's senior U.S. senator and the congressman, struggling to get a clinic built. They were successful. The federal legislators took up the cause, a line item made it into the budget, and the ribbon-cutting took place just days before Ombuds 4 joined this study.

Why did constituents approach Ombuds 4 instead of going directly to their senator or congressman? One reason might be proximity: neither of the officials who later took up the cause were likely to be seen in Ombuds 4's district. They did not travel home as often, neither lived in the district, and, as federal officeholders, they had much more territory to cover. Ombuds 4 seemed approachable due to his name recognition, frequent appearances at home, and person-to-person style. His close ties to the Republican party gave him access to the senator and congressman in question. In short, Ombuds 4 was in a position to help local veterans with their concerns.

Perhaps the largest concern of the district involved the ninety-mile stretch of highway connecting Lone Oak with Spruceville. Spruceville was the closest larger city. It was also the nearest point at which a driver could merge onto a major interstate highway. But in order to make the trek, commuters had to traverse *Highway 38,* which carried relatively heavy traffic for a two-lane rural road. Many accidents were caused by vehicles crossing the yellow center line into oncoming traffic, due to careless passing of slower vehicles, general inattention, or alcohol impairment. When I told Ombuds 4 that I was coming out to follow him around in Lone Oak, he said, "Don't get distracted by all those crosses [when you're] driving up." He was referring to the wooden crosses put up along the roadside at spots where fatal accidents had occurred. The road was a constant worry in the community, and Ombuds 4 struggled to get funding for road widening. Driving up, I saw many spots where the widening to a four-lane, divided highway had begun. Yet funding was another major worry. Constituents fretted that the money would not be there to finish the project, especially given the recent collapse of the state's "fifteen-year plan" to build new highways (it was revealed that the plan was based on faulty cost estimates).

Highway 38 came up at every meeting I attended in the district, both formal and informal. Sometimes Ombuds 4 brought it up, sometimes others did. At the "listening post" chamber meeting, a plan was discussed to create a special bonding district that would incur debt to widen the road. State and federal aid would help pay the bonds off later. The priority was to get the widening done as soon as possible. Constituents complained about the collapse of the fifteen-year plan and its consequences for Highway 38. The issue even came up at a private meeting with a Southern State University administrator. The administrator argued that the road was a dangerous one for students from the metropolitan areas to travel, and that its current condition was harming the university's recruiting efforts. He worried that students and faculty could be courted away to other schools that were more conveniently located. A recent issue of Southern State's glossy alumni magazine featured a cover story about the dangers of Highway 38, the struggle to widen it, and the volunteer effort to place crosses near the fatality sites. Constituents kept up the pressure on Ombuds 4 regarding this issue. Ombuds 4 even tried to co-opt me into helping: When he introduced me to the chamber, he said, "He's from a metropolitan area. Maybe he can help us raise awareness about how important this is."

Lone Oak had experienced modest growth in recent years due to Southern State's national recognition and the growth of a nearby private medical school. Though he did not live there, Ombuds 4 attended more meetings and functions in Lone Oak than anywhere else. He became a civic booster whenever called upon to do so. He told me, "I really and truly believe that I have the best district in the state" because of the mix of higher education, small town folksiness, and agriculture. He repeated this theme, almost word-for-word, when speaking to a group of children at a Christian high school. He often touted Southern State's national recognition as a prominent liberal-arts university and a good value in education. Still, he was aware that his own rural community, several miles away, was easy to overlook in an increasingly suburban state. Speaking to the aforementioned students, he mentioned that some small towns in the district had counters across the roads that measured the traffic flow. He entertained the students by saying, "I tell people, 'If you're not busy, could you please back up and run over that counter again?'"

In the rural communities away from Lone Oak, confinement hog farming had become a major concern. These indoor operations had more hogs than most family-farmer, open-pasture farms. The larger concentration of waste was a challenge. The state attorney general got involved in the controversy, aggressively prosecuting operations that violated the state's waste disposal laws. In Lone Oak, a loose coalition of environmentalists announced their opposition to confinement-feeding and their intent to fight it wherever possible. One tactic they used was to run a "hog radical" (Ombuds 4's term) against Ombuds 4. They tried to focus the campaign on that single issue, but they were not successful. Ombuds 4 presented himself as a moderate on the issue, stressed his incumbency, and was reelected easily. But even for the less "radical" constituents, the confinement-feeding operations remained a concern. Ombuds 4 struggled to address the issue without giving in to the radicals and their demand to "run these people [the agribusinesses operating the indoor farms] out of Dodge," as he put it.

Ombuds 4 stressed that non-farmers often misunderstand farming techniques. He took the radicals to task on this point. Waste leaks were a major concern around the confinement farms, but according to Ombuds 4, the radicals wrongly referred to these as "lagoon leaks." In fact, he told me, the problems were not in the waste lagoons, where the hog waste settles and solid sediment is collected as fertilizer. Rather, the problem stemmed from the pipes that carried the waste to these lagoons. Often, they would develop a block, back up, then blow out and leak. Ombuds 4 sponsored successful legislation requiring the confinement farms to enclose these pipes in earthen structures to contain leaks. His bill also mandated more-frequent state inspections. He prided himself on this and pointed to the legislation as an example of pragmatism instead of ideological extremism. This enabled him to fend off the challenge from the hog radicals. He also pointed out that the radicals were hurt in Lone Oak. Most residents there did not live on farms and were unconcerned about the hog farming issue. Further, some employees at the factory farms found that their wages and benefits were better than they would be at other jobs in this rural community. So Ombuds 4 argued that the new farms must be accommodated, even regulated, but not "run out of Dodge."

His approach on this issue seemed to have been politically successful. According to Ombuds 4, he merely needed to be effective in responding to local needs. Unlike Advocates 2 and 3, for example, he did not organize town halls with high turnouts and media publicity to confront a major issue. In fact, he saw the hog radicals as would-be advocates who had stirred up too much controversy already. He believed that his rural communities were better served by his own approach, which he felt was more responsive to farming needs and the district's interests. Both ombudspersons and advocates work hard on issues of concern to their district. The difference is that advocates often seek to raise more publicity and controversy in order to socialize the conflict. By contrast, Ombuds 4 presented his hog bill as a successful attempt to *defuse* the controversy raised by others while satisfying district needs. Much like Ombuds 3 on the eminent domain issue, he presented his stand on hog farming as a balanced approach that moderated the conflict.

Ombuds 4 once held town halls, then switched to the listening post format. The difference is this: in a town hall, constituents meet en masse; at a listening post, they come in one by one or in small groups. The chamber supplied a waiting room and meeting room at its building. If two different individuals or groups arrived at the same time, one waited while Ombuds 4 met with the other. He chose this format largely because of difficulties with one particular constituent whom he called a "guaranteed crackpot." This man often spouted strange or nonsensical ideas in public forums, and was almost certain to be at any public meeting in Lone Oak. He had disrupted many meetings, with the result that "other people don't want to be there," according to Ombuds 4. The listening post forum was a way around this problem. The eccentric fellow showed up there too, but Ombuds 4 had recently begun asking the chamber to escort him out the door without a meeting. It is remarkable that a single constituent can prompt a legislator to change the format for his district meetings. But Ombuds 4 was pleased with the listening post system, which generally brought out representatives from key interests in town. These included the chamber, an ad hoc committee formed to lobby for widening Highway 38, law enforcement agencies, and the schools. Obviously, by providing the space, the chamber insured itself especially good access to Ombuds 4.

Ombuds 4 faced relatively high-quality Democratic challengers in each election cycle. (He had not had a primary challenge.) According to him, his hog radical challenger was actually the weakest one. His toughest run was against a former Lone Oak mayor who also served as director of the local Planned Parenthood affiliate. Even then, he won with 62 percent of the vote. It should be noted that Ombuds 4 believed the district to be socially conservative, and that his pro-life stand might have helped him in that race.

Ombuds 4 had built a successful incumbency by presenting himself as the rural ombudsman for an area that might otherwise be forgotten. He involved himself not only in local legislation, but also in other levels of government regarding issues that were of concern back home. He often presented himself as a rural minority struggling for recognition in a metropolitan-dominated legislature. His constituents responded well. Name recognition was crucial. Ombuds 4 did his radio broadcasts and attended as many events as possible. He balanced all of this with his farming responsibilities. Even some of his committee choices reflected the ombudsperson's theme: he served on both higher education and agriculture committees (in one recent session, they met at the same time, forcing him to run back and forth between them). Like the United States as a whole, his state was becoming more and more suburban in its population growth and corresponding legislative power. Even so, when this outstate district needed some recognition, the rural ombudsman struggled to get it.

Conclusion

Jewell's four tasks are just as important to the ombudspersons as to the other representatives in this study. For the ombudsperson, *communication with constituents* often takes the form of simply listening to what constituents say. Some, such as Ombuds 1, focus on what local government officials tell them about local needs. Others, such as Ombuds 2 and 4, try to attend every meeting they possibly can, greet constituents, find out what is on their minds, and generally act responsive. Ombuds 3 believed that her constituents had fewer worries than many, but still listened carefully when issues arose.

For the ombudsperson, *policy responsiveness* means letting issues bubble up. When an issue comes onto the agenda, ombudspersons work to respond. However, they are less likely to actually place issues onto the agenda, preferring to let others do that. Ombuds 1 proposed ideas to meet district concerns and voted in accordance with local interests, for example, on taxes. Ombuds 2, in office only a short time when I shadowed him, was still working to find out what was happening at home. Ombuds 3 and 4 had sponsored substantial amounts of legislation in response to issues raised by constituents. Ombuds 4 also got involved in the struggle for a VA center—again, the theme was responsiveness to constituent demand, though this particular project did not require any legislation in the statehouse. Even so, constituents called Ombuds 4 first. He thought that was due to his responsiveness and name recognition in the district.

Allocation of resources for the district is important to the ombudsperson approach. For Ombuds 1, this simply meant "voting the district." Ombuds 2 worked closely with local chamber and school officials to find out what they needed from the state. Ombuds 3's constituents were generally well-off, and allocation of resources was not a major theme for her. Rather, she often worked to stop or change proposed state projects that might harm the community's well-being, such as the local university's proposed expansion. By contrast, Ombuds 4 saw his own district as easy to overlook, and felt it needed some major state projects, most notably for road widening. His constituents kept the pressure on him regarding money for Highway 38. Like in-district advocates, ombudspersons have a district-centered approach that often guides their actions both in struggling over resources and in doing casework.

Of all these ombudspersons, only Ombuds 3 downplayed the importance of *constituent service*. Her constituents were less needy, according to her. They were also more likely to approach local government instead of the state. Ombuds 1, 2, and 4, however, saw responsiveness to casework requests as an important facet of their district-centered focus. Urban Ombuds 3 and rural Ombuds 4 both believed that rural legislators get more casework requests than urban ones do.

On the whole, this group had fewer progressive ambitions than the in-district advocates. Ombuds 1 was unsure whether he would seek a state senate seat. Ombuds 2 had no intention of running for another office after his term limit. However, he did plan to seek reelection. Ombuds 3 was not too excited about seeking another office, though she added, "you never say never." Ombuds 4 planned to wait until redistricting to decide his political future.

Listening before responding is the ombudsperson's theme at home. The ombudsperson is there when the district needs new projects (or needs to alter or stop existing ones). Likewise, he pays close attention to constituent service needs: he is there to respond to district needs, whether they be district-wide or from just one constituent.

7

Districts, Ambitions, and Strategies
in a Term-Limited Era

Grounded theory is a methodology in which trends in data are developed during the data-collection exercise and subsequent analysis; the approach is discussed at length in Chapter 2. This chapter develops hypotheses from the data described and analyzed in chapters 3 through 6. In general, the results of my interviews and trips to the districts indicate that state representatives have concentric circles of constituency, much like Richard Fenno's congressmen. However, the circles themselves are different. This is due in large part to two factors. The first is the small size of the state legislator's constituency. The second is the larger role of progressive ambitions for higher office, which factors into many statehouse members' career-planning. Most of the representatives who expressed an ambition for a state senate seat were in-district advocates. Furthermore, "struggling" metropolitan districts with large proportions of working-class or poor residents were likely to be represented by in-district advocates. Those legislators with fewer political ambitions beyond the statehouse were more likely to be Burkeans or ombudspersons than advocates. Wealthier, politically competitive metropolitan districts tended to be represented by ombudspersons.

The first part of this chapter features a discussion of the concentric circles of constituency that I discovered. The second part presents four hypotheses, in which district characteristics and the legislators' ambitions are considered as independent variables and the legislators' home styles are considered as a dependent variable. The third part features a discussion of a new factor affecting legislators' career ambitions: term limits. These set constraints, but also provide new opportunities. Obviously, the constraints are on legislators' ability to make a career of serving in the house. The opportunities come when state senate incumbents are forced from office, opening up those seats for progressively ambitious house members.

Concentric Circles of Constituency

Figure 2 summarizes the concentric circles of constituency discovered by Fenno.[1] The constituencies represented by the smaller circles in the center are more immediate in their connection to the legislator. Those represented by the larger circles are more peripheral. The largest circle in Fenno's schematic is the entire district (the geographic constituency). Successively smaller are the reelection constituency, the primary (core) constituency, and the intimates (close friends and political contacts).

Fenno's circles can certainly be used to describe the state legislators in my study. For example, state legislators, like congressmen, have intimates in the district. Advocate 2, for one, had a close confidante in the district: a schoolteacher who lived at the other end of the community. She served as his political intimate, going to public events as his proxy when he could not be there. She also kept him posted on the goings-on he missed while in the capital. Advocate 5 had a similar confidante who announced her own candidacy for his seat shortly after Advocate 5 announced that he would not run again. Ombuds 4 also had such a contact, who died shortly before I started this study. Ombuds 4's friend had been particularly useful to him, because while he lived on a farm in another county, she lived in the district's population center and could keep tabs on local issues. Advocate 2's wife was his close political ally and even traveled with him to the state capitol during the session (both are retired from earlier careers); she is another good example of an intimate.

Figure 3 adapts Fenno's schematic to depict the concentric circles of constituency of the state representatives in this study. Again, the constituencies represented by the smaller circles in the center are

---

1. Fenno, *Home Style,* 1–30.

Figure 2: Fenno's Concentric Circles

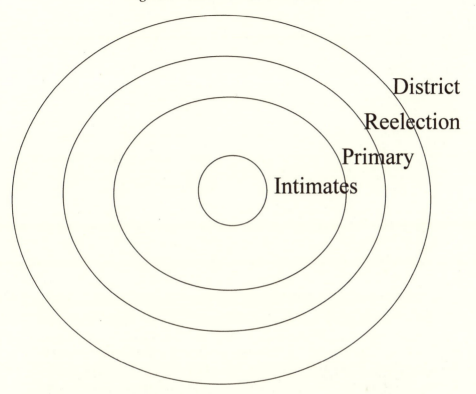

District
Reelection
Primary
Intimates

more immediate in their connection to the legislator. As Glenn Abney and Thomas A. Henderson have pointed out, different constituents have varying degrees of legitimacy in a legislator's eyes.[2] This depends on how closely and effectively these constituents have been identified with district interests. In my study, legislators' views of different groups or types of constituents varied from Ombuds 2's "good, solid citizens" to Ombuds 4's "guaranteed crackpot." Other characterizations occupied many points in between these extremes. All the representatives granted special consideration to local businesses, schoolteachers and administrators, and parents with children in the local public schools.

2. Glenn Abney and Thomas A. Henderson, "Role Orientations toward Subconstituencies: State Legislators and Local Officials," 299.

Figure 3: New Concentric Circles—State Representatives at Home

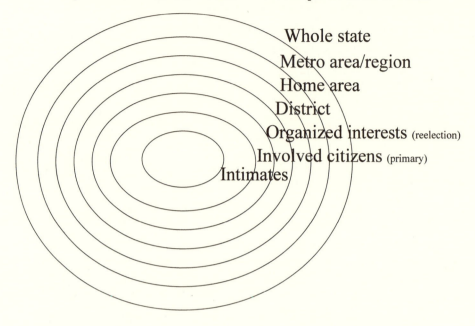

Whole state
Metro area/region
Home area
District
Organized interests (reelection)
Involved citizens (primary)
Intimates

All the legislators realized that many constituents do not vote or stay active in the electoral process. Advocate 5 was particularly frustrated about this. He told me that in an era of infotainment, it is hard for a state legislator to get name recognition. He predicted that if his own constituents were asked, "Who is your state representative?" they would be likely to respond with the name of their congresswoman or a U.S. senator—the one currently serving, or even one who retired twenty years ago. As Advocate 5 put it, when it came to name recognition, "I'm in competition with Tide [and] McDonald's. . . . and I usually lose." Yet he went door-to-door and used targeted direct mail in hopes of getting out the vote. He sought to help not only himself, but also the Democratic ticket.

For these state representatives, service to organized interests back home was central to an effective home style. Each of them faced both primary (core) constituencies who met with them regularly and reelection constituencies who were less involved in the political process but who nevertheless voted reliably to reelect their legislator. It is important to note that the term *primary constituency* refers to a core of

supporters, not to party primary elections. In fact, most of these legislators did not fear strong primary election challenges. They were
helped by state party organizations that usually backed incumbents
strongly if necessary. Each party seeks to ward off challenges that
might divide it. Thus, *primary* refers to a legislator's most organized,
active supporters. These supporters are often the leaders of organized
groups in the reelection constituency. Organized groups are the most
effective in gaining recognition from state representatives. For example, Advocate 4 depended on schoolteachers and business leaders to
articulate district interests. Ombuds 2 knew he could count on the
local chamber of commerce for support—he was the past president.
In another part of the state, the local chamber let Ombuds 4 use its
meeting room for his "listening post" sessions, thus ensuring their
own access to him. Organized labor was important to Advocate 5,
himself a union organizer. Labor leaders were part of the loose coalition that first recruited him to seek his house seat, and he kept in close
touch with them. School boards were crucial for Advocates 1 and 2,
both former board members.

The organizational advantage of teachers, school boards, and chambers gives them the best access to state legislators. This pattern was
consistent in every one of the twelve districts I visited. There were
only two possible exceptions. Very few of Ombuds 3's well-off constituents sent their children to the troubled local inner-city schools.
She therefore had less contact with the school district, and during the
course of this study, she emerged as a leading critic of those schools.
She successfully championed legislation to set up charter schools in
her school district and the state's other inner-city school district.
Turning to business, Advocate 3 had a well-organized chamber in his
district, but he was acutely aware that his inner-city constituents were
not among its members. The active chamber members in his downtown area were mostly commuters who lived in the wealthier neighboring county. Thus, Advocate 3 gave more priority to local church
and neighborhood organizations. But even he made the effort to be
at chamber sessions. One morning on which I observed him, he went
to a neighborhood meeting, then left early to make the last half of a
chamber session.

These legislators, like Fenno's congressmen, realized that certain
leaders will stand out within organized interest groups in the district.

Ombuds 4 called these people "totally politically plugged in." As Robert A. Dahl made clear in his seminal work on local government, resources to organize confer a crucial advantage in a pluralistic system.[3] Thus the strong, consistent organization of school boards, teachers' groups, and chambers of commerce gives these three types of organizations the best access to their state representatives. Some neighborhood associations are particularly active, too, such as those in Ombuds 3's district. A few people often stand out as the leaders of home-district organizations. These include chamber presidents and PR directors, school superintendents, school board presidents, local officials, and active citizens. At most meetings I attended, a handful of people did most of the talking, while others contented themselves with making social contacts and just voting "yes" or "no" on the questions presented by the leadership. Many chamber proposals were drafted by the leaders and then passed unanimously at the meetings with no discussion. Thus, those doing the drafting were making most of the decisions. The same was true at many suburban school boards. The individuals that invest time and energy into leading organized groups form still another circle of the home constituency.

In addition to the circles of constituency within the district, Figure 3 also features circles that stretch beyond the district's boundaries. Why so many circles beyond the entire district? The answer has to do with progressive ambitions versus long careers in the house. Many of these state representatives work to cultivate a constituency that will elect them to office in larger districts such as those represented by state senators. One circle takes account of the statewide orientation that Burkeans favor. Burke advocated a "whole-state" approach to representation, favoring national interests above all. The two Burkeans in this study presented themselves back home as legislators for the whole state. In their districts, they usually downplayed the local angle on pending legislation. Instead, they discussed their bills, votes, and committee service as the work of experienced men who had the best interests of the whole state at heart. As Burkean 1 said, "I don't get hung up on . . . 'how does this affect my district?'" In the beginning of Chapter 3, I explored this theme in detail, examining

3. Robert A. Dahl, *Who Governs: Democracy and Power in an American City,* 223– 28.

how Burke's concept of "virtual representation" exemplifies a concern for larger interests beyond the district. Thus the first circle to be added to Fenno's model is one that is broader and more encompassing than any other. That circle is the "whole-state" constituency stressed by Burkeans. Advocates beyond the district also stress this constituency.

State representatives must perform an enormous amount of boundary-crossing. Participant observation allowed me to see state representatives (and senators) working together in their home districts. Malcolm Jewell hypothesizes that this strategy occurs because of the small size of some districts, as well as overlapping municipal boundaries.[4] For example, many school districts cut across several legislative districts. Most of those districts' representatives appear at the schools' legislative forums. (Some states have multimember districts, though Missouri and Kansas are not among them.) These factors add a new dynamic to the ones Fenno observed among congresspersons. In Fenno's observations, legislators almost always appeared alone. Legislators interacting with one another in the home district is a subject for research that has been generally overlooked. Jewell does speculate about the role of cooperation among legislators who serve contiguous home districts. He finds that metropolitan legislators cooperate more with one another in their home districts than rural legislators do, because of the small size of the metropolitan districts and their interconnectedness as part of a larger urban area. Yet he acknowledges that more research is needed to find empirical evidence for his hypotheses. This study provides such evidence.

Appearing together, the state legislators in this study were much more likely to defend their legislative institutions than were Fenno's "lone wolf" congressmen. The latter, in Fenno's words, would "run for Congress by running against Congress," while the metropolitan state legislators I observed often worked together to tell constituents how bills move through the legislature and to explain why those processes are important.[5] Sometimes they would even defend each other, as when Advocate 1 spoke up for Rep 1, who represented a nearby suburban district. Advocate 1 was a strong Democrat, and Rep 1 an

4. Jewell, *Representation in State Legislatures*, 56–57.
5. Fenno, *Home Style*, 168.

equally strong Republican, but Advocate 1 told a chamber forum, "I've seen [Rep 1] up until 1 A.M., and by God, he's working." Advocate 4, a Republican, made a similar statement at a schoolteachers' meeting: "You're a wonderful citizen!" he told a Democratic legislator who represented a neighboring district. Some neighboring representatives worked together as a team. Burkean 1 and Rep 1, whose districts adjoined one another, were rarely seen apart in their home districts. They were close friends and often divided the labor when it came to making presentations to constituents. Ombuds 3 and Rep 3 had a similar relationship. Good friends from similar, bordering districts, they often sponsored legislation together. Rep 3 even sat in while I interviewed Ombuds 3.

Because legislators work together on so many boundary-crossing issues, still more circles must be added to Fenno's typology. These are also larger than the district, but they nest into the "whole-state" circle. The first is the metropolitan area represented. Obviously not all legislators are metropolitan, but even some of the small-town representatives I studied found themselves working with neighboring legislators on issues that cross boundaries, such as school districts, highways, and economic development projects. But such cooperation was particularly common among the metropolitan legislators. Some took a home-style approach that stressed the city and the entire metropolitan area. For example, Advocate 6, though a Republican, worked closely with the majority Democrats. For her, the well-being of the district was synonymous with the well-being of the entire city. She used her seat on the Appropriations Committee to ensure that projects for the city were funded. Many of these were only partially in her district, and some were located several miles away in other parts of the city. The "whole city" approach also tied directly into her political ambitions when she won her council seat. Advocate 6 discovered that her orientation toward the whole metropolitan area had prepared her well for a council run. Other legislators also focused on the entire metropolitan area, especially when seeking media publicity. For example, several representatives appeared at a televised event to present a state check to help restore a city landmark, the memorial honoring World War I veterans. Advocate 2 was featured prominently in this ceremony, even though his district was several miles away, in a different part of the city. At the event, he said he had worked hard to serve all the veterans of the state (a "whole-state" constituency) and to get the metropolitan area's fair share of state money.

As a result of these observations, the two additional circles to add are: the metropolitan area or region of the state, and the home area. *Home area* refers to a community that is smaller than the entire metropolitan area, but large enough to be split into at least two legislative districts. This could be a school district or a medium-sized suburb. The suburb of South Poplar, for example, was divided into two nearly equal-sized pieces. One was in Ombuds 1's district, the other was in Ombuds 2's district. While Ombuds 1 balanced the legislator's responsibilities with another job and was less likely to be seen at home district meetings, Ombuds 2 was retired and had a more person-to-person home style. Thus, Ombuds 2 often dealt with constituent service requests and home-district issues that came from throughout South Poplar, even those that originated in Ombuds 1's district. Ombuds 2 either resolved these or referred them to Ombuds 1's office. Similarly, Advocate 3, who had progressive ambitions to serve in the state senate, considered himself a servant for all of his home county when it came to casework. "I get a lot of calls," he said. (He did not, however, take casework requests from other parts of the metropolitan area or the state.) Again, a state representative oriented himself to a constituency which was not entirely contained within his district.

To sum up, the concentric circles of constituencies are groups whose support is cultivated by the representative. The legislator collects information about the district from these constituencies—particularly from the more intimate, smallest circles—and this information helps him to be responsive. A legislator's home style should be responsive to these constituencies' needs if he seeks to be reelected and/or pursue higher office. The next section discusses the impact that key district characteristics, and the legislators' own ambitions, have on their approaches to home style.

Hypotheses

Table 1 summarizes key district characteristics for the communities represented by the participants in this study, as well as the representatives' party affiliations, the competitiveness of their elections, and their political ambitions. Since this study is based on the representatives' perceptions of their constituencies, the information given in the table comes from what the representatives told me in their answers to my interview questions. "Income" refers to the legislator's perception of the median income level of district residents relative to the metropolitan area as a whole (or the state as a whole for the rural legislators). "Population change" accounts for whether the legislator saw the district as growing, staying the same, or contracting in recent years. "Property values" likewise refers to changes in the last several years of the 1990s. "Partisan leaning" is the representative's perception of party preferences in the district. I also asked the legislators whether they generally faced competitive elections. Finally, I collected information about each one's future ambitions. The hypotheses below relate a representative's choice of home style to both district characteristics and personal political ambition.

HYPOTHESIS 1

Financially struggling, metropolitan districts → *In-district advocate*

Struggling districts are easily overlooked, according to their own representatives. Because there is no significant population or property value growth, local revenues cannot be expected to automatically increase. Because the metropolitan area's growth has shifted elsewhere, these districts stand to lose resources unless their political officials are particularly effective at defending the district's interests. Thus, representatives from these areas tend to "socialize the conflict." They work hard to draw attention. They promote their own efforts to get resources to the district. Advocate 2's town hall meetings and Advocate 3's forum on violence in the media are cases in point. While many of the other representatives found town hall meetings to be a "waste of time" (as Advocate 6 said), those from financially struggling districts tended to develop an in-district advocate style, feeling that such an approach best fit the communities they served. These legislators acted as if political leadership, not growth, was the most effective way to bring resources to the community's roads, schools, and other projects.

Table 1: Districts, Ambitions, and Strategies

Reps	Where	Income change in 1990s	Population change in 1990s	Change in property values in 1990s	Partisan leaning	Rep's party	Competitive elections?	Future ambition
Burkeans								
Burkean 1	Outer-sub	Above avg.	Up rapidly	Up	Rep	Rep	No	State senate/Congress
Burkean 2	Rural	Below avg.	Same	Same	Even	Rep	Yes	Retire
In-district Advocates								
Advocate 1	Inner-sub	Average	Same	Same	Dem	Dem	No	State senate
Advocate 2	Inner-sub	Average	Same	Same	Dem	Dem	No	State senate
Advocate 3	Urban	Below avg.	Loss	Down	Dem	Dem	No	State senate
Advocate 4	Inner-sub	Average	Same	Up	Slight Dem	Rep	No	Insurance comm.
Advocates beyond the District								
Advocate 5	Urban	Average	Same	Same	Dem	Dem	No	Union organizer
Advocate 6	Outer-sub*	Above avg.	Up rapidly	Up	Even	Rep	No	City council
Ombudspersons								
Ombuds 1	Inner-sub	Above avg.	Up slightly	Up slightly	Even	Dem	Yes	State senate
Ombuds 2	Inner-sub	Above avg.	Up slightly	Up slightly	Slight Dem	Rep	Yes	Retire
Ombuds 3	Urban	Above avg.	Same	Up	Slight Dem	Dem	No	Retire
Ombuds 4	Rural	Below avg.	Loss	Down	Slight Rep	Rep	Yes	State senate

*Advocate 6's district is a growing suburban area, most of which has been annexed to the central city. The community maintains its own school districts separate from the inner-city schools.

Many of these districts featured neither decline nor growth in their populations and property values. At first glance, they appeared to be stable communities—districts that were not struggling. However, according to Advocates 1, 2, and 4, the metropolitan area continued to grow around them (see Appendix II: The Site of the Study). In growing areas with rising property values, the pockets that show no growth are likely to be left behind. It is not enough simply to maintain population and property values year after year. A district's place in the metropolitan area is not secure when its neighbors are growing more quickly. Advocate 3's district was the only one in this study to show significant decline in recent years, but Advocates 1, 2, and 4 all believed that the absence of growth was sufficient to put their communities in a struggling position. Each sought to counteract this problem with strong political leadership, focusing on the salient issues of the district and immediately neighboring communities.

HYPOTHESIS 2

*Politically competitive, higher socioeconomic status
metropolitan districts → Ombudsperson*

Those representing financially secure urban and suburban communities were likely to adopt an ombudsperson's approach. Ombuds 3 stressed the importance of local government in meeting her constituents' needs. With highly developed local governments in the city and county, constituents did not feel as dependent on their state legislators to address their concerns. Legislators from these well-off communities were likely to spend more time working closely with local government officials, letting those officials articulate the district's concerns to them. Ombuds 1 emphasized his close contacts with local officials. He often consulted them, especially when trying to decide if a particular issue was important enough to require statehouse action.

Ombudspersons often trace their home styles to the district's voters, whom they believe to be particularly well educated and politically savvy. Ombuds 3 told one group how "amazingly well connected" the people are in her city. Ombuds 1 said that "the voters are smart." Often, if a legislator perceives his constituents to be especially sophisticated or organized, he will not place himself in the position of raising new issues back home. Rather, he emphasizes a willingness to listen to what his constituents have to say. In such an environment, it makes more sense for him to attend meetings organized by others within the community than to organize them himself. This is how Ombuds 3 handled the university demolition proposal in her district, for example: she let the constituents take the lead, then came in to negotiate a compromise among the different groups. Rarely did a legislator from a well-off metropolitan district organize a forum on his own. In the few exceptional cases, the forum was a small one, held to solicit advice and feedback from a handful of local government and school district officials.

If a district is politically competitive as well as wealthy and metropolitan, the wise legislator avoids taking stands that might alienate some constituents. Here again, listening, responding, and compromising are the preferred approaches. In short, legislators from these well-off communities are expected to adopt the ombudsperson home style.

HYPOTHESIS 3

Ambition for a state senate seat → *In-district advocate*

Metropolitan state legislators inevitably find there is a "spillover effect" from their appearances at home. Their districts are so compact that spillover is inevitable. For example, a legislator speaking at a school district forum or local government event will find that these local jurisdictions cover several legislative districts. There is really no way to avoid reaching constituents in those neighboring districts. However, some legislators seek spillover more aggressively than others. Campaigning in local jurisdictions helps build name recognition in the district and nearby communities, which is enormously helpful in a state senate run. In the two states I studied, a state senate district includes approximately three times the population of a state house district.

To take an example, Advocate 2 was not content to just appear at the Grove City school forums organized by someone else. Noting that his home school district, Birchtree, did not have school district forums for state legislators, he took the lead in getting them organized and encouraged his supporters and neighboring state legislators to attend. Average turnout at the Birchtree forums was soon higher than the average turnout at the Grove City forums. Organizing legislative forums, rather than simply attending those organized by someone else, is a particularly aggressive way in which to develop spillover name recognition. Likewise, it is going above and beyond the call of duty to do service work for those who call from another part of the county, outside one's own district. Both of these approaches involve establishing an in-district style while also seeking opportunities to expand the scope of one's activities not only throughout the district, but also into immediately adjoining communities.

HYPOTHESIS 4
No political ambition after statehouse → Burkean or Ombudsperson

Not all representatives invest their time in socializing the conflict. Such publicity-building activities take time away from legislating, as well as from other important aspects of one's life such as family and outside career. Thus it should not be surprising that those who lack future political ambitions often shy away from the advocate approach. If a legislator's political ambitions stop at the statehouse, he is likely to invest less time than others in organizing forums, drawing huge crowds, and gaining media publicity outside the district. A Burkean approach, centered on making one's own judgments and later defending them to constituents, fits well with this strategy. The legislator still meets with constituents, but primarily to explain decisions after they are made, rather than involving constituents in pending public policy decisions. Likewise, the ombudsperson approach is a good fit with a less ambitious career, because it allows others in the district to take leadership roles while the representative listens and responds to constituents' concerns. Both Burkeans and ombudspersons prefer to attend meetings organized by somebody else, rather than organize their own forums.

It is clear from these four hypotheses that there are ample reasons to argue that both district- and ambition-related factors have a significant impact on representatives' choice of strategy. Legislators from struggling metropolitan districts are likely to prefer the in-district advocate approach. Those representing more prosperous urban and suburban communities are more likely to be ombudspersons. Those from politically competitive districts are also likely to adopt the ombudsperson approach. Regarding career ambitions, those seeking state senate seats are the most likely to be in-district advocates.

THE DISTRICTS
Socioeconomics, Party Leaning, and Competitiveness

In the metropolitan area, advocates tend to come from districts that are not growing. None of the in-district advocates in my study represented districts with any significant population or property value growth. Furthermore, advocates served all of the metropolitan districts in which population growth and property value appreciation were negligible. All of these except one were in-district advocates. The exception was Advocate 5, whose preference for a beyond-the-district strategy appeared to be directly tied to the division of his district between urban and neighborhood school districts. By stressing education generally instead of district-specific school issues, Advocate 5 was able to avoid confronting the deep split of his constituents over the matter. But in-district advocates served all of the other non-growing districts, including the one that showed substantial decline (Advocate 3's). Advocate 4 was the only in-district advocate who served a community where property values were slightly increasing. But even his community had no significant population or housing growth.

While the no-growth urban and inner-suburban districts preferred in-district advocates, the two rural districts did not follow this pattern. These communities were not experiencing much growth, and the most rural parts of Ombuds 4's district were truly struggling. Yet, though there was some party competition here—the rural legislators perceived their communities as either Republican-leaning (Ombuds 4) or evenly divided between the parties (Burkean 2)—neither of these districts was served by an advocate. Ombuds 4's district stood out as a particular anomaly: of the twelve districts in the study, it is the only one that experienced significant decline but was served by an ombudsperson. In short, rural districts appear to be different from their metropolitan counterparts, but more rural cases would be needed to explore these differences in depth. (This study was designed to focus on legislators from metropolitan districts.)

Legislators representing more prosperous urban communities tended not to adopt in-district advocate styles. Ombuds 1, 2, and 3 all told me that their voters were smart, and the representatives serving these communities could wait for information to bubble up from home. They did not need to work aggressively to place issues on the district's agenda. The two well-off communities not served by ombudspersons were Burkean 1's and Advocate 6's. Both these legislators believed that they had safe reelection margins and could turn their focus well beyond the district and neighboring communities, onto statewide and citywide concerns as well as their own (somewhat idiosyncratic) future ambitions. By contrast, Ombuds 1 and 2 believed that their upcoming elections were likely to be competitive and that they had to adopt a strategy to prepare for that. Ombuds 2 seemed especially cross-pressured. His "good citizen" inclinations seemed to push him toward a Burkean approach. But in order to be competitive for reelection, he concentrated on meeting and listening closely to community leaders in the chamber and the schools and working on their behalf—for example, by lobbying local government to halt rezoning for a trailer park. Ombuds 3 felt safer in her district than Ombuds 1 and 2 did in theirs, but she worried that redistricting could cut into her Democratic majority, and for that reason, she did not see her seat as safe.

Seven of these twelve legislators believed that their districts had voting majorities that leaned toward their own parties. Burkean 1 and Advocates 2 and 5 told me that their party label was enormously helpful in getting reelected. Two of the subjects told me they were partisan minorities in their district: Ombuds 2 and Advocate 4 were Republicans serving communities that they perceived as Democratic-leaning. Both took district-centered approaches, with Advocate 4 struggling against numerous proposals from other parts of the county or state that he saw as dangerous for his own area. Of those who saw their districts as evenly split between the two parties, Advocate 6 built up enormous name recognition and trust at home by stressing the broadly popular themes of economic growth and development and serving as an advocate beyond the district. Burkean 2 anticipated a close reelection margin in each race he ran. But given his personal background and proclivities, an imperfect "fit" with the district might have been the reason that he did not feel safe in his seat. Yet he argued that he had done a lot for the good of the state. In any case, he planned to retire after another term or two in the house.

CAREER PLANS

State senate was by far the most mentioned career ambition. All but one of the legislators who sought senate seats took district-centered approaches. Burkean 1 was the anomaly, and he was waiting for redistricting before deciding his political future. All the others considering a senate run were either in-district advocates or ombudspersons. In fact, all of the in-district advocates planned senate bids except Advocate 4, who decided instead to run for insurance commissioner. The in-district advocate strategy seems to work well with senatorial ambitions because of the spillover pattern discussed earlier. Spillover into adjoining house districts is excellent in building name recognition for a senate run. The ombudsperson's high visibility at local meetings and reputation for responsiveness also affects neighboring communities, and may also help build name recognition and political reputation for a state senate run.

The advocates tended to be more ambitious than the others. Advocate 5 was the only advocate who did not mention any future political ambitions. He retired from the house to work full-time for his union and spend more time with his young family. Advocate 6 had a particularly idiosyncratic ambition, moving from her long incumbency in the house to an at-large city council seat. She was the only one in the study to make such a move. Her "beyond the district" focus fit well with her plans; she had spent years presenting herself as a fighter for the whole city's interests. Advocate 5's own idiosyncratic ambition—a promotion at the teachers' union—was served well by his focus on statewide education and labor issues, particularly his sponsorship of the collective bargaining bill.

While the advocates showed a strong proclivity toward progressive ambitions, the Burkeans and ombudspersons were mixed. Some of them did have plans to continue in public life. But of the three subjects in this study who planned to retire completely after serving in the house, one was a Burkean and two were ombudspersons. None of the advocates planned to retire.

The pursuit of progressive ambition for state legislators is now constrained by a new phenomenon: term limits. Passed by voters in many states, these laws force legislators out of office after a specified number of terms are served. The next section considers the impact that term limits have on legislators' progressive ambitions.

Term Limits: Institutional and Individual Effects

Missouri voters have placed term limits on their state legislators, and many other states' voters have done so as well (though not in Kansas). Nine of this study's participants hailed from the Show Me State and they had strong opinions on term limits. Because incumbents were "grandfathered" into the eight-year limits, they did not take full effect until 2002, three years after I finished collecting data.

In order to understand how term limits are affecting legislators' ambitions, one must first see these limits as the legislators themselves see them. Not surprisingly, most of my subjects were opposed. They feared the loss of institutional knowledge in the capital. They suggested that this loss would leave policymaking in the hands of "lobbyists and bureaucrats," who, as Burkean 1 pointed out, "don't have term limits." However, there were a few dissenters to this viewpoint. This study offers slim anecdotal evidence that term limits do affect some legislators' progressive ambitions. However, it is too soon to tell if this is a one-time phenomenon. While I conducted the study, many legislators were making career decisions to leave the house, in apparent anticipation of the "day of reckoning," the first day when incumbents would be forced from office by the limits. But it will take a longer-term study to determine whether term limits have lasting effects on progressive ambitions. Other early evidence, though, also indicates that they do have some effect. Kevin O'Leary has found that California legislators responded to term limits by preparing to seek other political offices. They often began preparing to run for higher office after only a few years in office, even though they are permitted to serve six years in each house under California's term limit law (if reelected by the voters, that is).[6]

"LOBBYISTS AND BUREAUCRATS"

Most of this study's subjects consistently opposed term limits, and each one employed the "lobbyists and bureaucrats" argument. They presented this argument in clear, emphatic terms. Alas for them, the voters were not persuaded. But even though term limits are now state law in Missouri, many of the state's legislators continue to emphasize their concerns. Burkean 1 told me: "I've been here ten years and I'm already in the top 10 percent for seniority. You have a natural cleansing, so why impose some artificial limit there? And for those people that choose to stay longer, thank God for them, because of their institutional knowledge that they bring to the table. . . . I think it's beneficial to have people here . . . because otherwise, you know who's going to be running things? Lobbyists and bureaucrats, because they don't have term limits."

This representative used his discussion of term limits to reinforce his Burkean theme—representation based on wisdom, experience, and deliberation. His concern about lobbyists and bureaucrats was echoed by many other legislators, who added a second concern: the day of reckoning.

A DAY OF RECKONING

Advocate 1, a Democrat, disagreed with Republican Burkean 1 on many policy decisions. But he adopted a similar theme in discussing term limits: "The other part of term limits, let me add, is that I think we're going to find that come 2002, when 90 percent of everyone who's here is gone . . . we'll have no institutional history. This place, this capitol, will be dependent on the lobbyists and the bureaucrats.

6. Kevin O'Leary, "Time's Up: Under Term Limits, California's Legislative Engine Sputters."

Now if that's what the people back home want, fine. They've got it. I think government in this state is going to be crippled in 2002."

The "day of reckoning" theme was brought up by many of my subjects. Missouri's term limits took effect in 1994. They limited legislators to eight years each in the state house and state senate. Advocate 1 saw the day of reckoning coming in 2002. That was when voters would finally come face to face with the effects of the law they had passed. Legislators would also face the full consequences.

Even some legislators who once favored term limits had, in Ombuds 4's words, "totally reversed" themselves. Ombuds 4's perspective was unique for two reasons. First, he was one of only two rural legislators in this study, and he feared that term limits would hurt rural interests. Second, he found himself caught by a legal technicality. The term limits initiative counted even partial terms toward one's limit. Because he was chosen in a special election, Ombuds 4 faced a term limit after only three and a half terms in office, instead of the usual four. He told me:

> I would have supported [term limits] in '92. You know, I saw . . . what I thought was no turnover in Congress or Missouri legislature. And I've come to . . . totally reverse myself. . . . It's critical . . . especially to the rural areas, because . . . we're a little different animal than the suburban legislator. . . . I see . . . a lot more turnover in the city. The rural ones, if you're out there and you build up the seniority and . . . you build your numbers, and you get to know people, and they get to trust you, and you . . . get the seniority to get on [the] Budget [Committee], for example, . . . you can help your area. Whereas, you're swallowed up . . . if you're a rural person and you have no real contacts or relationships built. . . . You take the two cities, that makes the rest of us a real, real minority.

As Ombuds 4 explained, most legislators in his state hailed from suburban districts, reflecting the state's population. However, some rural representatives had so much seniority that they rose to positions of power. They used this power to help their constituents. The cycle was completed when grateful constituents returned these rural legislators to office, where they accrued still more seniority. I earlier quoted Ombuds 4 discussing his view that rural legislators have an advantage in the seniority-building process because they have better name recognition among their constituents than do their metropolitan counterparts. Most state representatives already serve less than eight years in office. But for those who would make a career of service in the statehouse, term limits will definitely alter their plans. This, in turn, may already be altering the processes of the statehouse.

ANTICIPATION

The 2002 elections were clearly the day of reckoning. However, most legislators already saw changes in the house due to term limits. Some incumbents were leaving in anticipation of the limits. People moved up to committee and party leadership positions more quickly—perhaps before they were ready. Some ran for other offices. New legislators had more power, but institutional knowledge was lost.

Only two of my twelve subjects reversed themselves on term limits. Besides Ombuds 4, the other "flip-flopper" was Advocate 6, who told me: "Term limits, I think, are one of the worst things that has ever happened in Missouri to the legislative [system and] to government. . . . [I] didn't even realize how bad this was going to be. . . . Now . . . I'm seeing the repercussions of this . . . which are that we're going to turn this body over to the bureaucrats."

Advocate 6 was more concerned with the empowerment of bureaucrats than that of lobbyists. But like Advocate 1, she referred to a day of reckoning. She also admitted to having changed her position on the issue now that she could see the consequences. Advocate 5 agreed that the repercussions had already begun. Noting that lawmakers now moved into leadership positions more quickly, with less experience, he told me:

> All those veterans who'd kind of been building careers started thinking about what they were going to do. So I think it's my opinion that some of the people who'd been around for, you know, twelve, fifteen, twenty years, left earlier than they would have, which has actually opened up leadership positions, chairmanships, and stuff like that. The speaker was elected in '92, the same year I was. All right, you know, he's been speaker three

years. That just . . . wouldn't have happened [before]. . . . I'm [a committee] chairman. I think I got at that chairmanship a little earlier than I would have. The bad part is, we've got a speaker who was elected in '92! I mean, I'm a big supporter of his, but he wasn't ready to be speaker.

Sitting in while I interviewed Ombuds 3, Rep 3 put this a little more concisely. He saw a "brain drain" occurring because people had "scrammed" from the house in the last election.

DISSENT

A few legislators dissented from the anti-term-limits view. When Rep 3 spoke of "brain drain," his friend Ombuds 3 countered that lobbyists would actually be an asset to the new legislators. She also believed that the legislative staff had enough institutional knowledge to carry on. She said:

> When people talk about term limits, there's a lot of fear that the lobbyists will take over, and that . . . you'll have . . . unexperienced elected officials [and] that the . . . lobbying corps will come and take over. And I don't have that fear. And the reason I don't have that fear is . . . since I've been here, we have never had a big issue that both sides haven't been camped on our doorstep. So, I think . . . the lobbying corps has gotten to the point that both sides of . . . most important issues are represented. . . . There is some fear that the bureaucrats [will] take over. And I think Missouri is a little bit better placed on this than some other states might be because we have, in both house and senate, quite a bit of staff that's for all of us. And I think those staff positions we have confidence in for the most part, and that they will stay stable. So we're not purely at the mercy of the rest of the bureaucracy.

Ombuds 3 agreed that it would be the lobbyists who would carry on institutional knowledge after term limits took effect. However, she did not fear this. Instead, she argued that lobbyists for opposing sides would balance one another and provide valuable information. Furthermore, she was the only subject in this study to mention legislative staff in this context. She believed that staffers would smooth the transition to a term-limited era.

Only one other legislator expressed support for term limits to me. Advocate 2 made the commonly heard argument for term limits: they allowed for new people and ideas. At the same time, he understood that his support for term limits put a constraint upon his own service. He told me: "I voted for term limits. I think term limits are a good thing. I think people are here too long. They get too powerful, and it doesn't give other people a chance in the district if they want to be . . . nominated for public office. They want to serve, and everyone's got different ideas. Just because I've got an idea doesn't mean the other guy doesn't have a better idea . . . I voted for term limits, and term limits will take me out."

While Ombuds 3 and Advocate 2 were outnumbered by the other subjects, their arguments show that the anti-term-limits view is not universal among state legislators. However, the majority of subjects in this study did oppose the limits. They feared the "lobbyists and bureaucrats" taking over. They saw the full effect of term limits as a "day of reckoning." And they saw changes already taking place, in anticipation of that day.

CAREERS

Term limits are a fact of life for many state legislators today. They must be confronted, regardless of one's support or opposition to the concept. This study provides some anecdotal evidence that the average legislator's career plans shifted in anticipation of term limits. But overall, the evidence is slight. More than half of the legislators in this study harbored some progressive ambition. That includes six of the nine Missouri representatives. However, it also includes two of the three Kansas legislators, who did not face term limits. Term limits primarily appeared to shift legislators' plans forward a few years. Those planning to run for state senate or other, higher office thought they might do so sooner. This occurred not only because house members were term limited and could not run again, but also because state senate seats were being opened up by term limits.

According to Burkean 1, the average tenure in the Missouri House is five and a half years. Thus, the average Missouri legislator would not see his time in the house cut short by an eight-year term limit. Burkean 1 and Advocate 1 believed that a handful of long-serving state legislators serve as repositories of institutional knowledge and help to socialize new members. They feared for the loss of these few "old-timers." But most house members do not stay so long.

So what impact do term limits have on progressive ambitions? A longtime incumbent, Advocate 6, decided to run for an at-large city council seat, a relatively unusual ambition for a state legislator. It is worth recalling that Advocate 6 "flip-flopped" from support to strong opposition of term limits. Her distaste for the impending changes may have influenced her plans. Advocate 1, Advocate 2, Burkean 1, Ombuds 1, and Ombuds 4 all discussed the possibility of state senate runs. They may have considered these higher offices somewhat sooner because term limits would force out the senate incumbents. Advocate 3, a non-term-limited Kansan, also harbored ambitions for a senate seat. He was elected to that seat shortly after I ended data-collection for this study. Also free from term limits, Advocate 4 was considering a run for state insurance commissioner. These two Kansans did not have a single date upon which to focus. By contrast, the Missourians knew that the day of reckoning was coming in 2002. Then they would have to make a decision to step aside or run for higher office. Thus term limits gave the Missourians a specific election on which to focus their future plans. The three non-term-limited Kansans could keep their plans more fluid, though their plans were dependent on the plans of others. Burkean 2, the third Kansan, did not seek higher office. His plans were heavily influenced by the ambitions of a young, politically ambitious constituent who would be likely to run against him in a few years. For the Missourians, term limits crowded out such traditional political calculations and substituted the day of reckoning.

TERM LIMITS: SUMMARY

This study indicates that the early effects of term limits were primarily institutional. Missouri legislators were able to point to many changes taking place in anticipation of the day of reckoning. Some of the "old-timers" were already leaving office during this study due to their impending term limits. As a result, institutional knowledge was lost among legislators. This shifted power to lobbyists, bureaucrats, and staff. New legislators moved into key party and committee positions more quickly. Rural areas, prone to reelecting incumbents for long periods, were possibly losing power as a result of these changes.

On balance, this study provides only limited evidence for any change in the average legislator's progressive ambitions due to term limits. For the term-limited subjects, the day of reckoning primarily served as a focal point: a sort of "put-up-or-shut-up" date by which decisions must be made regarding higher office. But the non-term-limited subjects were just as likely to display progressive ambitions as were the term-limited ones. Clearly, that particular conclusion would be more meaningful if tested with a larger dataset. But the qualitative data here do provide some insight into how legislators are coping with term limits. It is another challenge to be confronted while they carry out the task of representation.

Conclusion

The successful representative must fit the district. He must develop a style that is responsive to his circles of constituencies and to his district's overall characteristics. Strategy is partly a matter of personal proclivities and ambitions. But it also must be appropriate for the district one serves and the ambitions one holds. Those ambitions, in turn, are focused on a specific date by term limits.

None of the relationships described above are perfect. As with almost any data analysis, there are deviations from the pattern. In general, however, there is a congruence between certain types of districts and certain representational strategies. This conclusion fits nicely with the folk wisdom of the legislators in this study, as well as that of Fenno's congressmen. Specific strategies work better in some places than others. Furthermore, some approaches fit better than others with certain political ambitions beyond the statehouse. Whoever our new representatives are, if they are going to be effective, they will have to develop a home style strategy that fits both the district and their own ambitions.

Afterword

Here is the status of the twelve state representatives as of December 2002:

BURKEAN 1 left the house due to term limits in 2002. He narrowly lost the Republican nomination for his local state senate seat to a state representative who had served in office only two years. He is currently contemplating his future political career and continues to be very visible in his home district.

BURKEAN 2 served as house education chair until he was defeated by a Democratic challenger in 2002. His district had been redrawn to encompass part of the Democratic-leaning college town that previously had been just outside the district. The National Education Association backed Burkean 2's opponent, who went door-to-door while Burkean 2 did not.

ADVOCATE 1 left the house due to term limits. Redistricting had shifted all of Grove City and nearly all of Elmwood into a Democratic-leaning state senate district. He plans to seek the seat when the ailing incumbent retires or is forced from office by term limits, which will be within two years. He has already begun raising money for his senate bid.

ADVOCATE 2 was redistricted into a state senate district that is predominantly African American. The incumbent in that district will not be term-limited out for six more years. Term-limited in the house, Advocate 2 abandoned his senate run and plans to retire. In 2001, he won a major victory in his struggle against capital punishment. A substitute motion for his legislation became law. The bill banned capital punishment of the mentally retarded.

ADVOCATE 3 was elected to the state senate in 2000. He won his primary easily and faced no Republican opposition in the general election. He secured the Democratic nomination for secretary of state in 2002, but was defeated two-to-one by the Republican candidate. He remains a state senator.

ADVOCATE 4 was reelected to his house seat with no opposition in 2002. Shortly afterward, he resigned his seat to take a job as assistant to the newly elected state insurance commissioner. Per state law, a local party committee will choose his successor, who is likely to be a candidate recommended by Advocate 4.

ADVOCATE 5 left office after the 2000 session and went to work full-time as an organizer for the National Education Association. He and his family moved in order to live near the state capital. The candidate he endorsed as his successor won the seat easily in 2000 and again in 2002.

ADVOCATE 6 continues to serve on the city council, chairing a key committee. She has sought reelection to the council.

OMBUDS 1 also left the house under term limits. He filed for but then withdrew from the Democratic primary for the state senate seat. He then attempted to run for the senate seat as an independent candidate, but failed to secure sufficient signatures on his election petitions. His proposals for two petition initiatives—one to shrink the size of the house to one hundred members and the other to allow the fire department to provide the city's ambulance service—did not come to fruition.

OMBUDS 2 was defeated for reelection in 2000. His district had continued to trend Democratic. The close presidential election and strong union get-out-the-vote drives brought out many straight-ticket Democratic voters that year. The Democratic challenger who defeated him was a twenty-nine-year-old woman employed by the county prosecutor's office. She was easily reelected to the seat in 2002 against a new Republican opponent. Ombuds 2 became principal of a Christian school near his home. He does not plan to seek elective office again.

OMBUDS 3 won reelection to her house seat in 2002 after defeating a Democratic primary opponent. Her district had changed a great deal, because her friend Rep 3's district was eliminated and her district absorbed much of it. Her Democratic challenger argued that the new district should be represented by a member of the gay and lesbian community and by someone who would have supported the collective bargaining bill that Ombuds 3 had opposed. Labor unions backed her opponent. Ombuds 3 won with a large majority in the precincts that were part of her old district, but her victory was much narrower in those areas that had been part of Rep 3's district. She will be term-limited out of the house in 2004.

OMBUDS 4 did not seek reelection in 2000. Another Republican won his seat with his support and was reelected in 2002. Ombuds 4 has returned to farming.

Appendix

I. Data Collection

I spent two years observing and interviewing twelve state representatives. This study presents and analyzes the resulting qualitative data. Whenever possible, I conducted the interviews in the home districts, sometimes in connection with other home-district activities. However, this was not always feasible. In all, six interviews were conducted in state capitol offices, one on the house floor during the third reading of a bill, one in the representative's car as he ran campaign errands, one in a former campaign headquarters in the district, one in the representative's home, and two in public places in the home district (both of which immediately followed meetings with constituents).

In addition to tape-recording and transcribing my interview with each legislator, I traveled with them in their home districts: attending forums, meeting constituents on the street, watching consensus and conflict unfold, and struggling with local problems. Like Fenno, I often found myself talking to legislators "on the run"—usually riding with them as they drove from meeting to meeting.[1] Many were eager to talk as we drove, pointing out important points of local controversy as we passed them. I attended too many events to list, but they included numerous chamber of commerce meetings and school district legislative forums, community center receptions, classes in local schools, and interest-group-sponsored events. I visited with newspaper publishers, lobbyists, social workers, lawyers, candidates for office (a few of whom were elected during my study), teachers, school

1. Fenno, *Home Style,* 281.

administrators, community activists, schoolchildren, and businesspersons. I sat in a radio studio while one representative went on the air. With other representatives, I attended church services, passed notes scrawled on napkins during a formal reception, and helped load campaign brochures into a car trunk. I went to class with fourth graders, applauded the state high school wrestling champions (two years in a row), toasted the inauguration of Kansas City's first woman mayor, and ate countless sausage-and-egg breakfasts. I explained the purpose of my study to dozens of constituents, until the representatives finally reached the point where they could explain my study themselves, without my having to say anything. Through it all, I tried to see the home districts as the state representatives themselves saw them—the constituents, the controversies, the consensus, the history, and the future.

I worked hard to be balanced. Yet I did find myself spending more time observing some representatives than others. I saw at least a dozen public appearances each by Advocates 1 and 2, Burkean 1, and Ombuds 2 over the course of two years. Advocate 1 and Ombuds 2 each guest-taught a class for me. Advocate 2 and Ombuds 2 became personal friends of mine, and to this day we frequently exchange E-mail or stop to visit after a legislative forum. My mother lives in Advocate 2's district, only a few blocks from his home, and during our interview he invited her over to tour his garden and greenhouse. Ombuds 2 occasionally forwards me "funnies" via E-mail. I also have a little history that brings me closer to some of my subjects. Ombuds 4's nephew and I were best friends in grade school, where Advocate 2's wife worked as our school nurse. I had a natural tendency to observe Advocates 2 and 5, along with Ombuds 1 and 2, more often because they represented the area where I grew up. However, Ombuds 1 spent a great deal of time at his outside job, and I never had a true "day in the district" with him. Furthermore, I had only a few opportunities to observe Advocates 3 and 4 in their home districts. Ombuds 4's district was far from Kansas City and I traveled there for only one day, though it was indeed a full day of activities for him. Advocate 4 was added to my sample late in the study. For several weeks after our interview, he was attending "candidate school" in Washington, D.C., preparing to run for state insurance commissioner. But I did secure several observations at different types of events for each representative. Many of them seemed excited to be studied. They were pleased that academics were finally (in their minds) paying attention to state legislatures.

II. Site of the Study

Ten of these twelve representatives served districts in the Kansas City area. Two others represented rural districts in Missouri and Kansas. The metropolitan area sits across two states. Kansas City, Missouri, with approximately 450,000 people, is the central city. (Three other cities in the area have over 100,000 people each.) Though St. Louis is Missouri's largest metropolitan area, Kansas City actually has a larger city population due primarily to annexation. While St. Louis is "landlocked" by an unusual city-county relationship, Kansas City has aggressively used its prerogative to annex unincorporated land, particularly since the 1950s. Viewed on a map, Kansas City's hundreds of square miles look like a Rorschach blot. This reflects the city's pattern of annexing around previously incorporated suburbs. Many of these suburbs (Advocate 1's hometown, for example) are surrounded by the city on all sides.

Like virtually all U.S. metropolitan areas, Kansas City has experienced waves of suburban flight in recent decades. About a third of area residents live in Kansas. Suburban Johnson County is among the nation's wealthiest counties per capita. This suburban "sprawl" sometimes earns the wrath of those in the metropolitan area. Several suburban communities on the Missouri side have also grown significantly. Some of these, such as most of Advocate 6's district, actually lie within the Kansas City limits due to annexation. Others, such as Burkean 1's district, lie in suburban municipalities but share the same county as the central city. Across the border in Kansas, much of Wyandotte County (home of Advocate 3's district) has declined into inner-city poverty.

In general, Kansas City is known for low-density growth. The area's population is spread across seven counties in two states. There are innumerable school districts and local governments. Numerous political cleavages make it difficult for the metropolitan area to act as a single, coherent entity.[2]

Kansas City is known for a lower-key way of life than larger cities on the nation's coasts, as well as for lower housing costs and more-spread-out development patterns.[3] The area has more miles of freeway per capita than any other in the United States. It is intensely car-dependent. During the course of my study, I observed highways to be a major development issue for many state representatives (particularly Advocate 2).

Both the city and the metropolitan area were growing as of the late 1990s. Much of the city's growth was due to housing starts on annexed land, but there was also a wave of gentrification in older urban neighborhoods. This was centered in the adjoining districts of Ombuds 3 and Rep 3. The property values both in these gentrified communities and in the growing outer suburbs were rising rapidly, while those in the older inner suburbs were stable or declining slightly.

The Kansas City, Missouri, School District had long been a headache for the entire metropolitan area. Many suburban representatives told me their constituents had come to escape the city's troubled schools. The district has long been known for white flight and poor student achievement. The ire of outstate Missourians was raised to a fever pitch during the late 1980s and early 1990s when, as a result of court-ordered desegregation in the Kansas City School District, the U.S. federal courts ruled that the state must help pay for an expensive magnet school program. There was a good deal of legal action that followed the initial ruling, but the state's obligation to fund the program was upheld by the U.S. Supreme Court. Rural Missourians spoke often and angrily about the Olympic-sized swimming pool and other amenities built partly at state expense.

The city has allowed annexed communities to keep their own school districts, separate from the Kansas City School District. Though a part of Kansas City proper, these communities struggle to avoid any involvement with the city school district. Advocates 2, 5, and 6 and Ombuds 1 and 2 all represented parts of the city that have their own suburban schools. In 1998, Ombuds 3 and Rep 3 successfully cham-

2. G. Ross Stephens, "Politics in Kansas City," 383–84.
3. Neal R. Peirce and Jerry Hagstrom, *The Book of America: Inside Fifty States Today*, 602–3.

pioned legislation to create charter schools in the inner-city school districts of Kansas City and St. Louis. Several charter schools opened that may contribute further to the gentrification of certain city neighborhoods. A number of these schools have also opened to cater to the poorer inner-city students.

Missouri has a long history of both fiscal and social conservatism. Like other border and southern states, Missouri was controlled for years by a conservative Democratic party organization. Since the late 1960s, Republicans have become more competitive for statewide office. Today, the parties have nearly equal numbers of legislators in both the state house and senate. Missouri has long been torn by cleavages, particularly those that divide the metropolitan areas from the rural communities. Among the states, only Pennsylvania has as many lines of political cleavage.[4] The city and county of St. Louis often struggle at cross-purposes. Jealousies also flare between Kansas City and St. Louis. Legislators are under intense pressure to balance the needs of different parts of the state. Kansas City's interests have often been unpopular in rural Missouri, particularly since the aforementioned desegregation ruling. Central Kansas City's state representatives rank among the state's most liberal, but they must work with a more conservative state Democratic party to get things done. Like many metropolitan areas, Kansas City has both inner and outer suburbs. The inner Missouri suburbs tend to be represented by moderate, pro-union Democrats, but they occasionally elect a few Republicans—also moderates, such as Ombuds 2. Wealthier residents of the new outer suburbs prefer Republicans.

Kansas is no longer the rural state made famous in *The Wizard of Oz*. Though agriculture remains crucial in the Sunflower State, its population and growth have shifted to the suburbs. The state experienced population loss in the late twentieth century.[5] But as residents flee from stagnant rural economies, suburban Johnson County just keeps growing and growing. The Bureau of the Census estimates that Johnson County grew by over 20,000 residents in only twelve months from July 1997 to July 1998. The 2000 census confirmed that Johnson County had become the most populous in the state, having

4. Richard R. Dohm, "Political Culture of Missouri," 35.
5. Virginia Gray, "The Socioeconomic and Political Context of States," 8.

surpassed Sedgwick County (which is home to the slower-growing city of Wichita).[6] With nearly all of their elected officials Republicans, Johnson Countians had solidified their hold on many leadership positions in both houses of the state legislature.

Wyandotte County, by contrast, has experienced one of the most devastating population losses in urban America.[7] Declining into inner-city poverty, the community lost both residents and jobs while gaining a reputation for crime. In 1998, the state of Kansas merged the city government of Kansas City, Kansas, with the county government of Wyandotte County, in a closely watched attempt to overhaul the way business was done (see the section on Advocate 3 in Chapter 4). Wyandotte County was the only reliably Democratic county in the state. It had lost so many people that local government was struggling with vacant housing. The mayor-CEO of the Wyandotte County unified government spearheaded an aggressive drive to tear down vacant houses and redevelop the lots. In 1998, this county, the metropolitan area's poorest, showed its remaining political muscle. Wyandotte County votes were pivotal in allowing a Democratic challenger to defeat an incumbent Republican for the area's congressional seat. He drew nearly even with the incumbent in the older, less wealthy parts of Johnson County, and trounced him with a large majority in Wyandotte County. The victor became Kansas's only Democrat in the U.S. House at the time. In 1999, the entire seven-county Kansas City area was represented by Democrats in the U.S. House. (Missouri and Kansas each had two Republican U.S. senators.)

Metropolitan-rural cleavages continue to dominate these states, particularly Missouri. Both states have experienced recent controversies over legalizing concealed handguns. Urban area residents tend to oppose these proposals, while rural communities support them. In a 1998 Missouri referendum, an overwhelming defeat in suburban St. Louis County was enough to narrowly stop concealed-carry permits from being written into law (a majority of Kansas City–area voters also voted "no"). In Kansas, the state legislature passed concealed-

6. U.S. Census data for city and county populations is available on the World Wide Web at ⟨factfinder.census.gov⟩.

7. Ann O'M. Bowman and Richard C. Kearney, *State and Local Government: The Essentials*, 15.

carry legislation but the governor vetoed it, and the veto was sustained. Metropolitan and rural legislators in both states also struggle over the allocation of highway and education funding.

Kansas has recently gained national notice for the deep split in its Republican party. The moderate wing of the party is solidly pro-business and moderate on social issues. The conservative wing is more anxious to cut taxes and implement socially conservative programs. In 1999, the conservative-controlled Kansas state school board made international headlines by removing evolution from the state's recommended K-12 science curriculum. Many moderates, including the governor and Burkean 2, worried over what this would do to the state's reputation among potential new residents. The moderate-conservative split can turn nasty. At the end of the 1999 session, moderates solidified their hold by removing a noted conservative from the house Appropriations chairmanship. Democrats sometimes exploit this split to gain a few victories, but they remain badly outnumbered.

It is not unreasonable to view Kansas as a three-party state. Each GOP wing has its own leadership, fund-raising organizations, and ideology. Each acts essentially as a separate party. Often, the two factions refuse to share lists of party donors with one another. One moderate leader was reputed to have said recently that he would "squash conservatives like bugs." Repeated several times in newspaper accounts, this quote contributed to the climate of distrust.

One of the sharpest contrasts between Kansas and Missouri concerns the initiative-and-referendum process. Missouri has it, Kansas does not. Consequently, Missouri voters have passed both a tax lid and term limits on state legislators, while Kansas has neither. Missouri's Hancock Amendment is one of the toughest tax lids in the nation, limiting state and local revenues to a fixed proportion of the state's economy. As a result, Missouri ranks fiftieth among the states in per-capita state spending.[8] The amendment also limits local property taxes. In Missouri, some Kansas City–area school district leaders resent the Hancock Amendment. Residents complain that it limits their ability to compete with the wealthy, growing suburban districts in Kansas. In Johnson County, in contrast, controversy swirls around the periodic property reassessments. As property values ap-

8. Gray, "Socioeconomic and Political Context of States," 4.

preciate, so do local tax bills, leading to calls for some sort of cap or limitation on tax increases that result from reassessment. In 1999, the Kansas Legislature passed legislation requiring local government to either limit these increases or hold public hearings.

Finally, Missouri voters have limited state legislators in both houses to eight years apiece. Because longtime legislators were "grandfathered" into the limits, their term limit "clock" did not start until voters approved the initiative in 1994. The full effects of this change came in 2002, when the majority of current state legislators were forced out by term limits.[9] Some longtime legislators began running for other offices or leaving for other careers in anticipation of the new limits.

No metropolitan area is a perfect embodiment of the United States, but Kansas City is caught up in many of the major controversies that swirl through American state politics: school funding, highways, competition for jobs and growth, city versus suburbs, annexation, and migration from inner to outer suburbs, just to name a few. The two rural representatives I interviewed were intended to provide some balance and contrast to the metropolitan-area focus. But just as the United States has become a suburban nation (most Americans live in suburbs today), most of my subjects represented suburban or mixed urban-suburban districts. In short, this study is not based on a true representative, random sample, but the sample does provide the opportunity to hypothesize about similar communities across the country.

III. Coding Decisions: Distinguishing among Suburbs

The table on page 185 summarizes the effect that district characteristics and representatives' ambitions have on home style. There were some coding difficulties with the distinction among urban, inner-suburban, outer-suburban, and rural districts. Besides Advocate 6, whose district is described in a footnote to the table, Advocates 2 and 5 and Ombuds 1 and 2 all served districts that blended urban and inner-suburban characteristics. Advocate 5's district was almost entire-

9. Hamm and Moncrief, "Legislative Politics in the States," 168.

ly contained within the central city, though two of the three school districts he served were neighborhood districts separate from the city schools. I coded his community as urban. Advocates 2, 5, and 6 all served districts that lay partly within the central city's limits and part-ly in suburban cities. However, all three of these districts lay entirely outside the central city school district, which encompassed the urban core of an annexation-driven city. Because of the schools, I coded these districts as inner-suburban, though they could plausibly be cod-ed as urban instead. However, a glance at the table shows that the inner-suburban communities and the urban ones are coming to re-semble one another, so the distinction might not be particularly im-portant.

Most other coding distinctions were much easier to make when classifying the districts. It was particularly easy to distinguish be-tween the inner and outer suburbs in this study. As Myron Orfield points out, inner-suburban communities today have come to re-semble urban communities as much as, and perhaps more than, they resemble outer suburbs.[10] Like most inner-city communities, inner suburbs are becoming more racially diverse, they have flat property values, their populations are aging, and they are generally unable to annex any further. Some, such as Advocate 2's community, have gained a reputation for crime, though crime there is still not near-ly as high as comparable statistics from the inner city. Interesting-ly, Ombuds 1 and 2 each told me that property values were higher and population growth more rapid in the portions of their districts that lay within the central city's limits. In contrast, there is little growth of either population or property values in South Poplar, the suburb split into the respective districts of Ombuds 1 and 2. With its affordable housing, South Poplar has become a popular destina-tion for blacks fleeing the inner-city schools. It is beginning to re-semble the adjoining, diverse district of Advocate 2. This again shows the growing similarities between cities and inner suburbs. As Ombuds 2 put it, "In the past fifty years, this district has changed from rural [to suburban]. And now it's changing again, becoming more urban."

10. Myron Orfield, *Metropolitics: A Regional Agenda for Community and Stability,* 30–34.

IV. A Note on Grammar and Names

> Um, the transition . . . the transition from verbal to, to written communication, you know?

Verbal conversation is its own type of communication, very different from written language. My research vividly reminded me of this difference. A person's conversation might sound fluid, clear, and coherent to the ear, but it is often harder to understand when transcribed onto paper. As any contemporary playwright or screenwriter knows, our conversation is full of half-sentences, repeated phrases, slang, nonstandard grammar, and even profanity. In addition, certain key phrases come and go as part of the language. The phrase "you know" has virtually replaced "um" as a connecting phrase in verbal, modern American English. It also appears at the end of sentences, making a declarative statement into a question (that is, into a question, you know?). On some of my transcripts, the phrase "you know" appears at least ten times per page. It is the proper job of linguists, not political scientists, to study the origins of this phrase and probe how it came to play such a prominent part in spoken language.

I offer this note in lieu of placing "[*sic*]" after each example of nonstandard grammar. All subjects—including one former college president who holds a Ph.D.—used some nonstandard grammar in their interviews and informal conversations with me as we traveled around their districts. I used nonstandard English too. My conclusion is that even erudite, educated, and well-spoken people do not generally use the Queen's English for verbal communication. "[*sic*]" seems to indicate that the subject quoted is unknowledgeable or ignorant of proper grammar and must be corrected, but that is not the case here. Instead, the verbal conversations transcribed for this project are simply an informal means of communication. I have transcribed the quotes as accurately as possible. Occasionally I have inserted an ellipsis in place of sentences that were repetitive or were tangential to the point of the quotation. Also, a few of the subjects used mild profanity; this is included in quotations only when I deemed it necessary in order to appreciate the essence of what was said.

In places, I have elected to give the true names of the states involved (Missouri and Kansas) as well as that of the metropolitan area. In addition, certain counties are referred to by their real names. All individual representatives, along with most cities and school districts, are referred to by pseudonyms. Each pseudonym (except for Advocate 1, Burkean 2, etc.) appears in italics the first time it is used.

Curious minds may not be able to resist speculating on the true identity of some of the legislators. I have made the participants in my study aware of this possibility, but as a matter of professional responsibility, I will not confirm or deny any speculation as to the true identity of anyone or anyplace referred to by a pseudonym in this study.

Bibliography

Abney, Glenn, and Thomas A. Henderson. "Role Orientations toward Subconstituencies: State Legislators and Local Officials." *Polity* 15 (1982): 295–304.

Barker, Ernest. *Essays on Government.* Oxford: Clarendon Press, 1945.

Bibby, John F., and Thomas M. Holbrook. "Parties and Elections." In *Politics in the American States: A Comparative Analysis,* 7th ed., ed. Virginia Gray, Russell L. Hanson, and Herbert Jacob. Washington: Congressional Quarterly Press, 1999.

Bowman, Ann O'M., and Richard C. Kearney. *State and Local Government: The Essentials.* Boston: Houghton Mifflin, 2000.

Burke, Edmund. "Speech to the Electors at Bristol." 1780. In *Orations and Arguments by English and American Statesmen,* ed. Cornelius Beach Bradley, 89–140. Boston: Allyn and Bacon, 1895.

Cain, Bruce E., John A. Ferejohn, and Morris P. Fiorina. "The Constituency Service Basis of the Personal Vote for U.S. Representatives and British Members of Parliament." *American Political Science Review* 78 (1984): 110–25.

———. "The House Is Not a Home: British MP's in Their Constituencies." *Legislative Studies Quarterly* 4 (1979): 501–23.

Casey, Gregory, and James W. Endersby. "Funding for Education in the 1990s: A Case Study." In *Missouri Government and Politics,* rev. ed., ed. Richard J. Hardy, Richard R. Dohm, and David A. Leuthold, 258–72. Columbia: University of Missouri Press, 1995.

Cavanaugh, Thomas E. "The Calculus of Representation: A Congressional Perspective." *Western Political Quarterly* 35 (1982): 120–29.

Dahl, Robert A. *Who Governs: Democracy and Power in an American City.* New Haven: Yale University Press, 1961.

Dohm, Richard R. "Political Culture of Missouri." In *Missouri Government and Politics,* rev. ed., ed. Richard J. Hardy, Richard R. Dohm, and David A. Leuthold, 21–37. Columbia: University of Missouri Press, 1995.

Dolan, Kathleen, and Lynne E. Ford. "Change and Continuity among Women State Legislators: Evidence from Three Decades." *Political Research Quarterly* 50 (1997): 137–51.

Downs, Anthony. *An Economic Theory of Democracy.* New York: Harper and Row, 1957.

Eulau, Heinz, and Paul D. Karps. "The Puzzle of Representation: Specifying Components of Responsiveness." In *The Politics of Representation: Continuities in Theory and Research,* ed. Heinz Eulau and John C. Wahlke, 55–71. Beverly Hills, Calif.: Sage, 1978.

Eulau, Heinz, and John C. Wahlke, eds. *The Politics of Representation: Continuities in Theory and Research.* Beverly Hills, Calif.: Sage, 1978.

Fenno, Richard F., Jr. *Congress at the Grassroots: Representational Change in the South, 1970–1998.* Chapel Hill: University of North Carolina Press, 2000.

———. *Congressmen in Committees.* Boston: Little, Brown, 1973.

———. *Home Style: House Members in Their Districts.* Ontario, Calif.: Scott, Foresman, 1978.

Fishkin, James S. *Democracy and Deliberation: New Directions for Democratic Reform.* New Haven: Yale University Press, 1991.

Freeman, Patricia K., and Lilliard E. Richardson Jr. "Exploring Variation in Casework among State Legislators." *Legislative Studies Quarterly* 21 (1996): 41–56.

Glaser, Barney. *Theoretical Sensitivity: Advances in the Methodology of Grounded Theory.* Mill Valley, Calif.: Sociological Press, 1978.

Goffman, Erving. *The Presentation of Self in Everyday Life.* Garden City, N.Y.: Doubleday, 1959.

Graham, George J., Jr. 1972. "Edmund Burke's 'Developmental Consensus.'" *Midwest Journal of Political Science* 16 (1972): 29–45.

Gray, Virginia. "The Socioeconomic and Political Context of States."

In *Politics in the American States: A Comparative Analysis,* 7th ed., ed. Virginia Gray, Russell L. Hanson, and Herbert Jacob, 1–31. Washington: Congressional Quarterly Press, 1999.

Hamilton, Alexander, James Madison, and John Jay. *The Federalist Papers.* 1787–1788. Reprint, ed. Gary Wills, New York: Bantam, 1982.

Hamm, Keith E., and Gary F. Moncrief. "Legislative Politics in the States" In *Politics in the American States: A Comparative Analysis,* 7th ed., ed. Virginia Gray, Russell L. Hanson, and Herbert Jacob, 144–190. Washington: Congressional Quarterly Press, 1999.

Harder, Marvin, and Carolyn Rampey. *The Kansas Legislature: Procedures, Personalities, and Problems.* Lawrence: University Press of Kansas, 1972.

Howard, Philip K. *The Death of Common Sense: How Law Is Suffocating America.* New York: Random House, 1994.

Jewell, Malcolm E. "Legislative Casework: Serving the Constituents, One at a Time." *State Legislatures* 5 (November 1979): 14–18.

———. *Representation in State Legislatures.* Lexington: University of Kentucky Press, 1982.

———. "Trends in Research on U.S. State Legislatures: A Review Article." *Legislative Studies Quarterly* 22 (1997): 265–74.

Johannes, John R. "The Distribution of Casework in the U.S. Congress: An Uneven Burden." *Legislative Studies Quarterly* 5 (1980): 517–44.

Johannes, John R., and John C. McAdams. "Entrepreneur or Agent: Congressmen and the District of Casework." *Western Political Quarterly* 40 (1987): 535–53.

Key, V. O. *Politics, Parties, and Pressure Groups.* 5th ed. New York: Crowell, 1964.

King, Gary. "Replication, Replication." *PS: Political Science and Politics* 28 (1995): 444–52.

Loftus, Tom. *The Art of Legislative Politics.* Washington: Congressional Quarterly Press, 1994.

Loomis, Burdett R. *Time, Politics, and Policies: A Legislative Year.* Lawrence: University Press of Kansas, 1994.

Madison, James. "Federalist 10." 1787–1788. In *The Federalist Papers,* ed. Gary Wills, 42–49. New York: Bantam, 1982.

Mayhew, David R. *Congress: The Electoral Connection.* New Haven: Yale University Press, 1974.

Miller, Warren E., and Donald E. Stokes. "Constituency Influence in Congress." *American Political Science Review* 57 (1963): 45–56.

Moncrief, Gary F., Peverill Squire, and Malcolm E. Jewell. *Who Runs for the Legislature?* Upper Saddle River, N.J.: Prentice-Hall, 2001.

Moncrief, Gary F., Joel A. Thompson, and William Cassie. "Revisiting the State of U.S. State Legislative Research." *Legislative Studies Quarterly* 21 (1996): 301–35.

Muir, William K., Jr. *Legislature: California's School for Politics.* Chicago: University of Chicago Press, 1982.

O'Leary, Kevin. "Time's Up: Under Term Limits, California's Legislative Engine Sputters." *American Prospect* 17 (December 2001): 30–33.

O'Neill, Tip, with Gary Hymel. *All Politics Is Local and Other Rules of the Game.* New York: Random House, 1994.

Orfield, Myron. *Metropolitics: A Regional Agenda for Community and Stability.* Washington: Brookings Institute Press, 1997.

Peirce, Neal R., and Jerry Hagstrom. *The Book of America: Inside Fifty States Today.* New York: Norton, 1984.

Peterson, Paul E. *City Limits.* Chicago: University of Chicago Press, 1981.

Pitkin, Hanna Fenichel. *The Concept of Representation.* Berkeley: University of California Press, 1967.

Price, Kent C. "Instability in Representational Role Orientation in a State Legislature." *Western Political Quarterly* 38 (1985): 162–71.

Riker, William H. *The Art of Political Manipulation.* New Haven: Yale University Press, 1986.

Rosenthal, Alan. "The Consequences of Constituency Service." *State Government* 59 (1986): 25–30.

———. *The Decline of Representative Democracy: Process, Participation, and Power in State Legislatures.* Washington: Congressional Quarterly Press, 1998.

———. *Legislative Life: People, Process, and Performance in the States.* New York: Harper and Row, 1981.

Sanders, Lynn M. "Against Deliberation." *Political Theory* 25 (1997): 347–76.

Schattschneider, E. E. *The Semi-Sovereign People: A Realist's View of Democracy in America.* 1960. Reprint, Fort Worth: Holt, Rinehart, and Winston, 1983.

Schrag, Peter. *Paradise Lost: California's Experience, America's Future.* New York: New Press, 1998.

Searing, Donald D. *Westminster's World: Understanding Political Roles.* Cambridge: Harvard University Press, 1994.

Serra, George. "What's in It for Me? The Impact of Congressional Casework on Incumbency Evaluation." *American Political Quarterly* 22 (1994): 403–20.

Serra, George, and Albert D. Cover. "The Electoral Consequences of Perquisite Use: The Casework Case." *Legislative Studies Quarterly* 17 (1992): 233–46.

Siegel, Roberta S., and Wolfgang Pindur. "Role Congruence and Role Strain among Urban Legislators." *Social Science Quarterly* 54 (1973): 54–65.

Songer, Donald R., James M. Underwood, Sonja G. Dillon, Patricia E. Jameson, and Darla W. Kite. "Voting Cues in Two State Legislatures: A Further Application of the Kingdon Model." *Social Science Quarterly* 66 (1985): 983–90.

Sorauf, Frank J. *Party and Representation: Legislative Politics in Pennsylvania.* New York: Atherton Press, 1963.

Squire, Peverill. "Legislative Professionalization and Membership Diversity in State Legislatures." *Legislative Studies Quarterly* 17 (1992): 69–79.

Stephens, G. Ross. "Politics in Kansas City." In *Missouri Government and Politics,* rev. ed., ed. Richard J. Hardy, Richard R. Dohm, and David A. Leuthold, 375–86. Columbia: University of Missouri Press, 1995.

Strauss, Anselm, and Juliet Corbin. "Grounded Theory Methodology: An Overview." In *Handbook of Qualitative Research,* ed. Norman K. Denzin and Yvonna S. Lincoln. Thousand Oaks, Calif.: Sage Publications, 1994.

Strøm, Kaare. "Rules, Reasons and Routines: Legislative Roles in Parliamentary Democracies." *Journal of Legislative Studies* 31 (1997): 155–74.

Thurber, James A. "The Impact of Party Recruitment Activity upon Legislative Role Orientations: A Path Analysis." *Legislative Studies Quarterly* 1 (1976): 533–49.

Wahlke, John C., Heinz Eulau, William Buchanan, and LeRoy C. Ferguson. *The Legislative System: Explorations in Legislative Behavior.* New York: Wiley, 1962.

Yiannakis, Diana Evans. "The Grateful Electorate: Casework and Congressional Elections." *American Journal of Political Science* 25 (1981): 568–80.

Index